Settlements, Social Change
and Community Action

Of related interest

Social Workers, the Community and Social Interaction
Intervention and the Sociology of Welfare
John Offer
ISBN 1 85302 731 6

Therapeutic Communities
Past, Present and Future
Edited by Penelope Campling and Rex Haigh
Foreword by John Cox
ISBN 1 85302 614 X

The Essential Groupworker
Teaching and Learning Creative Groupwork
Mark Doel and Catherine Sawdon
ISBN 1 85302 823 1

The Working of Social Work
Edited by Juliet Cheetham and Mansoor A. F. Kazi
ISBN 1 85302 498 8

Research in Social Care and Social Welfare
Issues and Debates for Practice
Edited by Beth Humphries
ISBN 1 85302 900 9

Introduction to Therapeutic Communities
David Kennard
ISBN 1 85302 603 4
Therapeutic Communities 1

Social Work with Children and Families
Getting into Practice
Ian Butler and Gwenda Roberts
ISBN 1 85302 365 5

User Involvement and Participation in Social Care
Research Informing Practice
Edited by Hazel Kemshall and Rosemary Littlechild
ISBN 1 85302 777 4

Practice Teaching – Changing Social Work
Edited by Hilary Lawson
ISBN 1 85302 478 3

Settlements, Social Change and Community Action

Good Neighbours

Edited by Ruth Gilchrist and Tony Jeffs

Jessica Kingsley Publishers
London and Philadelphia

First published in the United Kingdom in 2001 by
Jessica Kingsley Publishers Ltd
116 Pentonville Road
London N1 9JB, England
and
325 Chestnut Street
Philadelphia, PA 19106, USA

www.jkp.com

Library of Congress Cataloging in Publication Data
A CIP catalogue record for this book is available from the Library of Congress

British Library Cataloguing in Publication Data
A CIP catalogue record for this book is available from the British Library

ISBN 1 85302 764 2

Printed and Bound in Great Britain by
Athenaeum Press, Gateshead, Tyne and Wear

Contents

Preface

It is the intention of the editors of this collection to bring the work of the settlements both past and present to a new and wider audience in order that they can learn from its history as we have.

It was while we were researching the needs of the growing numbers of students in Newcastle and their impact on the local population, in order to see how as an organisation the YMCA could respond, that the early university settlement movement seemed a likely place to look for ideas about students and community.

Through visiting settlements and talking to people about their early history we were encouraged to find out more. In Liverpool for example, we found others were also exploring the idea of residential projects, whilst Toynbee Hall is researching the potential of renewing its links with the universities and offering residential work in the East End.

In Newcastle, while the issues affecting universities and communities are very different today, similarities can be found. The principle of bringing people together to learn from one another; the notion of service and association; the role of social research for a purpose other than meeting the funders' demands, and the value of living and learning together in community, have all been borrowed from the university settlement in a proposal for a new student settlement.

In our journeys around the country visiting projects and exploring archives we had many people to thank for making us welcome. People have embraced the notion of creating something new out of a history; of reviving the past in a way relevant to the future. Whether it was in the housing department of Newcastle Civic Centre or at the BASSAC Headquarters, someone has always been able to recount their days at such and such a settlement when they were a student; or, like the Vice Principle of the University of Northumbria, when they stayed at the settlement where Ghandi slept. We hope this small contribution will add to the growing interest in the movement and revive memories for those who have been involved. Certainly the sense of excitement and enthusiasm for the future has convinced us that the settlement movement is on the brink of a renaissance.

Thank you to all our contributors. Sadly John Matthews died before this book was published. When I met him at BAASAC he was very enthusiastic about recording the history of the movement and hoped one day to write one himself. We hope this has gone some way towards meeting his ambition.

Ruth Gilchrist
Tony Jeffs

Introduction

Ruth Gilchrist and Tony Jeffs

A professor of social work recently asked one of the contributors to this book what she was currently researching and was told 'settlements'. The response produced a blank look and an enquiry along the lines of 'What are they?'. Our author subsequently told us that for her the comment encapsulated the extent to which the contribution of settlements to the development of social work in particular and social policy, in general, was now disregarded in Britain. The anecdote did not surprise either of us although it did prompt one of us to comment that it would be rare to encounter such ignorance among welfare professionals in the United States. There the contribution of the settlement movement and the names of pioneers still resonate. Indeed one of us recalled not long ago teaching a first year undergraduate class and asking each of the students towards the end of the first session to nominate the American they most admired. One selected Jane Addams and another Sophonisba Breckinridge. During the discussion that followed it appeared the whole class had heard of the former and apparently knew what a settlement was. Whether this experience would have been replicated in other colleges we cannot second-guess, but there appears to be a wide variation in terms of awareness regarding the contribution of the settlements between Britain and the United States. It is one that requires some redress on this side of the Atlantic and it is hoped this text will make some contribution towards achieving this.

This book emerged from the involvement of one of the editors in moves to establish a new settlement in Newcastle-upon-Tyne. The idea was initially to gather material that would help participants in the project gain an insight into the past and present contribution of settlements. Subsequently the intention became to help resuscitate the collective memory of welfare professionals and others regarding the historic role of settlements while simultaneously celebrating contemporary successes. The resulting chapters are therefore a mix that mirror these twin aims.

A simple idea lay at the heart of the first settlements: that all should share in community. That if men and women from universities and privileged backgrounds came to live for some time among the poor of London and other cities, they could do something to reduce the inequalities of life. As Barnett explained:

> A settlement is simply a means by which men and women may share themselves with their neighbours; a club house in an industrial district, where the condition of membership is the performance of a citizen's duty; a house among the poor, where residents may make friends with the poor. (1898, p.25)

Scott Lidgett, a pioneer of the movement, worked and lived for almost half a century in the settlement he helped establish in Bermondsey, one of the poorer districts of London. He composed a set of aims to help newcomers secure a better grasp of what the settlement sought to accomplish. These were:

1. To bring additional force and attractiveness to Christian work.

2. To become a centre of social life, where all classes may meet together on equal terms for healthy intercourse and recreation.

3. To give facilities for the study of literature, history, science and art.

4. To bring men together to discuss general and special social evils and to seek their remedy.

5. To take such part in local administration and philanthropy as may be possible.

6. And so to do all this that it shall be perfectly clear that no mere sectarian advantage is sought, but that it shall be possible for all good men to associate themselves with our work. (Lidgett 1936, p.117)

Once allowance is made for Bermondsey Settlement being initiated by Methodists and the self-proclaimed religious commitment this fostered, it is possible to recognise within these aims aspirations common to virtually all settlements. Also it is important to stress that the masculine emphasis is somewhat misleading. Bermondsey Settlement within a short space of time established a women's house alongside the original building. Women members and activities lay at the heart of the enterprise. Indeed, settlements from the outset led the way in many respects by allowing women the space to create new forms of community intervention and to work alongside men as equal partners.

As Michael Rose (Chapter One) shows, the settlement movement was influenced by a rich array of thinkers. In particular social idealists such as Green, Ruskin and Carlyle (Picht 1914, p.9), Christian Socialists such as Maurice, Hughes and Kingsley (Kelly 1970: Wilkinson 1998) and social reformers such as Octavia Hill and Mary Ward helped the pioneers identify three key needs. These were for scientific research concerning poverty; the furthering of wider lives through education; and an enhancement of leadership in local communities (Pimlott 1935, p.11). As Mina Carson (Chapter Two), John Matthews and James Kimmis (Chapter Three) and Jon Glasby (Chapter Five) communicate, the early settlements made significant progress on all three fronts.

First, they attracted a number of very able and committed settlers, many of whom became deeply involved with social inquiry and the development of thinking and policy around the alleviation of poverty. Toynbee Hall, for example, gained an early reputation as a 'training ground for bright, young, reform-minded civil servants' (Meacham

1987, p.85). The residents list reads like a roll-call of key figures in the making of the welfare state: William Beveridge, R. H. Tawney, Clement Attlee and Kenneth Lindsay all spent time there. Indeed, Evans (1984) very persuasively argues that perhaps the greatest contribution of the settlements in Britain up to the present has not been their influence on the poor but on the thinking of the middle-class politicians and administrators who subsequently shaped the welfare state – settlers such as Attlee, who went on to become a Labour Prime Minister. In later years he recalled the following:

> When I was a young barrister just down from Oxford, I engaged in various forms of social work in East London. The condition of the people in that area as I saw them at close quarters led me to study their causes and to reconsider the assumptions of the social class to which I belonged, I became an enthusiastic convert to socialism. (Attlee 1949, p.25)

In passing, though, it should be noted that some promulgated the more cynical view of George Lansbury, Attlee's predecessor as leader of the Labour Party. Lansbury, who lived in east London and was politically active there for almost 40 years, believed the settlements too often served as a conduit for the sons and daughters of the better-off, enabling many such individuals to find municipal and government appointments after a brief sojourn, their stay allowing them within the space of a few short months to become 'experts on social affairs' (Lansbury 1928, p.130).

Second, the settlements made a considerable contribution to working-class education, providing a great range of evening and extension classes, debates and discussions, and facilitating a significant number of cultural clubs and associations. Part of Barnett's initial vision placed Toynbee Hall as the core of an east London 'working man's university'. Elementary and vocational classes were seen initially in that context as a temporary phenomena that would fade away as other provision emerged, allowing Toynbee to become a university college. This did not come to pass, however, as Mark Smith (Chapter Seven) recounts. Toynbee instead, like other settlements, came to make a decisive and sustained contribution to the adult education movement in Britain and elsewhere. In addition the settlements and their residents were energetically involved in school reform, getting themselves elected to school boards and highlighting gaps in provision via research and innovation. In particular they were in the forefront of reform providing after-school clubs, holiday programmes, education for those who would nowadays be assessed as requiring 'special needs', literacy classes, as well as play and youth work (see Chapter Eight). Throughout, though, what has so often set them apart from mainstream educational services has been a desire to cater for the whole person. As Henrietta Barnett recognised, 'Children need to be taught to enjoy as much as they need to be taught to work' (1909, p.319).

Lastly, Samuel Barnett, like Beatrice and Sidney Webb, George Bernard Shaw and other Fabians 'saw the immense possibilities of local government' (Pimlott 1935, p.106) and believed that settlements could provide some civic leadership. This was to be achieved through the education and stimulation of electors, and the participation of residents with local people in local government. This was often achieved from small beginnings. For example, Sunday afternoon teas at Hull House, Chicago, brought together women from the neighbourhood, trade unionists, social philosophers and political activists; as one young participant later recalled, they led them 'to feel that we were part of something that was more important than just our own problems' (quoted Kennedy 1979, p.142). Some like Jane Addams, subsequently became major political figures locally, nationally and internationally. In this they were aided by the links described by Christian Johnson (Chapter Four), which the settlement movement forged between units both locally and internationally. Within Britain residents like Attlee and Salter became Members of Parliament, as did wardens such as J. H. Whitehouse of Ancoats and Percy Alden of Mansfield House, Canning Town.

It is clearly difficult to quantify the impact of settlements at local and national levels. However, Stocks suggests it has been substantial, to the extent that by the mid-1940s there was

> ...scarcely any field of social legislation or any statutory instrument of social service which does not owe something if its inception or direction to the recorded observations or voluntary experiments of settlers who, year by year, followed the call of Samuel Barnett to those mean streets where their fellow-citizens led anxious meagre lives. (Stocks 1945, p.3)

Furthermore, as Ruth Gilchrist (Chapter Nine), Mark Smith (Chapter Seven) and Tony Jeffs (Chapter Eight) indicate, in those areas of welfare provision that have been traditionally under-resourced the contribution of the settlements has often been disproportionately greater. Social and material conditions have improved since the early years and consequently the settlements have had to change their roles and structures accordingly. This has not always been an easy process, as Martin Walker's account (Chapter Six) of how Toynbee Hall has changed during the last 20 years shows. Nevertheless, the contribution of the settlements remains significant and innovative, as Crescy Cannan and Chris Warren in their chapter on the development of family centres (Chapter Ten) show. In addition Sarah Banks (Chapter Eleven) portrays a picture of extensive and varied activity within the contemporary settlement movement. Although in some respects the settlements' role has diminished, many of the chapters indicate the extent to which they continue to play a crucial role in localities and influence policy nationally.

However, contemporary settlements rarely bring people together in the way Barnett and others envisaged. It is unusual for them to mix people from varying social and educational backgrounds to learn from each other, collaborate and find solutions to common problems. For this reason they are no longer crafting a vibrant constituency committed to social reform and radical change, at least not on a scale sufficient to 'make a difference'. Few settlements now act as catalysts obliging individuals from different classes and backgrounds to meet, except, that is, as 'professional' and 'client'. The decline in the model which valued residency as an essential ingredient has removed a defining characteristic which set the movement apart from the bulk of community initiatives then and now. Perhaps it is important therefore to recognise the significance of the decision of some, notably Toynbee, to re-emphasise the value of living with 'your neighbours'. The concept of service remains, indeed Gedge might well have been writing of many settlement workers today when he noted half a century ago the tendency for such individuals 'to work themselves to death' (1937, p.149) but that is an altogether different type of service to that which lay at the heart of the movement. These criticisms may seem somewhat harsh and unfair, because after all it is almost impossible to identify any organisation, except a few religious groupings, that does so. The difference, though, is that settlements, unlike other welfare and educational agencies, were founded on a belief that meeting needs was important, but equally so was the fostering of friendship and less exclusive forms of community. In this sense the imperatives that pushed the settlement movement forward remain tantalisingly and intractably in place. Today as much as in the past we still have to find ways of encouraging a meaningful sense of mutual responsibility and solidarity, of stimulating and sustaining a meaningful dialogue between rich and poor, the powerful and the powerless, professionals and their clientele. Imagine for a moment what benefits might accrue for us all if those controlling our great retail conglomerates were involved in the sort of settlement experiment recounted by G. D. H. Cole:

> In 1902 the Sunderland Co-operative Society opened its Coronation Street Branch, in a poor part of the town as a People's Store. The new Store included grocery and butchers' shops selling along with the normal range of goods cheap soup by the cup and bowl. In addition to the shops there was a hall for meetings, and a miniature 'Settlement' with two resident social workers, club-room facilities, and arrangements for voluntary help from women members of the parent Society. National

leaders of the Women's Co-operative Guild took it in turns to take up temporary residence in the Settlement. The welfare side was a great success and the shops paid a dividend of 20d in the £. (Cole 1945, p.122)

It is not only the better-off and influential that would benefit from revisiting the settlement tradition. For we all have still to address the sad paradox that as higher education has expanded throughout the industrialised world, so it has in the main become more, not less, isolated. Physically our universities increasingly come to resemble fortresses protected by perimeter fences, security guards and closed circuit television, all the paraphernalia of the high-security state being employed to keep the public, who after all fund higher education, at arm's length. Universities may in many instances be located in city centres, often low-income areas, to take advantage of cheap labour and land rents, but they are as cut off physically and intellectually as they ever were in Barnett's day. The case made over a century ago for eradicating the barriers between universities and the wider community still resonates today. The knowledge-rich and the knowledge-poor remain remote from each other. Ways still need to be found to bring them together if the problems and needs of the latter are to be given a fraction of the attention lavished on servicing the wants of the rich and powerful. Those once labelled the mendacious poor are now designated the underclass. Labels may have altered, but this class remains in the eyes of respectable society a group to be feared, avoided and occasionally pitied. For academics it constitutes a profitable source of research income but little else. Neither academics nor the rest of society seem to have any desire to engage with the socially excluded and poor as equals. Without such a dialogue, however, we have no hope of finding a solution to many, if not most, of the intractable problems that beset us. Nor will we be able to create a democracy comprising free and equal citizens. The enforced passivity of the poor still makes a mockery of almost every democratic political system and will continue to do so until their engagement is encouraged in the way the settlers anticipated it would be, and not merely tolerated.

It is hoped the following chapters will stimulate in some small way wider reflection upon the contemporary manifestations of those problems that stimulated the emergence and growth of the settlement movement. In putting together this book we hope to encourage a deeper appreciation of the merits and strengths of the remedies and programmes developed by generations of settlement workers and their neighbours. Those settlers bequeathed us a rich legacy of ideas and policies that we would all do well to revisit regularly. We can learn so much from their endeavours, thinking and 'failures'. As Violet Markham, founder of the Chesterfield Settlement stressed in a letter written in 1894, ultimately 'there is of course only one remedy: that is education and plenty of it' (Jones 1994, p.30).

Perhaps that in the final analysis best summarises both the motivation and ambition of the settlements and the settlers.

Bibliography

Attlee, C. R. (1949) *The Labour Party in Perspective and Twelve Years Later.* London: Gollancz.

Barnett, H. (1909) 'Town children in the country.' In S. and H. Barnett (eds) *Towards Social Reform.* London: T. Fisher.

Barnett, S. (1898) 'University settlements.' In W. Reason (ed) *University and Social Settlements.* London: Methuen.

Cole, G. D. H. (1945) 'Mutual aid movements in their relation to voluntary social service.' In A. F. C. Bourdillon (ed) *Voluntary Social Services: Their Place in the Modern State.* London: Methuen.

Evans, T. (1984) 'The university settlements, class relations and the city.' In G. Grace (ed.) *Education and the City: Theory, History and Contemporary Practice.* London: Routledge and Kegan Paul.

Gedge, P. M. (1937) 'Charterhouse in Southwark.' In E. M. Jameson (ed) *Charterhouse.* London: Blackie and Son.

Jones, H. (1994) *Duty and Citizenship: The Correspondence and Papers of Violet Markham 1896–1953.* London: The Historians' Press.

Kelly, T. (1970) *A History of Adult Education in Great Britain.* Liverpool: Liverpool University Press.

Kennedy, S. E. (1979) *If All We Did Was to Weep at Home: A History of White Working Class Women in America.* Bloomington: Indiana University Press.

Lansbury, G. (1928) *My Life.* London: Constable.

Lidgett, J. Scott (1936) *My Guided Life.* London: Methuen.

Meacham, S. (1987) *Toynbee Hall and Social Reform 1880–1914.* London: Yale University Press.

Picht, W. (1914) *Toynbee Hall and the English Settlement Movement.* London: G Bell and Sons.

Pimlott, J. (1935) *Toynbee Hall: Fifty Years of Social Progress 1884–1934.* London: Dent.

Stocks, M. (1945) *Fifty Years in Every Street,* (2nd edition). Manchester: Manchester University Press.

Wilkinson, A. (1998) *Christian Socialism: Scott Holland to Tony Blair.* London: SCM Press.

The secular faith of the social settlements

'If Christ came to Chicago'

Michael Rose

> Let combination and brotherhood do for the newer and simpler
> faith what they once did for the old – let them give it a practical
> shape, a practical grip on human life... Then we too shall have
> our Easter – we too, shall have the right, to say 'He is not here, he
> is risen'. Not here – in legend, in miracle, in the beautiful outworn
> forms and crystallisations of older thought. He is risen – in a wiser
> reverence and a more reasonable love; risen in the new forms of
> social help inspired by his memory, called afresh by his name.
> (Mrs Humphry Ward 1888, p.480)

Such sentiments, though well suited to the sermonising of a late
twentieth-century Anglican bishop, form the climax to a lengthy
novel by the late nineteenth-century writer, Mrs Humphry (Mary)
Ward. In it, the eponymous hero, Robert Elsmere, an Oxford graduate
inspired by the teaching of T. H. Green, experiences doubt in the
doctrines of the Church of England into which he has been ordained.
Leaving his comfortable rural living, he goes to work in the inner city,

addressing meetings of sceptical working people on the tenets of a new faith of humanity and brotherhood.

Published early in 1888, the novel was a runaway success, selling 40,000 copies in Britain, 200,000 in the United States, and being reviewed by Gladstone in *The Nineteenth Century*. Its author, Mary Ward, was an Arnold, grand-daughter of the eminent Victorian, Thomas, of Rugby School, and niece of Matthew, poet, professor and inspector of schools. Two years after the publication of *Robert Elsmere*, she founded a settlement, University Hall, in Gordon Square, Bloomsbury. It was, however, a settlement with an intellectual purpose, that of popularising the radical critique of the Bible through public lectures by leading British and Continental scholars. Despite the best efforts of its warden, the Unitarian minister, Phillip Wicksteed, it proved to be a failure. Even Bloomsbury, it seemed, had no great desire for Biblical scholarship, whether radical or not. Some of the younger members of the settlement, themselves perhaps tiring of Bible lectures, moved a little to the northeast of Gordon Square, and started a boys' club in Marchmont Street. Other social activities among the poor of St Pancras followed, and Mary Ward abandoned the cerebral University Hall to concentrate on founding a new settlement. Relentless bullying of the Duke of Bedford and of the wealthy newspaper proprietor and publisher, John Passmore Edwards, produced both land and capital. In 1897, the Passmore Edwards Settlement was opened in a purpose-built Art Deco building in Tavistock Place. On Mary Ward's death in 1921, it took the name of its foundress. While atypical in some ways, its origins illustrate the interweaving of religious idealism and practical social activity which was a central feature of the settlement movement on both sides of the Atlantic (Rodgers 1931; Sutherland 1990; Trevelyan 1923; Ward 1918).

Although the concept of living among the poor in their own neighbourhoods, and not merely visiting them from afar, was not uncommon in the nineteenth century, particularly among clergymen who often had no choice in the matter, the idea of a collegiate-style residential settlement house, or social settlement, is usually credited to the Reverend Samuel Barnett and his wife, Henrietta. Raising funds in Oxford and Cambridge through a Universities Settlements Association, Barnett opened a pseudo-Oxbridge college, Toynbee Hall, in his own Whitechapel parish in 1884. Here young Oxbridge graduates could reside, pursue their careers in the City or the Inns of Court, but return to the settlement at evenings and weekends to give their spare time to philanthropic, social and political activities among their East End neighbours. In doing this, they would raise the cultural level of the 'mean streets' of East London, develop communities not severed by class or sectarian conflict, and give back some of that cultural privilege which their university studies had given them (Briggs and Macartney 1984; Pimlott 1935).

Americans came, and saw, and copied. In 1886 the first American settlement, Neighborhood Guild, was established in New York City. Three years later America's most famous settlement, Jane Addams' Hull House, opened in West Side Chicago. By 1900, there were more than 100 settlements in the United States, many of them in New York City, Boston and Chicago, and some 45 in Britain, over 30 of these being in London. By 1914 American numbers had increased four-fold, but the British remained relatively static in number despite the entry of non-metropolitan English cities, notably Manchester, Liverpool, Bristol and Birmingham into the ranks (Davis 1967; Woods and Kennedy 1922). The settlement movement in Britain has been, like Lucky Jim's shipbuilding techniques, a strangely neglected topic, with its historiography focused heavily on Barnett's Toynbee Hall. In the United States, by contrast, the movement has featured centrally, and often critically, in social historians' debates on gender and ethnicity in the nineteenth- and twentieth-century city (Crocker 1992; Karger 1984; Lissak 1989; Lasch-Quinn 1993; Philpott 1978). One of the best accounts of the origins of the British movement remains that of Inglis (1963), who sees it as one of the failed attempts to reconcile the working classes to organised religion in the late nineteenth century, 'The settlements were religious in impulse', he claims (ibid, p.174). It is the aim of this chapter to examine this claim and its consequences for both the British and the American settlement movements.

Religion and the settlements

Settlement leaders like Barnett, or Albert J. Kennedy in the United States, fiercely proclaimed the non-sectarian nature of their enterprise. Both drew a line between settlements, with their ideal of community formation, and missions, with their aim of converting the poor. The American National Federation of Settlements (NFS), founded in 1911, carefully scrutinised all applications from settlement houses for membership, and rejected any which appeared to have sectarian missionary activities in their programmes. Even sectarian foundations, Anglican Oxford House, Methodist Bermondsey, Congregational Mansfield House, or Chicago's Presbyterian Olivet Institute, stressed the secular nature of their work and made no attempts to proselytise. Such rejection of missionising increased the attraction of the settlement ideal to the young, educated and socially conscious men and women of late Victorian Britain and America.

The settlement creed attracted because it enabled the living-out of an ethical existence in deprived areas, expressing the immanence of God without having to trouble the mind with the literal truth of scripture, or the paraphernalia of virgin birth, resurrection and ascension which nineteenth-century science, historical as well as natural, had seriously challenged. 'It took the Life to make God known', Barnett insisted, and a practical, ethical Christianity, shorn of superstition, could be put to practical purpose. 'What,' W.T. Stead asked its leading citizens in 1893, 'if Christ came to Chicago?' 'What would Jesus do?,' Stead's brother's Browning Hall Settlement advised its neighbours to ask themselves, when pondering how to cast their votes in a London County Council Election (Harris, 1993; Barnett, 1921; Schults, 1972; Robert Browning Settlement, 1912). The life and activity of the settlement helped purge the resident of religious doubt. Stanton Coit 'passed through fires of religious doubt' on his way to founding America's first settlement in 1886, while Charles

Stover, his colleague at Neighborhood Guild, found the 'key to his theological perplexities' in settlement work. Graham Taylor, head-hunted from his college post in Hartford, Connecticut to become the first professor of sociology at the Chicago Theological Seminary in 1893, agreed to the move only on the condition that he could found and live in a settlement house, Chicago Commons, close to Hull House, on the city's West Side. Here he developed a 'practical theology' which 'dealt only with the application of religion to life, not at all with theological theory', tracing his spiritual and social heritage 'from Thomas Chalmers, Charles Kingsley, F. D. Maurice and John Ruskin away back to Thomas More of Utopia, to Francis of Assisi, to the Seer of Patmos and above them all to Jesus of Nazareth' (Taylor, 1928). Such a mix of mid-Western Liberal Protestantism, local involvement and concern for social problems created, as Martin Bulmer has shown, a powerful school of sociology at the new University of Chicago, to which the city's leading settlement houses, Hull House, Chicago Commons, the University of Chicago and North Western, all made important contributions. The social gospel expressed itself in and through the settlement movement (Davis, 1967; Taylor 1930; Bulmer 1984).

Though the settlement ideal might satisfy the need for an active, non-mystical or prescriptive faith, guilt remained present within it as within conventional religions. Beatrice Webb wrote of a 'consciousness of sin' among the young of her generation. Why were deprived areas so deprived? What had created such areas of poverty and wretchedness in the inner city? The answer would seem to lie in that wave of industrialisation and urbanisation that had swept over Britain and, later, over parts of the United States in the late eighteenth and nineteenth centuries – a process still called by some the 'Industrial Revolution'. In March 1883, the young Balliol scholar and tutor Arnold Toynbee died suddenly at the age of 31. The lectures on English economic history which he had been delivering at Oxford, together with some of the addresses on political economy which he had been giving to working-class audiences in northern industrial towns, were collected together and published posthumously under the title of *Lectures on the Industrial Revolution*. Toynbee portrayed the Industrial Revolution as a catastrophic event which had destroyed the mutual bonds of an older, more closely-knit society. While political democracy had gone some way to alleviating the consequences of this, there needed to be also an economic democracy to bring capitalist and worker together and create a new united community of mutual trust and obligation. The social Humpty Dumpty had to be put together again.

Toynbee's early death made him into a martyr figure for the embryo settlement faith. Stories spread of his begging forgiveness of his working-class audience for the wrongs done to them by industrialisation; of his collapsing after his last lecture, and being borne from the room on the sturdy shoulders of working men to die in his wife's arms. He became an idealised, secular, Christ-like figure with the homo-erotic attraction of a proto-Rupert Brooke. Despite Mrs Toynbee's reservations, Samuel Barnett insisted on making his new settlement house Toynbee's memorial. 'Our conscience felt the rebuke of the contrast between the wealth of inheritance and opportunity stored up in Oxford and the poverty of the life lived amid the mean streets and monotonous labour of East London. In a vague way we felt the claim of that poverty upon our wealth,' wrote Cosmo Gordon Lang, later to be Archbishop of Canterbury, but in 1883 one of a group of young Oxford men who had heard Barnett's plea for university settlements in the year of Toynbee's death (Fraser 1973; Kadish 1982, 1986; Toynbee 1884).

Toynbee clarified historically the claims of poverty on wealth, and historians were prominent members of the early British settlements. R. H. Tawney was an early resident at Toynbee Hall, and T. F. Tout a founder of Manchester's Ancoats Settlement in 1895. Gonner at Liverpool, Lodge at Edinburgh and Leonard at Bristol were active in the founding of their university's settlements, and Paul Mantoux's name appears briefly as a resident at Passmore Edwards. Graham Taylor, head resident of Chicago Commons, included in the bibliography for his lecture course on 'Social Teaching in the Scriptures' not only Seeley's *Ecce Homo* and Ward's *Robert Elsmere* but also W. J. Ashley's *English Economic History*. Economic history or 'industrial history' became, along with ethics and law, a compulsory subject for social work trainees at E. J. Urwick's School of Sociology, many of them residents at the Women's University Settlement in Southwark. If 'guilt' was an item in the secular faith of the settlements, it was one which was defined historically.

Community and neighbourhood

Geography as well as history had a part in the formation of the settlement creed. Central to the ideal was the concept of residence in a community. A settler must set up house as 'neighbour of the working poor' in Barnett's words. This might be done by renting an ordinary terraced house or tenement in the district, by occupying a larger house in the area for communal living, or, in a few cases, by the provision of a purpose-built settlement house for both residential and communal activity. 'Neighbourhood as springboard puts us into a position to assess every aspect of living from pre-natal care to dotage, to get into the family as an operating unit and into society also as an operating unit', wrote Albert Kennedy (1958) who began his long settlement career in Boston in 1906 in close association with Robert Archie Woods, 'Boston's male Jane Addams' and founder of South End Settlement House.

Kennedy, Woods, Graham Taylor, Mary Simkovitch of Greenwich House, New York City and many other American settlement founders centred their faith on 'neighborhood' as a unit of community building. A neighbourhood of a few blocks, no larger, in Kennedy's view, than a child's legs would carry it to school, shops or settlement clubs, would be a place where everyone knew everyone. Class and ethnic divisions could be overcome by middle-class, Anglo-American settlement residents living as neighbours to working-class Irish, Poles, Lithuanians or Greeks. The model they had in mind was that of the American small town in which many of them had been raised, Kennedy in Rosenhagen, New Jersey; Taylor in Shenectady,

New York; Simkovitch in Newton, Massachusetts (Davis, 1967). Mary McDowell, head resident of the University of Chicago settlement, wrote lovingly of her upbringing on the Ohio River near Cincinnati. Her grandfather, a carpenter and boat builder, presided over a democratic household where guests at table might be a fellow craftsman or the President of the United States. She attended the Methodist class meeting led by old Father Sherer, a 'Lincoln like figure', who 'laid his old hands on my young head (and) stamped upon my imagination a pattern to follow and consecrated me to a religious life of right relationships'. When her family moved to the 'comfortable, complacent Christian' Chicago suburb of Evanston, she rapidly became bored, went to live 'Back of the Yards' in South Chicago and founded the University of Chicago Settlement (McDowell, 1928).

The British settlement faith was inspired less by the small town than by the rural parish, that ideally cohesive and socially balanced community with squire and parson at its head. Barnett had the task of trying to revive a defunct East End parish, St Jude's, Whitechapel – an experience he shared with supporters and mentors like J. R. Green, the historian, and Rev. W. H. Fremantle, whose curate Barnett had been (Addison 1941; Barnett 1921). 'Come and be the squires of East London' pleaded the High Anglican clergyman, Henry Scott Holland, seeking residents for the new Oxford House in Bethnal Green in 1884 (Ashworth, 1984).

A formative influence on settlement believers in their search for this ideal community was the Rev. Thomas Chalmers, the early nine-teenth-century Scots minister. His writings about his work in the parish of St John's Glasgow profoundly influenced nineeenth-century philanthropic reform, despite the relatively poor success rate with which historians have credited his contribution (Brown 1982; Cage and Checkland 1976; Checkland 1980; Hilton 1988). In the first volume of his *Polity of a Nation*, Chalmers described the means of 'assimilating a town to a country parish'. A minister, unable to 'bring the personal influence of his kind and Christian attentions to bear upon all families' as in the small country parish, should divide the densely populated city parish into 'small manageable districts', appoint friends to acquire an intimate knowledge of each one and to act as an intermediary between the inhabitants of the district and the minister. Such a system, popularised later by the Elberfeld scheme of poor relief administration in the Rhineland, might seem redolent of early nineteenth-century schemes of visiting the poor and of the 'managed' philanthropy of the Charity Organisation Society, whose methods and ideals have been seen (wrongly) as the antithesis of the settlement ideal (Hunter, 1912; Rose, 1981, 1986; Gilbert, 1966; Fraser, 1984). For a late nineteenth-century generation concerned with the contrast of *Gemeinschaft* and *Gesellschaft*, the settlement house seemed an ideal vehicle for realising the faith of Chalmers in converting the crowded, squalid and featureless inner city into active and coherent neighbourhoods. While Chalmers was not, to the modern mind, such an intellectually fashionable guru of the settlement movement as F. D. Maurice or John Ruskin, his *Christian and Civic Economy of Large Towns* had an honoured place in settlement house libraries. Jane Addams might rebuke the over-enthusiastic 'neighborhood' believer, Robert Woods, with the comment that she 'did not believe in geographical salvation', but belief in 'community' was an essential article of settlement faith.

Clubs and classes

If the settlement movement contained all the elements necessary to make it a secular faith well suited to the needs of the educated young in the late nineteenth and early twentieth-centuries, it also developed from its foundation many of the features (and weaknesses) of organised religion. To realise their faith in community revival, settlement workers developed a range of clubs and classes, camps and playschemes, mothers' meetings and infant welfare clinics, 'at homes', dances and dramatic societies. Like most churches and chapels, they became a focus for a variety of activities which gave them a general purpose rather than a specialist image within the increasingly professional world of twentieth-century social work. Children, married women and later the aged were their most numerous clients; adult males, except in the depths of the interwar depression, the least. Strenuous attempts were made to retain the support and interest of the adolescent, and youth work became a prominent feature of many settlement programmes. Their own young residents and workers entered with gusto into the collegiate activities of the settlement house. Manchester's Settlement Associates in the early 1900s argued questions of the day in their Toynbee and Fawcett Debating Clubs, rambled in the Derbyshire hills, put on Shakespearean plays, courted, married and supported progressive causes from women's suffrage to the abolition of the sweated trades. Leighton Hall, Stanton Coit's attempt to launch a neighbourhood guild in Kentish Town in 1892, foundered at an early stage. To judge from its journal, *The Moscheles Review*, its members appear to have been cheery young things, more interested in the tennis club, fancy dress balls and rather fatuous debates, than in serious social regeneration (Coit, 1891; Stocks, 1945).

By contrast perhaps with this hedonistic amateurism, settlement houses also experienced that trend in most new religions which leads from prophetic cult to professional institution. As the founding mothers and fathers died, Barnett in 1913, Addams in 1935, McDowell in 1936, Taylor in 1938 ('Sister Mary McDowell, divine St Jane, and now blessed Father Taylor, have all three crossed the Great Divide' wrote Raymond Robins in a letter of condolence to Taylor's son), they were succeeded, often not without internal disruption, by professionals rather than prophets. Settlement houses themselves, especially those with university connections, began to play an important role in the field training of those entering the new profession of social work. Settlements were also ideally placed to become observation platforms or laboratories for scientific social investigation, and as a result distanced themselves from the working-class neighbours that they were putting under the microscope.

'Who can doubt' wrote Arthur Foley Winnington-Ingram, head of the Oxford House Settlement and later Bishop of London, 'that working people are apt to look on the parson's work as a business as much as their own.' The same was true of the 'secular parsons' in the settlement house. No one could doubt the commitment to settlement ideals of later leaders like Hilda Cashmore and Gordon Kidd in Manchester, Helen Hall in New York City or Jimmy Mallon at Toynbee Hall. But between them and their neighbours on Every Street, Henry Street or the Commercial Road, there was always a gulf. 'Settlement ladies' is the term older inhabitants of Barton Hill and Ancoats persistently use of the female settlement workers they remember in the Bristol and the Manchester of the 1930s (Briggs and Macartney 1984; Hall 1971; Inglis 1963; Jennings 1971; Lubove, 1965; Stocks 1945; Winnington-Ingram, 1940).

It was not only in its personnel that the social settlement experienced some of the contradictions of older established creeds, but also in its fixed capital, its buildings. Despite the example set by Barnett of obtaining sufficient funding to place a purpose-built, pseudo-Oxbridge college in Whitechapel's Commercial Road, such largesse was not a requirement of settlement faith. Residence could be achieved merely by renting an apartment in a tenement block or a workman's cottage in a bye-law street. Activities, however, particularly those of club or meeting, required more spacious premises, hard to come by in an inner-city district without breaching the ideals of temperance or of non-sectarian activity by renting space in pub or chapel. With the failure of Coit's neighbourhood guild scheme for cells of settlement residents in each street or apartment block, settlements increasingly turned to the idea of larger premises to house both residents and club activities. Where no sufficiently generous benefactor could be found for a brand new building, as it was, not only for Toynbee, but for Passmore Edwards in 1897 and for Chicago Commons in 1901, then a larger, old house in a previously fashionable area proved an acceptable substitute. The former home of the Chicago merchant Charles P. Hull, at Polk and Halstead on the city's West Side, provided the beginnings for Hull House, which then expanded to cover several blocks by the 1930s. The Mosley family's Ancoats Hall was, once its sanitary arrangements had been improved, the base for Manchester University Settlement in 1895, although it was soon to move along Every Street and add the disused Round Chapel to its building stock. While such expansion might be seen as a mark of success, it added considerably to the financial strains on the settlement. Capital funding was not usually a problem. Wealthy benefactors could be found to provide the funds for a new building, or for an extension or refurbishment of the old, particularly if their name was to be carved over the door. Gymnasia were a particular favourite of wealthy American philanthropists.

Much more problematic was the day-to-day maintenance of such building stock, given harsh wear and tear, the heavy environmental pollution of most settlement neighbourhoods and, in the British case, the severe damage wrought by German bombs in the 1940s. Day-to-day finance was, and remains, a regular nightmare for settlement treasurers. A slender regular income was provided by the annual contributions of subscribers, fees paid by residents for board and lodging, and the small sums in pennies or cents paid by neighbours for membership of clubs and use of settlement facilities. The occasional small windfall might come from a bequest, a student rag, a jumble-sale, or grants from the public or private welfare sector in support of a specific social programme, but day-to-day financing was precarious. The state of the boiler or the roof bulked large in the minds of settlement directors, a situation all too familiar to parish clergymen. As costs rose and donations dwindled after 1945, many settlement houses had to be abandoned to join the Victorian chapels and churches whose empty shells littered the inner city. Residence as an item of settlement faith was diminishing rapidly by the 1960s, its demise due as much to financial strain as to a weakening of belief in its efficacy.

The social settlement story can therefore be told in terms of the rise of a new secular religion, assuaging guilt by living out a life of service on the streets of an inner-city community or neighbourhood – a religion perhaps weakened by its too rapid institutionalisation in the form of a professional clerisy and over-elaborate building. As with institutional Christianity itself, however, it is perhaps too early to declare the settlement ideal a corpse ready for historical dissection. Many of its institutions, though transformed into community, drop-in or social action centres, still confront the problems of homelessness, delinquency and drug addiction in the inner city. Toynbee Hall still stands, a place of regular social work and of occasional penance for politicians. Manchester's University Settlement has passed its centenary year, housed in a new building and tackling the old ills of East Manchester. The ideal of community is scarcely a redundant one in a late twentieth-century facing the collapse of both state regulated socialism and market regulated capitalism as panaceas for the sins of the world.

Bibliography

Addison, W. G. (1941) *John Richard Green.* London: SPCK.

Anon (1918) *Eighteen Years in the Central City Swarm.* London: Robert Browning Settlement.

Ashworth, M. (1891) *The Oxford House in Bethnal Green.* London: Oxford House.

Barnett, H. O. (1921) *Canon Barnett, His Life, Work and Friends.* London: John Murray.

Briggs, A. and Macartney, A. (1984) *Toynbee Hall: The First Hundred Years.* London: Routledge.

Brown, S. J. (1982) *Thomas Chalmers and the Godly Commonwealth in Scotland,* Oxford: Oxford University Press.

Bulmer, M. (1984) *The Chicago School of Sociology.* Chicago and London: University of Chicago Press.

Cage, R. and Checkland, E. O. A. (1976) 'Thomas Chalmers and Urban Poverty. The St John's Parish Experiment in Glasgow, 1810–1837.' *The Philosophical Journal* 13, Spring 1976, 37–56.

Checkland, O. (1980) *Philanthropy in Victorian Scotland: Social Welfare and the Voluntary Principle.* Edinburgh: John Donald.

Coit, S. (1891) *Neighbourhood Guilds. An instrument of social reform.* London: Swan Sonnenschein.

Crocker, R. H. (1992) *Social Work and the Social Order. The Settlement Movement in Two Industrial Cities, 1889–1930.* Urbana: University of Illinois.

Davis, A. (1967) *Spearheads for Reform. The Social Settlements and the Progressive Movement, 1890–1914.* New York: Oxford University Press.

Fraser, D. (1973) *The Evolution of the British Welfare State.* (Second edn. 1984) London: Macmillan.

Gilbert, B. B. (1966) *The Evolution of National Insurance in Great Britain. The Origins of The Welfare State.* London: Michael Joseph.

Hall, H. (1971) *Unfinished Business in Neighbourhood and Nation.* London: Macmillan.

Harris, J. (1993) *Private Lives, Public Spirit. A Social History of England 1870–1914.* Oxford: Oxford University Press.

Hilton, B. (1988) *The Age of Atonement.* Cambridge: Cambridge University Press.

Hunter, H. (1912) *Problems of Poverty. Selections from the Economic and Social Writings of Thomas Chalmers.* London: Thomas Nelson and Sons.

Inglis, K. S. (1963) *Churches and the Working Classes in Victorian England.* London: Routledge.

Jennings, H. (1971) *Sixty Years of Change – the University Settlement, Bristol 1911–1971.* Bristol: University Settlement Bristol Community Association.

Kadish, A. (1982) *The Oxford Economists in the Late 19th Century.* Oxford: Clarendon Press.

Kadish, A. (1986) *Apostle Arnold. The Life and Death of Arnold Toynbee 1852–1883.* Durham N. C.: Duke University Press.

Karger, H. J. (1987) *The Sentinels of Order: A Study of Social Control and the Minneapolis Settlement House Movement, 1915–1950.* Lanham, MD: University Press of America.

Kennedy, A.J. (1958) Unpublished letter to J. McDowell. Social Welfare History Archive, SW56, Box 36, University of Minnesota.

Lasch-Quinn, E. (1993) *Black Neighbors. Race and the Limits of Reform in the American Settlement House Movement, 1890–1945.* Chapel Hill: University of North Carolina.

Lissak, R. (1989) *Pluralism and Progressives: Hull House and the New Immigrants 1890–1919.* Chicago: University of Chicago.

Lubove, R. (1965) *The Professional Altruist: The Emergence of Social Work as a Career.* New York: Atheneum.

McDowell, M. (1928) 'How the living faith of one social worker grew'. *Survey Graphic* April 1, 1928.

Philpott, T. L. (1978) *The Slum and the Ghetto: Neighborhood Deterioration and Middle Class Reform, Chicago, 1880–1930.* New York: Oxford University Press.

Pimlott, J. A. R. (1935) *Toynbee Hall. Fifty Years of Social Progress.* London: J. M. Dent.

Robert Browning Settlement (1912) *Eighteen Years in the Central City Swarm.* London: Robert Browning Settlement.

Rodgers, J. (1931) *Mary Ward Settlement. A History 1891–1931.* London: Passmore Edwards Settlement.

Rose, M. E. (1981) 'The Crisis of Poor Relief in England, 1860–1890'. In W. J. Mommsen (ed.) *The Emergence of the Welfare State in Britain and Germany.* London: Croom Helm.

Rose, M. E. (1986) *The Relief of Poverty 1834–1914.* London: Macmillan.

Schults, R. L. (1972) *Crusader in Babylon: W.T. Stead and the Pall Mall Gazette.* Lincoln: University of Nebraska.

Stocks, M. (1945) *Fifty Years in Every Street. The Story of Manchester University Settlement.* Manchester: Manchester University Press.

Sutherland, J. (1990) *Mrs Humphry Ward. Eminent Victorian, Pre-Eminent Edwardian.* Oxford: Clarendon Press.

Taylor, G. (1928) 'Response to Jane Addams'. *The Chicago Theological Seminary Register* XVIII, 4 November 1928.

Taylor, G. (1930) *Pioneering on Social Frontiers.* Chicago: University of Chicago Press.

Toynbee, A. (1884) *Lectures on the Industrial Revolution of the 18th Century in England.* London: Rivingtons.

Trevelyan, J. (1923) *Life of Mrs Humphry Ward.* London: Methuen.

Ward, Mrs Humphrey (1918) *A Writer's Recollections* Vol. 2. New York and London: Collins.

Woods, R. A. and Kennedy, A. J. (1922) *The Settlement Horizon.* New York: Russell Sage Foundation. New edn. ed. Judith Trolander (1990), New Brunswick: Transaction Publishers.

Winnington-Ingram, A. F. (1940) *Fifty Years' Work in London 1889–1939.* London: Longmans Green.

2

American settlement houses

The first half century

Mina Carson

Like their English counterparts, the American settlements were called into existence to serve the needs of two populations: the urban poor and a particular group of middle-class college graduates. To this latter collection of motivated, skilled and restless women and men, the swelling of United States commerce and industry in the late nineteenth century, drawing millions of immigrants from Europe, triggered a response conditioned by their immersion in the social literature of English modernity and American liberal Protestantism. Their response to America's social and political growing pains was at once proprietary and inclusive. These young people had been brought up to have a stake in their society. As they became aware, through the ministry or religious mission, through college social work, through the reports of friends or their own travels, of the dimensions of human impoverishment, and what they saw as the spiritual and social grimness of life in the industrial slums, they framed an indictment of existing welfare institutions and ideologies that led them to discover an English innovation – the settlement house. Quickly – so quickly that settlements were founded within a few years in New York (Neighbourhood Guild 1886, College Settlement 1889) Chicago (Hull House 1889), and Boston (Andover

House 1891, Denison House 1892), often with only hearsay knowledge of each other – these young men and women adapted the English settlement to their perception of the social needs of immigrant residents of American cities. In doing this, they created for themselves new social roles predicated on their privileged social positions: their educated speech, family connections, mobility and ability to open doors was dedicated to facilitating for others the same access to the better things, the same sense of belonging, the same range of choices.

Motives of the founders

The earliest American settlement founders, and many of their peers and colleagues, were steeped in the language and literature of Victorian Britain. They read Carlyle, Ruskin and Dickens at home, in school or at college. They took in ideas of social organicism, the inter-dependence of all parts of society, that functioned in the nineteenth century as both a conservative and liberal ideology, both from these authors and from their own upbringings. They also learned the language of pathos and rage regarding the impersonal cruelties of laissez-faire or state-sponsored industrialisation from the writers of Britain, France and Germany, and later their own countrymen (Carson 1990, Davis 1967).

Religious ideas and feelings were part of virtually all the American settlement founders' motivations for pursuing social service (Crocker 1992). For some, religious issues ran through the fabric of their thinking as threads woven into the subculture they grew up in. This was true of Lillian Wald, for example, a Jewish woman whose religious traditions were never a salient part of her life, but for whom service to others and sensitivity to cultural difference were family and group values (Siegel 1983, Wald 1915). For others, religious vocation itself led to the settlement movement. Graham Taylor and Robert Woods offer variants of this narrative: Taylor a Congrega-tional minister who pioneered liberal social teachings in a seminary before he himself founded a Chicago settlement; and Woods a (lay) graduate of Andover, a liberal theological seminary that funded and gave its name to his Boston settlement house. And for still others, such as Stanton Coit, Vida Scudder, Jane Addams and Ellen Gates Starr, religion was a live entity, a set of issues in constant evolution, a way of creating identity for self and as part of a 'humanity', their obligations and relations to which all three were at pains to understand.

The liberal Protestantism that fuelled both Graham Taylor's and Robert Woods's ventures into social service was the most intellectually potent site for the fusion of social spirituality and social science in the United States in this period. Influenced by theologians such as the American Horace Bushnell and the Anglican clerics Frederick Denison Maurice and Frederick W. Robertson, post-Civil War liberal Protestants changed the spirit of their social teachings from an emphasis on restrictive personal and familial conduct dictates geared to personal salvation to a 'social gospel' based on an imitation of Christ. Compatible with a broad range of theological positions, this social gospel or social christianity was the American version of the English Christian Socialist movement of the 1880s, with its openness to social initiatives and panaceas of all kinds (Abell 1962, Ahlstrom 1972, May 1967). Both Taylor and Woods were well-read and well-travelled advocates of a gospel of philanthropic giving of the self, in the spirit of Christian mission but with a new and broader content. Graham Taylor became Bushnell's ideological heir at the seminary in Hartford, Connecticut, teaching courses in practical theology that pulled together the burgeoning literature of the social gospel. In the early 1890s Taylor moved from Hartford to Chicago, a noisy and noisome industrial city and one of the great American laboratories of social experimentation, and founded the Chicago Commons, a settlement affiliated to the Chicago Theological Seminary. Robert Woods chose Andover Theological Seminary in Masachusetts for his postgraduate study, compelled by a vocation within organised religion, but never able to discern a call to the ministry *per se*. When his mentor at Andover suggested that the young Woods head the seminary's proposed settlement, Woods plunged into preparations, including a six-month tour of England to observe the settlements and other social movements first hand (Taylor 1930, Tucker 1919, Wade 1964, Woods 1929).

There were differences between the motives of the men and women settlement founders that reflect experiential differences determined or shaped by gender. Most obviously, men could choose to be ministers while women could not. More generally, in American culture, with only a few exceptions, the expression of women's spirituality was limited to the domestic sphere: women were expected to serve as religious exemplars for their children and even their mates, but were not expected to take positions of spiritual leadership in the larger society. However, the sentimental conventions of middle-class culture did allow, and in fact demand, the leakage of women's religious and moral example into social life, and images of women 'ministering' to the material and spiritual needs of strangers as well as family filled popular literature and art. Women's mothering function was too culturally compelling, we may hypothesise, to allow its complete 'walling off' in some fictitious private realm. Equally speculative is the function of women's colleges, increasingly popular at the turn of the century, in providing the kind of monastic moratorium from home and family claims that had earlier been served for a few by Catholic sisterhoods. Freed from parental supervision, and not yet burdened with major household responsibilities, middle-class women college students of this period were liberated not only to spiritual musings but also to new real-life applications of their social and religious ideals (Rosenberg 1982, Solomon 1985).

For young women like Jane Addams and Ellen Gates Starr, college friends from middle-class backgrounds, religious ideas became part of their most intimate exchanges, in person and (fortunately for us) in their correspondence. Through their letters we can follow Starr's questing after a strong emotional and spiritual component to her religious practice, a questing that led her to Episcopalianism and ultimately to Catholicism, while Addams rather early left her abstruse theological musings for a more personally satisfying 'religion' of individual potency (amounting to Carlylean heroism) in human relations (Addams 1910, Davis 1973). Vida Scudder, one of the founders of the College Settlements Association and a major link between the colleges and the women's settlements, chose a path similar to Starr's in following an increasingly mystical 'High Church' religious bent in tandem with political and social radicalism. Scudder graduated from Smith College and then took her place as a 'special' student at Oxford, where she was of course barred by her sex from full participation in the formal life of the university. Like Woods and Addams, Scudder had direct contact with the social movements enlivening British politics and education at the end of the nineteenth century (Scudder 1937).

It may be argued that these, and a handful of others, were the exceptional individuals needed to spark a national movement: interested, articulate, visionary, uncomfortable. The literature of the American settlement movement also suggests that the influences affecting these young women and men impacted upon the lives of the hundreds of other participants in the first decade of the settlement movement. British and American social literature, religious ideals of service, a sense of adventure or 'out-of-placeness' in the 'normal' young adult pursuits, coupled with the young settlement movement's real continuity with previous social service alternatives, formed the mass of ideas, individual circumstances and social currents that brought young people into the settlements.

Settlement contributions, innovations and limitations

So what brought the neighbours into the settlements? What made the settlement houses attractive enough to draw in enough people, in many locations, to justify continued private funding of their programmes? The ideology of the American settlement movement as it was expounded in the early years both followed the British in stressing the mission of the settlements in melting away class distinctions in the industrial cities, and struck out on its own in tackling the specifically American issue of social service in neighbourhoods of multiple ethnicities and languages.

The reader will not be surprised to find historians have chosen varying emphases in explaining the persistence of the settlement houses. The issue turns mainly on how good a fit there was between the (imposed) programmes of the settlement houses and the (self-identified) needs of the settlement neighbours. Many historians, this writer included, have singled out Jane Addams as the American settlement leader with the most elaborated philosophy of liberal pluralism in the cultural 'absorption' of the immigrant population. As part of her conviction that Americans would be enriched by a genuinely reciprocal exchange with immigrant cultures within their borders, she founded the Hull House Labour Museum, whose centre-piece was a living exhibit of seven traditional modes of spinning and weaving, arranged in a supposedly chronological sequence culminating in contemporary factory processes. Her plan included not only demonstrating the continuity and differences in these processes for the benefit of visitors, but also giving meaningful employment to craftsmen and -women, and allowing them, and by extension their peers, to reconnect with the second generation of immigrants, who were beginning to scorn the ways of their parents (Addams 1910).

Lissak (1989) argues that Hull House in fact missed the point when it came to honouring the cultures of the immigrants. The Labour Museum, viewed in the context of the other class and club programmes of the settlement over several decades, was just part of a larger assimilatory vision promulgated by the settlement. Rather than fostering a genuine cultural and linguistic pluralism in Chicago, the settlement philosophy and policies encouraged assimilation in the tacit belief that superior Anglo-American cultural practices would eventually absorb – and incidentally, be enriched by – less sound 'New Immigrant' cultures. Perhaps more importantly, and as a demonstration of this argument, Lissak points out the differential attendance of various immigrant subgroups at Hull House activities. She analyses the relationship between the East European Jewish community and Hull House, for example. When an 'able second-generation Americanised leadership' emerged in this Jewish community, this group established separate gathering places for Jewish clubs and Jewish youth. They perceived Hull House as condescendingly inclined to put German Jews in charge of any Jewish-oriented activities instead of respecting the abilities of the quite different Eastern European Jewish immigrants to manage their own political and social affairs.

Exposing the subtle but important differences between Americanisation and Liberal Progressive philosophies of immigrant blending, Lissak points out that while Americanisers thought of Anglo-based American culture as complete, the Liberal Progressives pictured American culture as a still-evolving blend of vital classical and modern cultures: Greek, Roman and Egyptian as well as English. This philosophy made room for the incorporation of the 'best' elements of more recent additions to American life; however, as Lissak argues, while this philosophy included respect for the right and ability of any individual from any culture to make the most of him- or herself, it did not offer the same 'equality of opportunity' to entire cultures, and this failure put it 'in conflict with the Hull House democratic principles' indeed 'Hull House's concern became the cultural 'elevation' of newcomers, rather than the selection and culti-vation of immigrant cultural contributions in their own right' (Lissak 1989 pp.90–91).

Despite their liberal departure from prevailing patronising and discriminatory views of immigrants' assimilation into American society, even the most 'democratic' settlers probably failed to hold or convey the institutional view that immigrant languages and social practices were something other than remnants to shed at the first opportunity. Starker, even, were the settlement workers' attitudes and actions toward African Americans. Most historians would agree with Lasch-Quinn's observation that the settlements succumbed in important ways, in both theory and action, to the prevalent racism of the progressive era, and thus missed opportunities to interact in helpful ways with black communities and to critique, through action, the dominant racial views of their day. She points out that the settlement theorists, even the most liberal and race-conscious, distinguished between immigrants and African Americans to the detriment of the latter, characterising blacks collectively as morally inferior to other Americans, and less competent in all realms of life. Thus calls for the 'advancement of the race' were generally tempered or moderated by the explicit or implied belief that blacks were made of different stuff inside as well as outside. Settlement houses into the 1940s behaved institutionally in ways that affirmed general American practices of racial separation and discrimination, either ignoring growing colonies of African Americans in their neighbourhoods, or helping black or white leaders to establish separate programmes or houses for blacks in the belief that they had special needs and that their presence in existing settlement programmes simply would not be tolerated by the white clientele (Lasch-Quinn 1993).

While most of the early American settlements did not move into their neighbourhoods with the primary expressed intention of serving local children, not surprisingly that is what they did most successfully and consistently over the first 100 years. Mothers of infants and younger children quickly helped the settlement workers identify an area in which they could offer needed support and services. One of the first visitors to Hull House was a woman wanting them to watch her baby while she moved to a new home; soon Starr and Addams found themselves assisting at births (Addams 1910). The main impetus behind the founding of the Henry Street Settlement in Manhattan was Lillian Wald's desire to extend nursing services to the indigent population of the Lower East Side, services that at Henry Street and elsewhere often had at their core the urgent medical needs of women and children in childbirth, infancy and early childhood (Wald 1915, Duffus 1938). From survival to development was a direct link for the settlement workers in these decades of new theorising about the educational needs of the child. Well Baby clinics and milk stations were soon joined by childcare centres and kindergartens in the settlements. Besides filling local needs, these programmes offered structured opportunities for young residents and volunteers, particularly the women.

Older children stormed or were wooed into the settlements, depending on the chemistry between neighbourhood and house residents. The neighbourhoods of the early settlements held few charms for children, and the industrial culture they inhabited militated against a working-class family life that could function in either 'Old World' (authoritarian, corporate) or 'New World' (nurturing, companionate) ways. Few provisions for adequate childcare in families of working parents could reasonably be made. Children not in school spent their days in locked tenements or on the streets. The fortunate ones might be watched by grandparents or adult neighbours; the less fortunate, by older siblings or each other. Young children were constantly at risk from runaway horses, pedlars' carts, trolley cars, rickety fire escapes and unbarred upstairs windows, toxic water supplies, inadequate nutrition and contagious diseases against which there was little prophylaxis or medical attention available. Not surprisingly, children flocked to the settlements' playgrounds, playgroups, after-school clubs and summer camps. As the settlements' programmes became more elaborate, the better-endowed houses offered music lessons and dramatic activities, and, even more attractive to most, gymnasia with organised sports programmes, and swimming pools. As children found their ways to these interesting activities, many of their parents overcame whatever distrust of these do-gooders they might have to take comfort in knowing their kids had somewhere to go after school, and a relatively safe place to meet their playmates (Addams 1910, College Settlements Association 1901, Riis 1901, Wald 1915).

The settlement workers as Progressives

One of the shared characteristics of the first generation of settlement leaders was a propensity to social analysis that transcended the immediate task. The settlers' experiences with children brought home, so to speak, some of the fault lines in the social structure of industrial cities. Many school-aged children were not in school, not because they were lounging on tenement stoops, but because they were working: as newsboys, pedlars, shop assistants, pieceworkers, and in certain regions, as breaker boys in the mines or 'hands' in the textile mills. Concern for the health and futures of children led the settlements to some of their earliest and most enduring political involvements. Several settlements, including Hull House in Chicago, the University Settlement and the Friendly Aid House in New York, and Lincoln House in Boston, attempted sometimes disastrous leaps into urban electoral politics, often with the result that they made more enemies than friends in high places. A more productive kind of involvement was that of Robert Woods of Andover (later South End) House in Boston, who accepted appointment to several city commissions concerned with public health and recreation. Making friendly connections with progressive politicians paved the way for many more such appointments for settlement workers, particularly those who understood discretion as the better part of political valour and who were willing to do the public's work for no compensation – both of which qualifications were family legacies for many of the settlement workers (Carson 1990, Davis 1967).

As the Progressive movement heated up at state and then national levels, the settlement leaders became players in lobbying for public health and recreation facilities, child labour laws, and protective legislation for female workers (an issue of some contentiousness both then and later, for different reasons). The social scientific orientation of the settlement philosophy, in which the Americans followed the British and may actually have gone one better, created a fine cradle for the development of individual expertise in social problems. Some settlement workers were pioneers in the new careers of independent consultant and lobbyist for some special cause. Hull House harboured a whole nest of these new 'professionals'. Florence Kelley devoted years of travel and research to labour and immigration issues. Dr Alice Hamilton turned her medical background to becoming the nation's leading consultant in industrial toxicology. Julia Lathrop was the first head of the Federal Children's Bureau, established in 1912 (Addams 1935, Bryan and Davis 1990, Hamilton 1943, Sklar 1985, 1995).

Addams herself became a social philosopher respected and consulted by intellectuals of the rank of John Dewey and William James (Deegan 1988, Feffer 1993). Her own ventures into politics culminated (though did not end) in the remarkable 1912 presidential election, when Theodore Roosevelt stood on a Progressive platform against Wilson the Democrat and Taft the Republican. Though only Roosevelt was a Progressive in label, all three were progressives in action and intent. Addams was one of Roosevelt's nominators at the 'Bull Moose' convention of 1912, almost a decade before the constitution removed state bars to female suffrage. Later vilified as a pacifist who resisted the war fever of 1917–18, Addams never entirely lost her public lustre, and was sufficiently resuscitated to receive the Nobel Peace Prize in 1931 (Davis 1973).

Addams's career offers in fact a nice entree to the issue of the kind or kinds of politics the settlement workers practised. Addams characteristically acted as a go-between, labouring often vainly to moderate between the radical and the moderate wings of the settlement leadership in favour of what she felt was a larger vision of human well-being. In her view, the radicals not only risked the financial support of well-to-do donors but, more importantly, emphasised division at the expense of a vision of unity. At the same time she feared the tendency of some of the more moderate leaders to focus parochially on settlement structure and programme at the risk of the earlier humanitarian and generalist thrust of the movement.

There was indeed a small but important segment of the Progressive era settlement personnel, among them Ellen Gates Starr, Vida Scudder, and Helena Dudley (of Boston's Denison House) who may fairly be called radical, with socialist or pacifist ideals. For these and some less prominent settlement workers, exposure to the troubles and living conditions of the settlement neighbours deepened their political indignation and the radicalism of their social analysis. To these settlement workers democracy and equality meant not just fellow feeling with individuals in dire straits, but identification with groups of oppressed people and a class analysis of their persistent oppression. For sound historical reasons, these individuals were by and large most comfortable with settlement work in its early years.

The 1890s in the United States, like the 1880s in Britain, saw a real fluidity and openness in rhetoric about social ideas. Along with repressive concerns about race and immigrant inferiorities came creative engagement with some of the most intriguing radical ideologies of Western thought, particularly socialism and anarchism. The early settlements not infrequently hosted speeches and meetings devoted to expounding the reform schemes and philosophies of the time – meetings in which both settlement workers and local people participated. Writers and thinkers like John Dewey, Henry Demarest Lloyd and Upton Sinclair visited the settlement residents, as did foreign celebrities like the Fabians Beatrice and Sidney Webb and the Russian revolutionaries Peter Kropotkin and Catherine Breshkovsky (as the Americans rendered her name).

Not long after the turn of the century, however, as the channels of American progressivism flowed deeper and more predictably in moderate and managerial solutions to social problems, and the world-wide 'threat' of anarchism seemed not inconsiderable with a rash of assassinations, including their own President McKinley, Americans' tolerance of radical thought began to narrow. Settlement leaders in all the primary settlement cities began capitalising on their successes (naturally), elaborating their own programmes, joining reformers city-wide to lobby for amenities, and forming alliances with mainstream progressive politicians. Rather than linger defiantly on the outskirts of accepted urban institutions, the settlements stepped inside.

Settlement work and social work

One major trend that helped institutionalise the settlements in their particular form was the movement's central role in the professionalisation of social work. This occurred in several ways simultaneously. One was the involvement of settlement personnel in the first formal training courses for social workers, in particular the New York Charity Organisation Society's summer courses in philanthropy (after 1898); the Boston School for Social Workers (founded in 1904); and the Chicago Institute of Social Science and Arts, which began under the direction of Graham Taylor and evolved into the University of Chicago's Graduate School of Social Service Administration. These programmes used speakers and instructors from the settlements, placed settlement leaders in board or director positions, and sent students into the settlements as at least one option for direct social service experience (Lubove 1965, Richmond 1897, Trolander 1987, Woods 1923).

The settlements' interest in training programmes for social workers grew from their own burgeoning need for trained staff as certain programmes expanded. Youth workers and programme administrators were the most commonly needed. There were niches for individuals with experience in other settlement houses or similar philanthropies or organisations, and who knew the language and 'culture' of the settlements. Some began fashioning careers of this type even before training was widely available. Although settlements continued to draw heavily from nearby colleges and universities for volunteers and short-term staff, long-term administration was increasingly offered by these new quasi-professionals.

Another way in which the settlements contributed to the professionalisation of social work was through heavy participation in the writing and editorial direction of the magazines *Charities, Charities Review* and *The Commons*, which first merged and then mutated in 1909 into *The Survey*, a magazine offering exposes and analysis of United States social welfare issues, covering topics from immigration and ethnic rivalries to labour conditions, to racial issues, to various reform movements and leaders (Devine 1939, Chambers 1971). From the sweep of concerns addressed by *The Survey* and its predecessors we may discern several philosophical biases that came to characterise a significant sector of settlement opinion. One was symbolised by *The Survey* itself, with the bold photographs, the attractive presentation of difficult issues that claimed attention alongside any other periodical of the day. Social welfare issues deserved the attention of anyone who might pick up a compelling magazine. Hand-in-hand with this insistent leap into modern publicity came a bent or bias toward professionalism and 'efficiency'. Voluntarism of the nineteenth-century flavour was no longer sufficient or even preferable. Edward Devine, editor of *Charities* and *The Commons* in the era of its transformation to *The Survey*, presented this new view of social service by publishing excerpts from the economist Simon Patten's *The New Basis of Civilisation* between 1907 and 1909. Relax, Patten seemed to argue: in an era of abundance like the current one, the puritanical regimentation of leisure and the marshalling of good works to be brought to bear upon deprived people were far less effective than the provision of economic opportunities – opportunities which would motivate workers to discipline themselves in the work setting in order to get ahead. Better work habits would mean more money for fun, which in turn would evolve from primitive to more advanced recreation as people naturally discovered the 'higher pleasures' of music and art (Patten 1968, Fox 1967).

Patten's ideas embodied a new liberal challenge to the original settlement idea. As he criticised charity organisation societies, his words could be read to apply as well to the settlers: 'Mere goodness', he argued provocatively, 'must be replaced by efficiency and the paid trained agent must replace the voluntary visitor who satisfies her curiosity at the expense of those she meets, and in the end loses her faith in humanity or turns socialist' (Patten 1908, p.1045). Patten's faith in the cultural beneficence of a thriving capitalist economy not only carried an odd indictment of the settlements' philosophy of social reform through human contact – that it would promote (destructive) radicalism or pessimism among middle-class volunteers – but also came down squarely for the formal elaboration of settlement programmes as a modern and constructive substitute for the 'neighbours among neighbours' approach of the early settlements. In addition, Patten's *laissez-faire* attitude toward working-class recreation – that movies and dance halls would give way in time to galleries and symphonies – flew in the face of some of the repressive and controlling efforts of community reformers and settlement workers fearful of the maleficent effects of new forms of entertainment on urban youth. 'Progressive reform', Judith Trolander trenchantly observes, 'had its moralistic overtones', and a number of settlement leaders participated in campaigns to regulate or eliminate a mixed bag of 'evils' such as prostitution, movie theatres, dance halls and saloons (Trolander 1987, p.17, Addams 1909, Davis 1915, Nasaw 1985).

Changes and challenges 1914–1940

Criticism from both right and left – far left to barely left – fertilised discussion among settlement leaders about their continuing mission as times changed and city residents faced the challenges of large historical events: World War I and the Great Depression. The free-flowing discussion of radical ideas that tapered off in the height of the Progressive years was squeezed to nothing by American entry into the war and postwar repressive movements against organised labour, immigrants, African Americans, and the sparse remnants of articulate protest that survived wartime repression, prosecution or deportation.

The settlements settled down after the war to discussions of programme and funding. No rest for the weary: the settlers found themselves caught in postwar dislocations that gave way to apparent public complacency and unwillingness to fund facilities like the settlements. The brave new alternatives to the patchwork of resources available before the war were corporate sponsorship and Community Chest support. Interestingly, national settlement leaders were almost united in their suspicion of and opposition to settlement dependence on the new Community Chest movement. After several years of monitoring the Chest nation-wide, Charles Cooper, a Pittsburgh leader and hardly a rabble-rouser, wrote privately in 1928:

> The urge of the Chest movement is to conformity and standardisation, and the settlement movement stands in the way of this. We must have some general free agencies in social work, and I think the lot has fallen to the Settlement movement, but it will mean

trouble with the Chest group. (Carson 1990, quote p.183, Trolander 1975)

Just as Community Chest boards tended to dole out funds based on their preferences and expectations of social work in their communities, so even more pointedly particular corporations offered support to settlements doing the kind of work that furthered their own corporate goals. Among the examples Ruth Crocker offers is Neighbourhood House in Gary, Indiana, one-third of whose budget in 1924 was met by the Illinois Steel Company. Interestingly, this was at a time when European immigration had fallen away, and US black and Mexican migration into the city was on the rise. As the settlement made the momentous decision to serve these new populations, 'Americanisation' of immigrant homes became the primary focus of the settlement's activities. While Neighbourhood House programmes offered some practical advantages to immigrant women, like sewing classes in which they could make new clothes inexpensively. These programmes also purposely 'corrected' immigrant women's child-rearing and nurturing practices and put forth an ideal of housebound wives and mothers that flew in the face of the realities of working-class family finances, which often required the woman to go out to work or take in boarders. The steel executives that underwrote so much of the settlement budget, like US Steel in its support of the Gary Alerding Settlement, clearly believed they got good value for their money in promoting a contented and tractable labour force through improving home life and teaching 'American' values (Crocker 1992).

Other settlements also discovered that funding was easier to secure for discrete programmes that appealed to the ideals of the donors, rather than visions of the settlements as reform beacons in an urban landscape. Paradoxically, while family-oriented philosophies ruled settlement rhetoric, age- and sex-segregated activities often dominated settlement programming. Because girls' and boys' needs and development were seen as dramatically different, girls' and boys' programming were planned distinctly. This was most obvious in athletic activities, in which boys were taught to be competitive, while girls were encouraged not to be. Child guidance programmes reflecting a quasi-psychiatric as well as developmental approach to children's problems found some of their first host institutions in the settlement houses in the teens and 1920s; more generally, a number of settlement leaders touted the 'psychological' approach to youth work (Horn 1984, Reid 1981, Taft 1922). In some settlements, the 'headline' programmes for youth were in the arts. Albert Kennedy, a Boston leader who became prominent in the National Federation of Settlements (founded in 1911), became the most important advocate of arts programmes as the centrepiece of settlement contributions to their cities. In 1917 Kennedy enlisted personnel of Boston's Museum of Fine Arts to help him establish an independent Children's Art Centre in the South End. In its heyday, the art centre served both as a gallery for works of art of special interest to children, and a creative studio for their own artistic activity (Boer 1966, Carson 1990).

Clubs, games, sports, swimming, arts and crafts, cooking, music: successful settlements offered a palette of after-school and evening activities for youth that stabilised their position in their neighbourhoods even as populations shifted. The National Federation of Settlements recognised the coming economic crisis even before its full force hit, with a study of unemployment in 1928 subsequently used by Congress in researching the extent of depression hardships (Hall 1971, Trolander 1975). The terrible decade of the 1930s brought the settlements new workers, in Works Progress Administration assignments, and new internal struggles, in terms of decisions regarding how to respond to some of the local initiatives, including radical groups and unionisation campaigns, springing up to deal with local suffering. The 1930s also brought American settlements a renewed opportunity to open their doors and their efforts to black Americans, which by and large (that is, with some notable exceptions) they failed to do (Trolander 1975).

In their first half-century the American settlement houses steered a middle way through marginalized radicalism and ineffectual conformity to chart a unique, recognisable place for themselves in the landscape of American social welfare institutions and practices. The settlements certainly 'failed' in their first articulated ambition, to eliminate class barriers by fostering neighbourly understanding and community. In United States history, war and prosperity have done more than any combination of deliberate policy initiatives, public or private, to 'eliminate' or alter class divisions. On the other hand, they certainly did provide a place where young middle-class adults could gain a first-hand exposure to the roiling urban neighbourhoods of their period. A number of humane Progressive era reforms – nurseries, kindergartens and playgrounds, child labour laws, and extended school-leaving ages, to name a few – were fertilised in the settlement houses. And in their true liberal vision, their first leaders' hope of extending the 'higher things' of life to the largest number of people – the great American dream of individual opportunity set in Victorian language and then carried into the twentieth century – the settlements may claim some measure of success.

Bibliography

Abell, A. I. (1962) *The Urban Impact on American Protestantism*. Hamden, Connecticut. Archon.

Addams, J. (1909) *The Spirit of Youth and the City Streets*. New York: Macmillan.

Addams, J. (1910) *Twenty Years at Hull House, with Autobiographical Notes*. New York: Macmillan.

Addams, J. (1935) *My Friend Julia Lathrop*. New York: Macmillan.

Ahlstrom, S. E. (1972) *A Religious History of the American People*. New Haven: Yale University Press.

Boer, A. (1966) *The Development of USES. A Chronology of the United South End Settlements 1891–1966*. Boston: United South End Settlements.

Bryan, M. L. M. and Davis, A. F. (eds) (1990) *100 Years at Hull House*. Bloomington: Indiana University Press.

Carson, M. (1990) *Settlement Folk. Social Thought and the American Settlement Movement, 1885–1930*. Chicago: The University of Chicago Press.

Chambers, C. (1971) *Paul U. Kellogg and the Survey: Voices for Social Welfare and Social Justice*. Minneapolis: University of Minnesota Press.

College Settlements Association (1901) *First Annual Report of the College Settlements Association, 1901*.

Crocker, R. (1992) *Social Work and Social Order: The Settlement Movement in Two Industrial Cities, 1889–1930*. Urbana and Chicago: University of Illinois Press.

Davis, A. F. (1967) *Spearheads for Reform: The Social Settlements and the Progressive Movement 1890–1914.* New York: Oxford University Press.

Davis, A. F. (1973) *American Heroine: The Life and Legend of Jane Addams.* New York. Oxford University Press.

Davis, P. (1915) *Street-land: Its Little People and Big Problems.* Boston: Small, Maynard.

Deegan, M. J. (1988) *Jane Addams and the Men of the Chicago School, 1892–1918.* New Brunswick, New Jersey: Transaction Publishers.

Devine, E. T. (1939) *When Social Work Was Young.* New York: Houghton Neighbour.

Duffus, R. L. (1938) *Lillian Wald: Neighbour and Crusader.* New York: Macmillan.

Feffer, A. (1993) *The Chicago Pragmatists and American Progressivism.* Ithaca: Cornell University Press.

Fox, D. M. (1967) *The Discovery of Abundance: Simon N. Patten and the Transformation of Social Theory.* Ithaca: Cornell University Press.

Hall, H. (1971) *Unfinished Business in Neighbourhood and Nation.* New York. Macmillan.

Hamilton, A. (1943) *Exploring the Dangerous Trades: The Autobiography of Alice Hamilton, MD.* Boston: Little, Brown.

Horn, M. (1984) 'The moral message of child guidance, 1925–1945.' *Journal of Social History* 18, Fall, 25–36.

Lasch-Quinn, E. (1993) *Black Neighbours: Race and the Limits of Reform in the American Settlement House Movement 1890–1945.* Chapel Hill: The University of North Carolina Press.

Lissak, R. S. (1989) *Pluralism and Progressives: Hull House and the New Immigrants, 1890–1917.* Chicago: The University of Chicago Press.

Lubove, R. (1965) *The Professional Altruist: The Emergence of Social Work as a Career.* Cambridge: Harvard University Press.

May, H. F. (1967) *Protestant Churches and Industrial America.* New York: Harper Torchbooks.

Nasaw, D. (1985) *Children of the City: At Work and at Play.* New York. Oxford University Press.

Patten, S. N. (1908) 'Who is the good neighbour?' *Charities and The Commons,* 19, 29 February, 1045.

Patten, S. N. (1968) *The New Basis of Civilisation.* Cambridge: Belknap Press of Harvard University Press.

Reid, K.E. (1981) *From Character Building to Social Treatment: The History of the Use of Groups in Social Work.* Westport, Connecticut: Greenwood Press.

Richmond, M. (1897) 'The need of a training school in applied philanthropy.' *Proceedings of the National Society of Charities and Corrections,* 181–186.

Riis, J. (1901) *The Making of an American.* New York: Macmillan.

Rosenberg, R. (1982) *Beyond Separate Spheres: Intellectual Roots of Modern Feminism.* New Haven: Yale University Press.

Scudder, V. (1937) *On Journey.* New York: E. P. Dutton.

Siegel, B. (1983) *Lillian Wald of Henry Street.* New York. Macmillan.

Sklar, K. K. (1985) 'Hull House in the 1890s: A community of women.' *Signs* 10, 658–77.

Sklar, K. K. (1995) *Florence Kelley and the Nation's Work: The Rise of Women's Political Culture, 1830–1900.* New Haven: Yale University Press.

Solomon, B. M. (1985) *In the Company of Educated Women: A History of Women and Higher Education.* New Haven: Yale University Press.

Taft, J. (1922) 'The social worker's opportunity.' *Proceedings of the National Conference of Social Work,* 371–75.

Taylor, G. (1930) *Pioneering on Social Frontiers.* Chicago: University of Chicago Press.

Trolander, J. A. (1975) *Settlement Houses and the Great Depression.* Detroit: Wayne State University Press.

Trolander, J. A. (1987) *Professionalism and Social Change: From the Settlement House Movement to Neighbourhood Centres, 1886 to the Present.* New York: Columbia University Press.

Tucker, W. J. (1919) *My Generation: An Autobiographical Interpretation.* Boston: Houghton Neighbour.

Wade, L. C. (1964) *Graham Taylor: Pioneer for Social Justice.* Chicago: University of Chicago Press.

Wald, L. (1915) *The House on Henry Street.* New York: H. Holt.

Woods, E. H. (1929) *Robert Woods: Champion of Democracy.* Boston: Houghton Neighbour.

Woods, R. (1923) *The Neighbourhood in Nation-building.* Boston: Houghton Neighbour.

3

Development of the English settlement movement

John Matthews and James Kimmis

In 1991 one of us was invited to speak at the first voluntary sector conference to be held in Eastern Hungary since the end of Communist rule. It took place in the university town of Debrecen, and he was given the chance to visit local community centres. As he walked into the Czapokert Centre it felt as if he was in a settlement house and said as much to the warden. The warden took his hand and rushed him upstairs to her office, where she removed a book from the shelf. The text was entirely in Hungarian except for the words 'Toynbee Hall 1884'. The centre, it emerged, had been founded as a settlement in 1918 and had served that community through all the subsequent changes of regime. The link between 'Toynbee Hall 1884' and Czapokert Community Centre is the theme of this chapter.

No movement that has survived for over 100 years and spread so widely remains unchanged by factors of time or culture. But there are some elements that have transferred and remain recognisable wherever settlement houses are encountered. First, from the outset, those who lived in settlements were encouraged to work with, not for, local people. There was always direct service from one to the other in the form of education, advice and personal development. However, the core principle was that people worked together across social divisions for the improvement of their neighbourhood. Today we call this 'community development'. It is no accident therefore that in 1998 Czapokert Centre came to the International Federation of Settlements (IFS) Eurogroup with a proposal for a trans-national project on neighbourhood regeneration. This was immediately recognisable to all the delegates present as being within the settlement tradition.

Second, settlement houses were and remain more than community centres. They are places where people come together to bring about social change. Much of the work that goes on in them has been and is still about making sure people have skills to lead a more full and independent life. Early settlement houses were therefore drawn into work on sanitation, schools and labour relations, as well as adult education and youth clubs. The number of international social movements that have grown from the settlements is testimony to this drive for social change. For example, at present in Luthuania centres founded and helped by the international settlement movement are in the forefront of initiating community work training and standards. This is an entirely new development. Elsewhere action to relieve direct poverty has led to the development of social policy initiatives and campaigns designed to tackle the causes of poverty as much as to relieve it. It is an approach which is truly in the tradition established by the Barnetts all those years ago.

The first generation

Samuel Barnett once challenged students at Oxford with these words:

> Do you realise that all our social system is based on the tacit assumption that there is a leisured class in every locality who will see that the laws are carried out and generally keep social life going? Do you realise that there is no such class in London where it is most wanted? Come and be that class not in a patronising spirit but in a spirit of neighbourliness. You will find that there is more for you to learn than to teach. (Ashworth 1984, p.7)

Toynbee was built on the model of a residential university college with rooms for students, a dining hall, library and meeting room.

Students were offered community life and in return expected to engage with local people in a range of activities. Perhaps the nearest contemporary equivalent to this model of working is Voluntary Service Overseas (VSO), where those who are privileged in education and skills go to work in economically poorer areas. Subsequent experience shows Barnett to have been right – most students gain more than they give. One commentator, writing of the first generation, said:

> The importance of the settlement lies largely in the educational influence which it exercises on the Residents, and which in many cases has given the direction to their whole life. But even where the later calling has no direct relation to settlement work, the teachings of Toynbee Hall are not forgotten; in no-one who has lived there does the social conscience again go to sleep. From this point of view it is interesting to follow the career of the residents. There are three Members of Parliament, one of whom is Parliamentary Secretary to the Prime Minister, Mr Asquith, who himself takes a keen interest in Toynbee Hall. (Picht 1914, pp.31–32)

The diversity of activities undertaken in the early years was impressive. Children's holidays in the countryside, art exhibitions, literary and dramatic societies, clubs for young women and men all formed part of the staple diet. Alongside the relief of poverty and the advancement of social policy, personal development was one of the aims of this work. Some settlements developed specialisms, for example, the Albany in South London was home to a School of Domestic Economy covering such subjects as cookery, dressmaking and hygiene. Birmingham Settlement was one of a number founded by and for women; its activities included health care, education and play provision for children with disabilities, as well as a Provident Society savings scheme.

Of those opened before the First World War in the UK, 25 were for women residents, 11 for men and the remaining 10 were mixed. Many were established by Christian people and organisations. It is important to distinguish between settlements and missions. An example of a mission is Charterhouse-in-Southwark, founded with strong support from the public school of the same name. Until the 1960s the work was led by Christian priests and lay people and based at St Hugh's Church. For many years attendance at church was a precondition of membership of the mission's clubs and involvement in their activities. An unpublished history by Shirley Corke confirms that the fundamental purpose of the mission was conversion. By contrast Cambridge House in Camberwell was deliberately founded and operated in a way which distinguished it from the nearby University Mission. Another, Mansfield House in East London, founded by Mansfield Theological College in Oxford, combined features of both mission and settlement, for it was part established to give ordinands experience of working in deprived areas. However, theologically it came from a non-conformist tradition which held social justice to be a prerequisite for the creation of the Kingdom of God on earth.

Those foundations that came from the English public schools sought to forge friendships across social classes. Both Charterhouse-in-Southwark and St Hilda's East, founded by Cheltenham Ladies' College, set out to build bridges between young people through summer camps and exchange visits. It is doubtful if these were ever successful. A history of one East London family notes how two of the sons who were involved in a Boys' Club run by Oxford House felt this was their last chance; the two Sanders boys are quite clear: 'Of course not. They were a different class altogether. There were a few friendships but I never had any that lasted and don't know anybody who did' (Sanders 1989 p.154). However, if these organisations failed in this aim the same writers hold that their brother George's move into criminal activity was a by-product of his lack of involvement in the Boys' Club.

It is simplistic to regard early settlement houses as merely examples of Victorian philanthropy which allowed the wealthy to 'do good to the poor' – not least because no single founding model applies to all. They were certainly products of their time, yet to dismiss them as outdated and irrelevant is to miss the fundamental social purpose underpinning their work. For settlements were founded to promote social change, and the problems they sought to alleviate and overcome remain with us, albeit sometimes in new forms. As an early document explained, they were created

> ...to provide education and the means of recreation and enjoyment for the people of the poorest districts of London and other great cities; to inquire into the conditions of the poor and to consider and advance plans calculated to promote their welfare. (Quoted by Briggs and Macartney 1984, p.9)

An example of how the settlements exploited the talents of members to serve the community was the decision by Mansfield House to launch a free legal advice scheme. It established the Poor Man's Lawyer scheme in 1891, and Toynbee Hall soon followed. These were the forerunners of agencies such as the Citizen's Advice Bureaux (CAB), law and welfare advice centres which became a crucial point of access to the law for deprived communities.

Stead of Browning Settlement in South London provided much of the early evidence of the need for the old age pension and campaigned vigorously for it until its introduction in 1909. The Women's Settlement founded in 1899 worked with the University of London School of Economics to establish social work training for young women and provided both supervisors and lecturers for the programme. Cecile Matheson, warden from 1908 to 1916, researched social work training in Britain, Holland, Germany and the United States and pioneered a practice-based model which was subsequently adopted in Britain.

From the outset social policy reform and social action were among the key objectives of the settlement movement. Residents acted as managers of elementary schools, sanitary inspectors and members of various committees of enquiry set up to influence welfare policy. They also endeavoured to foster social harmony. This resulted in, for example, Toynbee Hall actively mediating in the 1889 dockers' strike and the busmen's strike two years later. Personal improvement was never the sole or even the most important aspect of the work. Rather the purpose was change – improving the conditions of neighbourhoods and learning from those neighbourhoods what needed to be achieved nationally.

Federation and association

By 1900 there were 36 settlements in Britain. The first *Handbook of Settlements in Great Britain* was published in 1922 and lists over 60 of which more than 20 are currently active. Initially most were linked to the Oxbridge public school network and the idea spread largely through personal knowledge and inspiration. The civic universities were not far behind in establishing their own settlements, but the model was different. These were based in poorer areas of the same city as the university itself and were secular from the start: Manchester Settlement led the way, being founded in 1895, Liverpool followed in 1898 and Birmingham in 1899. Overall a general impression gained from perusing the early minutes of English settlements is that their relationship to each other was that of a circle of friends with many wardens, linked via involvement in shared sporting, social and religious activities.

The First World War had a profound impact on the settlement movement. It seemed to generate a need to associate in a more formal way, perhaps reflecting a common dynamic within social movements, which often change direction and form when pioneers retire. It is possibly no accident that both the British Association of Residential Settlements (BARS) and the IFS were founded in 1920 and 1922 respectively. In England the residential and educational settlements formed separate associations although they kept in close contact, and the 1922 and 1928 Handbooks list the members of both. Residential settlements maintained the core concept of a community of people living together and committed to contributing to neighbourhood social action. Educational settlements, however, were part of the adult education movement and their focus was on providing a venue for courses, programmes and lectures for those who had left school. Eventually the national association changed its name to reflect shifting alliances. BARS became the British Association of Settlements (BAS) in 1967, at which time it also made an overture, which was rebuffed, to the Educational Centres Association for a closer working relationship. The first use of the term Social Action Centre is minuted by the executive committee in 1972. This reflected the number of newer multipurpose and resource centres being established at this period. Eventually BAS became the British Association of Settlements and Social Action Centres (BASSAC) in 1978. The question of changing the name was considered again in 1998 but research showed that respondents knew what BASSAC did and recognised its key role therefore it was decided to leave well alone.

During the 1920s attention turned to establishing settlements or community centres in non-traditional locations. BARS set up a Coalfields Settlements Committee in 1926 and a New Estates Community Committee in 1929. Examples of these developments were the settlements established at Elvington in Kent and Spennymoor in Durham. Basil Henriques, who was associated with several settlement houses in London, including those founded for the Jewish community, seems to be the originator of this response to the collapse of the coal industry. Henriques knew a 'resting' actor who was staying at Toynbee Hall and persuaded him to found and be the first warden of Spennymoor Settlement. Funding was secured from the Pilgrim Trust and it opened in 1931. Within ten years it had a branch of the county library, its own theatre, a children's playcentre, a CAB and a Poor Man's Lawyer, an adult education programme, plus a range of clubs catering for different groups.

The Coalfields work was not sustained and the committee was wound up in 1936. The New Estates Committee, however, generated a movement of voluntary managed neighbourhood community centres. One of the pioneers of that movement was Sewell Harris, who had previously worked in educational settlements. Of the new development he wrote:

> Looking back at the beginnings of the National Federation of Community Organisations (NFCO), I think it all began to grow

from a June 1929 conference which set up the New Estates Community Committee. I was a member of that, and so involved almost from the beginning. The term Community Association was in use by 1930 and by 1939 associations came into existence in many districts. By 1937 the New Estates Committee changed to the Community Centres and Associations Committee, of which I was the Chairman. That went on until 1945 when we founded the National Federation of Community Organisations. Sir Wyndham Deedes who had been connected with the Bethnal Green Settlement (Oxford House) was chairman for a year. Then I became chairman for six years from 1946. (Harris 1983, p.17)

The NFCO eventually became a completely independent association and subsequently changed its name to Community Matters, with a membership comprising many hundreds of neighbourhood associations and community centres. The NFCO is the second UK-based member of the IFS. It is often difficult to make clear distinctions between the work of settlements, social action centres and community associations. Members of BASSAC are drawn from neighbourhood-based community development agencies, with a number of paid staff. Community Matters, on the other hand, is more likely to attract members from volunteer-led agencies.

The Second World War and its aftermath

Following the Second World War the English settlement movement entered a period of crisis. During the war the settlements had been active in their support of local communities, especially in areas affected by bombing. After the war, however, they found it difficult to adjust to a new age and government.

Some felt the settlement model lacked relevance and needed to be replaced, others that it could now cease operations as Beveridge and Attlee (both of whom had been active in the early settlement movement) could be relied upon to ensure that the state would now provide for all. In a foreword to a survey of residential settlements in 1951 G. E. Haynes took this up:

It is sometimes said that the Residential Settlements should now merge in a younger movement which they did so much to foster... I believe there is room for both, working together as important elements in neighbourhood organisation. The Community Association seeks to be representative of the life of its district and to provide a basis for co-operative action between neighbours and local organisations... The Settlements on the other hand accept the existence of divisions and stratification in life as a special challenge to be met by securing leaders beyond the boundaries of its neighbourhood... Both have attendant dangers. The Community Association must be on its guard against parochialism and the Settlement against patronage – and there are plenty of examples to show that both pitfalls can be avoided. (Haynes 1951, pp.2–4)

The 1951 Survey from which the above is quoted identifies 48 settlements in the BAS. Their range of activities was substantial, with the focus on children's work, holiday clubs, play schemes, legal advice centres and educational courses. The impression gained from reading this survey is that they had retreated into the provision of clubs and leisure activities at the expense of policy work. Moreover, BAS seemed to be increasingly preoccupied with its own funding and survival. This is an impression confirmed from a reading of individual settlement histories. For example, the warden of Oxford House saw little hope for the future and resigned with a farewell message which warned, 'As far as money is concerned the situation becomes graver and graver each month' (Ashworth 1984, p.28). Similarly grand plans to re-launch Cambridge House after the war were unrealised due to a shortage of resources. The history of Blackfriar Settlement confirms that the nature of their activities in this period meant it was 'very much a hostel for women students and trainees who lived very cheaply in return for help with the clubs' (Barrett 1985, p.23).

The 1951 survey gave details of the work of 42 settlements, of which 26 still operate today or have merged with others. Their work was listed according to four categories. The first was 'Group activities for different ages'. Under that heading they ran over 160 clubs. The common denominator was that these were seen to strengthen family life by drawing together people of different ages for a wide variety of purposes. The second was 'Personal service work': here 30 offered some form of legal advice, for example, a CAB or law centre, or both. There were also 58 different schemes offering care for specific groups. The third category was 'Work with children' which incorporated 27 play centres, 38 children's clubs, 22 uniformed organisations and 23 holiday schemes and camps. The fourth grouping was 'Adult education' and between them there were nine Workers' Educational Association or University Extension groups, alongside over 80 classes including anything from dressmaking to drama to dance. With regards to staff, 36 had resident students and a total of 141 volunteer residents, while between them they had 155 paid employees. Despite evidence of a great deal of activity the text which accompanies the survey has a strangely old-fashioned ring, especially the conclusion:

> To sum up the Survey has shown that Residential Settlements have remained true to their original aim of uniting the human family through the conception of the 'good neighbour'. Their organisation and activities have continued to spring from their knowledge of human needs rather then any pre-conceived pattern. Their ideal has been strong enough to enable them to surmount the difficulties of industrial depression, war and financial stringency, and to find new methods to meet changing conditions. They have only to look round the old and new neighbourhoods today to see their testimony to unchanging values and their task of social integration are still essential. Wide fields lie waiting for the harvesters.
>
> (British Association of Residential Settlements 1951, p.36)

Rediscovering social action

The last 30 years have witnessed a renewal of a commitment to developing a social policy orientation within the work of the British settlement movement. William Beveridge was President of BARS until his death in 1963, and his passing seemed to provide a symbolic turning point for the association, which thereafter began to look anew at its role and future development.

This rethink was initiated by a group of radical settlement directors who were adopting a social action agenda and founded their own federation in South London. It was a time when social policy and community work in the UK were beginning to take note of the issues raised by the civil rights and other liberation movements in the United States, Africa and Latin America. The South London group was especially influenced by the ideas and practices of these movements and it was their concept of the 'social action centre' that incorporated this thinking, which was to revive the settlement movement in Britain.

Two important campaigns in the 1970s symbolised this shift. First, the Right to Read campaign which had its origins in literacy work undertaken at Cambridge House and led to a presentation at the 1972 BAS Annual Conference. The campaign grew until it consumed most of the time of the only paid worker. Eventually this work attracted government interest and in 1974 the Department of Education and Science funded BAS to develop a national literacy programme. However, in 1976 the government set up the Adult Literary Resource Agency, which took over this developmental role. The second was the Right to Fuel campaign which grew from work at the Birmingham Settlement on fuel debt. BAS formed an Energy Research Group in 1975 and published *A Right to Fuel* the same year. By 1977 the campaign had led to the appearance of 20 national and nearly 200 local organisations whose work was initially co-ordinated jointly by BASSAC and Friends of the Earth. Subsequently this also became a separate agency, although Birmingham Settlement remained an active participant. As recently as 1994 The Right to Fuel campaign, with BASSAC's support, initiated further work which helped to ensure that VAT was not added to fuel bills.

The way the Community Association movement grew to independence from its founding agencies, of which the settlements were one, is typical of how the settlement movement has worked over the years. Time and again, work pioneered in settlements has been 'handed over' to other agencies or encouraged to develop as an independent entity. Mary Ward House in Central London developed play-schemes for over 250,000 children. In 1925 this work, then taking place all over London, was handed over to the London County Council. This is a consistent theme in this story with childcare, children's holidays and playschemes programmes, free legal advice and meals-on-wheels all growing from settlement initiatives. Adult literacy and the Right to Fuel campaign subsequently joined that list of social movements. In 1979 the Latchkey Project was started and became the Out of School project before being handed over to the National Out of School Alliance.

There is a downside to the focus on social action. BASSAC became associated in the mind of government with campaigning, and for a time the funding for its work was called into question. But throughout, the settlements and their national agency remained key partners in discussions about community work training, the establishment of a national centre for community development, the development of community care and the problems of Britain's inner cities. Currently it is this focus of work that gives the British settlement movement a new direction and a public role. At its 1992 annual conference BASSAC adopted a new three-year programme entitled 'Tackling Poverty and Injustice'. Members agreed that since all settlements and social action centres were urban based this imposed a responsibility on them to contribute to debates on urban issues. At the time there was a membership of just over 70, the highest in the history of the organisation. Between them they employed over 1000 full- and part-time workers running nearly 1000 programmes. In addition many thousands of regular voluntary workers and hundreds of thousands of users were linked to BASSAC, whose members had a combined annual turnover in excess of £18 million.

'Tackling Poverty and Injustice' mixed policy initiatives with a programme to build the capacity of individual settlements and social action centres for engaging in partnerships with public and private bodies to regenerate their local neighbourhood. Between 1993 and

1998 the settlement movement became a key participant in urban policy formation and in what subsequently became known as community-based regeneration. For example, in 1995 the National Urban Forum was founded with help from BASSAC, who provided its first chairperson. More recently a major government contract for urban regeneration in London was given to a consortium of organisations led by BASSAC and based in its offices.

BASSAC has been committed to helping settlements and social action centres adjust to new funding and programme requirements. The move from grant-aid to contracts has been followed by the development of public, private and voluntary sector partnerships established to assist in the regeneration of local communities within areas of acute social need. Over half of the settlements and social action centres are now engaged in these partnerships. BASSAC itself in 1997 held over £500,000 each year for distribution to its members.

Together with other key agencies BASSAC has an acknowledged role in making submissions to government on urban policy. But by their very nature settlements and social action centres are multipurpose and therefore tend to engage in a wide range of social and community activities. The most recent shift in emphasis finds BASSAC members becoming closely involved in what has become known as social economy. Here the transferability of the settlement model works to the advantage of BASSAC members.

In earlier sections of this chapter reference was made to how the original idea of settlements travelled rapidly from the UK to the United States. However, the transfer was not merely between these two countries. For example, Siegfried Sirenius, a Lutheran Minister in Finland, anxious to create a social movement to overcome the deep cultural divisions in his country, drew on his friendship with Stead of the Browning Settlement and founded Kalliola settlement in Helsinki, and eventually the Finnish Federation of Settlements. Likewise in Central and Eastern Europe, following the collapse of communism, some drew on the settlement movement and its community-based neighbourhood house as a way of contributing to the reconstruction of civil society. But the movement is no longer one-way. It is now cyclical and what is learned in one country is now more readily available to all. So it is that our colleagues in the United States have pioneered community finance initiatives that have taken the concept of the credit union and turned it into a developmental tool. The rural development experiments in India and Bangladesh on micro-credit and community loan schemes have also been taken up by settlement houses in other countries. In the UK, for example, it has been Birmingham Settlement that has adopted these ideas and incorporated them within their own regeneration programmes, such as the Aston Reinvestment Trust (a pioneer community banking concept). Through Birmingham Settlement's work and enthusiasm BASSAC has been drawn into the whole process of establishing community businesses, loan schemes, micro-credit initiatives, all of which are aimed at improving the local economy in the most deprived areas.

When Barnett called upon students to come and 'settle' in East London in 1883 the area was the poorest neighbourhood in the metropolis. It remains so today, and is an area of economic and social transition. Near Toynbee Hall there is a church that was built for Huguenot refugees over 100 years ago. Gradually as they improved their situation they moved out. The building then became a synagogue as the area acquired a large Jewish population who were also predominantly refugees. They too became more prosperous and moved on. The building is now a mosque serving the religious needs of a mainly Muslim area, many of whose residents, like their predecessors, are refugees. Social and demographic movements such as this seem to provide those who work in settlements and social action centres with a never-ending challenge, raising questions such as: Will there always be areas that are poor? Where, if you get on, will you get out? Is it possible to break the cycle of deprivation, improve the local economy, the environment and social infrastructure so that those who live there can share the benefits of an integrated society without having to re-locate?

BASSAC believes it is possible to bring renewal to the local economy, give people work, sustain local businesses, make changes which improve the quality of housing, schools and community life, and create healthy and vibrant neighbourhoods everywhere – even in those areas where so often little hope is to be found. That has always been the vision which has inspired the settlement movement and remains so today.

Bibliography

Ashworth, M. (1984) *The Oxford House in Bethnal Green. 100 Years of Work in the Community*. London: Oxford House.

Barrett, G. (1985) *Blackfriars Settlement: A Short History 1887–1987*. London: Blackfriars Settlement.

Briggs, A. and Macartney, A. (1984) *Toynbee Hall, the First Hundred Years*. London: Routledge and Kegan Paul.

Harris, S. (1983). Full reference untraceable.

Harrow, J. (1998) Lecture given to Voluntary Action History Society – South Bank University, 12 May.

Haynes, G. E. (1951) *Residential Settlements: A Survey. Toynbee Hall*. London: British Association of Residential Settlements.

Rimmer, J. (1980) *Troubles Shared: The Story of the Settlement*, Birmingham: Phlogiston Publishing.

Picht, W. (1914) *Toynbee Hall and the English Settlement Movement*. London: G. Bell and Sons Ltd.

Sanders, P. (1989) *The Simple Annals: History of an Essex and East End Family*. Oxford: Alan Sutton Publishing.

4

Strength in community

Historical development of settlements internationally

Christian Johnson

Towards the end of the nineteenth century a new movement for social justice emerged. Its approach was straightforward: men and women who wanted to do something about poor social conditions went to settle in the worst affected areas and worked with their neighbours to improve the situation. Today the settlement movement can look back over more than a century of practical experience and achievement at local, national and international level, and is well equipped to continue its work of strengthening communities into the twenty-first century.

This chapter offers a brief introduction to the history and impact of the organisations which belong to the International Federation of Settlements and Neighbourhood Centres (IFS). IFS member organisations describe themselves as community-based and multipurpose, but only a few still use the name 'settlement'. There is a wide range of other names in different languages and countries, from *centre social* to *Nachbarschaftsheim*, and from *hemgard* to *sentro di barrio*. In this chapter the terms 'settlement', neighbourhood centre' and 'community organisation' are used.

Membership of IFS currently consists of 20 federations and 37 single centres, as well as corporate and individual associates, in 44 countries. Among them they represent thousands of local organisations, from small self-help groups to agencies with over 100 staff, and they are active across the full range of social, economic, cultural, educational and environmental needs in their communities (Table 1). Their work covers all age groups, from prenatal classes to activities for seniors.

In terms of age groups, members worked with pre-school children, school-age children, youth/teenagers, and elderly people/pensioners, and all but one with young adults. There were also pre-natal classes.

This vast range of activities is the result of over 110 years of development and adaptation to changing circumstances, and it also reflects the strength of the underlying ideas and goals.

The attempt by generations of volunteers and professionals to implement these ideas and goals within changing social and economic conditions since the late nineteenth century has created a fascinating pattern of activities and achievements. The emphasis of settlement work has always been on the immediate locality and this is where the dynamics and diversity of the movement have been most in evidence. However, from the beginning the activities in the local neighbourhood have been part of, and guided by, a global vision, and people from local and national organisations have taken an active role in promoting international links and co-operation. Tracing the history of the international movement from its origins until today therefore provides a unique introduction to the challenges and opportunities encountered by settlements and community organisations in the late nineteenth and twentieth centuries.

The origins of the settlement idea

In the late nineteenth century industrialised countries experienced social problems and mass poverty on an unprecedented scale. Large parts of the urban population experienced very poor working

Table 4.1 In a 1993 survey of IFS member federations, the areas of activity they mentioned as existing within their membership included:

- represented in all federations: child welfare and child services; youth services and youth welfare; services for elderly people; multicultural projects; projects for unemployed people; recreation/pleasure and social clubs.

- represented in more than three-quarters: housing, especially low-cost housing; housing associations/tenants and residents groups; family services; services for disabled people; self-help and other personal services; community enterprise/business; poverty issues; media and communication services; play; sport; performing arts; community education; adult/continuing education; pre-school playgroup; community care; race issues/anti-racism work; women's organisation/group; disability/access issues; immigration issues/work with refugees; community development policies/strategies; community participation/consultation; local management committees – roles and responsibilities; volunteer involvement/unpaid work; community newspapers; community work training/skills; advice work/advice centres.

- represented in more than half: welfare rights; visual arts, architecture, ceramic arts; public health projects; in-patient nursing-home services; alcohol abuse; social science/policy studies; black/minority ethnic organisation; learning difficulties; equal opportunities practice; tower blocks/high-rise buildings; homelessness/squatters; environmental/green issues; campaigning/community action; work against child abuse; work with offenders and their families; information technology and media projects (TV, video, radio, etc.).

conditions or unemployment, bad housing and serious health problems. The problems were particularly acute in large industrial towns and especially in London, which at that time was the world's largest city with about four million inhabitants. In the United Kingdom awareness of poverty as an issue was growing among concerned citizens, especially in religious groups and universities, and there were various attempts to counteract the negative social effects of urbanisation and industrialisation.

The most influential attempt with regard to the settlement movement began in 1873, when the newly married Samuel Augustus Barnett, a 30-year-old Church of England curate, and Henrietta Barnett (nee Rowland) went to live in St Jude's parish in the East End of London. In this poor neighbourhood the Barnetts organised practical parish activities and worked to alert others to the dismal conditions in the area. Barnett

> ...became increasingly concerned with the causes of the poverty about him. They were, he decided, basically moral. His reason for turning to the universities for help in meeting the larger issues of poverty was because ... their resources of human power and enjoyment represented what he wanted for everybody. (Kennedy 1986, p.15)

His aim was not to attract philanthropic gifts but to attack the root causes of poverty which Barnett saw emanating from the division of society into classes: he proposed the establishment of a settlement in his parish so that privileged students and disadvantaged local residents could live as neighbours and improve local conditions together.

The Universities Settlement in London was established in 1884 and named Toynbee Hall, in honour of the historian Arnold Toynbee, a key supporter at Oxford University, who had died prematurely in 1883. Early work included adult education courses and university extension lectures, children's country holidays, art exhibitions, literary and dramatic societies, assistance to Jewish immigrants, and the training of teachers and social workers. The underlying idea was that

> ... university men might get to know workmen and their problems through contact and discussion, and through teaching, research, public service and sociability, contribute something in return... Toynbee Hall was oriented, not to the parish or district, but toward the institutional structure of the nation... The residents came 'to learn as much as to teach, to receive as much as to give'. They lived in the neighbourhood in order to know as much as possible about it, as a spring board bringing about changes in the mores and the institutional structure of the nation. (ibid. p.16)

The importance of the mutuality of the relationship between people from different backgrounds within the settlement framework cannot be overstated: through direct personal encounter people were enabled to go beyond appearances and preconceptions and to get to know and value the individuality and humanity of each other, thus leading to greater respect for others and for themselves while building a stronger sense of community. Barnett wrote: 'A settlement is simply a means by which men or women may share themselves with their neighbours' (1895, p.14). He also explained the underlying principles: 'The equal capacity of all to enjoy the best, the superiority of quiet ways over those of striving and crying, character as the one thing needful, are the truths with which we have become familiar and on those truths we take our stand' (quoted Kennedy 1986, p.10).

The settlement approach can be summarised in three key points:

- every person has a right to grow and 'enjoy the best'

- effective change is evolutionary

- strong communities and positive social reform depend on personal communication across the social and economic divisions.

Each settlement was to adapt the approach to the circumstances encountered in its own times, culture, country, and above all neighbourhood, but all sought to work with local people to improve the quality of life for themselves, their families and neighbours.

The settlement approach spreads

Already by the end of 1884 London had two settlements, Oxford House and Toynbee Hall. In the next two decades over 20 settlements were established in the United Kingdom, most of them by the Church of England but some also by Wesleyans, Presbyterians, the Christian Socialist Movement, and by university groups on a secular basis. In a significant move at the time, several women's settlements were established. In the United Kingdom (as later elsewhere, for example, in the Netherlands and Scandinavia), there were early and continuing links to adult education which in some cases resulted in the foundation of specific educational settlements.

Several Toynbee Hall residents and visitors came from abroad and in this way the settlement idea soon spread to other industrialised countries. In 1886, Stanton Coit founded the Guild (later renamed University Settlement) in the lower East Side of New York; one year later alumnae of Smith College formed the College Settlements Association; and in 1889 Jane Addams established Hull House in Chicago. As large-scale immigration was a more important issue there than in the United Kingdom, many of the early United States settlements were established specifically to provide services for immigrants and refugees. By the turn of the century there were more than 100 settlement houses in United States cities and 10 years later the figure had risen to over 400. Even more than in other countries, women took the leading role in very many cases and initiated a new concept for settlement houses based on the value of 'living-in'. The early settlements were established in houses with live-in facilities or residences. There the 'poor and uneducated' could have free or low-cost housing and food and would be taught good social practices and manners by their benevolent social superiors. United States settlements were also more active than many others in fighting for reform and change on the issues which they and their neighbours faced within their neighbourhoods.

Settlements were started very soon in industrial towns and also in rural areas elsewhere in Europe and North America:

- The *Centres Sociaux* in France had forerunners in *Maisons Sociales* like *L'Union des Familles*, which emerged from the work of Madame de Pressencé with the wives of the Paris Communards in the 1870s, and in *L'Oeuvre Sociale* of Madame La Fer de la Motte (Lestavel (undated) A, p.3).

- In the 1880s and 1890s Canada saw the foundation of settlements responding to the poverty of people moving into large cities as industrial workers. Most of the early Canadian settlement houses were begun by women and several had church connections.

- In 1890 a 'Workers' Home' was founded in a working-class area of Helsinki by Aili Trygg-Helenius, and the Finnish settlement movement started in 1918 with the foundation of the Evangelical Society of Industrial Areas and Kalliola Setlementti in Helsinki by Reverend Sigfrid Sirenius, after a stay at Robert Browning Settlement in London.

- In 1892 Ons Huis (Our Home) was established in Amsterdam by school inspector Tours, and various Toynbee Associations and people's houses were started in other towns before the turn of the century.

- The first settlement in Japan was Kingsley-Kan (Kingsley Hall) in Kanada, Tokyo City, established by Sen Katayama in 1897 on the model of Toynbee Hall.

- In Germany, 1901 saw the foundation of the Hamburger Volksheim by Professor Walter Classen. Further neighbourhood centres emerged elsewhere and in 1910

Professor Friedrich Siegmund-Schultze established the
Soziale Arbeitsgemeinschaft Berlin-Ost in Berlin.

- In Austria, Wiener Settlement was founded by Viennese
  women in 1901.

- In 1905 the first community centres were established in
  Moscow.

- After early settlement activities by Natanael Beskow
  following a visit to Robert Browning Settlement in London,
  Birkagården was founded in Stockholm in 1912 to increase
  the self-reliance of the local working-class population.

- In Hungary, after a stay at Toynbee Hall, Rezsö Hilscher
  started a settlement in the Ujpest district of Budapest in
  1913 following the foundation of a first rural settlement
  two years earlier.

In various countries including the United Kingdom, Germany,
Austria and the United States there were also, from around the turn of
the century, Jewish Toynbee Halls and settlements which maintained
links with the wider settlement movement and carried out similar
work (Oelschlägel 1994).

Early achievements

The basic approach of building bridges between different social
classes and groups through common effort in poor neighbourhoods
was the same in all settlements which sprang up in the late nineteenth
and early twentieth century. They could only be effective, however, if
the methods and contents of the work were adapted to suit the
specific neighbourhoods. This made settlements into fertile places for
practical work, thinking and discussion. Perhaps the supreme
example of how working with the poor affected educated incomers
was free legal advice – those who were lawyers discovered the poor
had no access to the law and so started the free or 'penny lawyer'
schemes. In this way settlements became the starting point for many
wider developments that gained a life of their own and are often no

longer remembered as originating in settlements. This went in line with a philosophy, in many cases inspired directly by Quaker founders, that service took precedence over personal advancement. Because of this same philosophy, the contribution of Quakers to the origins and development of settlements is very difficult to document, as they did not want their contribution publicised and recorded.

Some examples of early achievements include:

- Toynbee Hall was instrumental in encouraging some of the earliest British surveys into poverty and unemployment, lobbied for better water supplies and other improvements to its neighbourhood, played a mediating role in several strikes, and established a model garden suburb to show what a modern urban neighbourhood might look like. Samuel Barnett, warden until his death in 1913, and Henrietta Barnett, who lived until the 1920s, both lectured and published widely about their values and the need for social and political change.

- Hull House was at the forefront of the women's movement from the late nineteenth and during the twentieth century. Examples of achievements of women who stayed at this settlement included the first American child labour legislation, the first juvenile court law, and the establishment and leadership of the Federal Children's Bureau. The outstanding achievements of Jane Addams were recognised with the Nobel Peace Prize in 1931.

- United States settlements as a whole made great early contributions in several fields. Settlement workers saw the neighbourhood as the client, advocating with their neighbours for reform at the local and federal levels. They also showed a strong commitment to volunteerism.

The list of reforms settlement workers helped to further is long. It includes inducing the public schools to add kindergartens, English and citizenship classes, home economics and industrial education. Settlement workers encouraged their local governments to establish playgrounds, laws to regulate low income housing, and mother's pensions. They supported the juvenile court, other child welfare measures, and occasionally, the labour movement. (Trolander 1987, p. 47)

- In the United Kingdom the work of Toynbee Hall and other settlements, apart from their direct impact, was to lead to the formation of a long list of organisations associated with settlement work at their inception, which have since achieved independent status. These include the Youth Hostels' Association, the Workers Educational Association, the Workers' Travel Association, the Children's Country Holidays Association, the National Federation of Community Associations, Community Service Volunteers, the Legal Aid Scheme, and the Child Poverty Action Group (Ely and Mundy 1980, p.53).

- Wiener Settlement was the first institution in the Austro-Hungarian Empire to introduce co-education to assemble children of different age bands into small family-size groups, and it was a leading force in gaining the right for mothers to become legal guardians of their children, which became especially important following the death of so many men in World War I (Kretschmer-Dorninger 1987).

Settlements also had, and continue to have, an important longer-term influence through the individuals whose lives were affected, and often changed, by their direct experience of them. Settlements made a great contribution to training, initially of volunteers and also after the Second World War of students in social work and social administration, who went on to become welfare professionals, especially in the United States, the United Kingdom, Scandinavia and the Netherlands. In addition, settlements provided formative experiences for many residents and users, especially in the case of young people. There are thousands of settlement volunteers and board members, individuals in government, academia or business, whose early experience as a settlement camp counsellor or club leader changed their outlook and values.

Increasing national and international activities

In the early years of the twentieth century settlements began to establish closer links with each other, and the first formal associations started to emerge. A key aim was to influence local and national government which, especially after the First World War, took an increasingly active role in social protection and welfare. In the United States, where a first meeting of settlement workers had taken place in 1892 in Plymouth, a national federation was formed in 1911 with Jane Addams as President. In the United Kingdom the first national federation was formed in 1920 and in France two years later. A first international conference of settlement workers was organised at Toynbee Hall from 8–15 July 1922, chaired by Henrietta Barnett. The International Association of Settlements was founded at a second International Conference from 30 June–5 July 1926 at the Cité Universitaire in Paris. After a period of increasing activity and expansion in many countries, settlement work was effected adversely by the economic crisis from the late 1920s onwards. In the United States settlements served as work sites for publicly funded jobs in the arts, recreation and education, and as advocates for those in need of jobs, housing and entitlements. Settlements, along with other youth-serving or 'character building' agencies, were in the vortex from which social group work emerged in the late 1920s and early 1930s. Although it combined a background in adult education, recreation and social work, it made its home in, and developed in, schools of social work. Settlements were also at the forefront of campaigning for better welfare programmes as the government took on an active role in the welfare field during the New Deal.

In the United Kingdom, the National Federation was involved in the New Estates Community Committee which resulted in the formation of the Community Association Movement.

> Given the basic concept of the settlement movement, that of living in the inner city as 'neighbours of the working poor', it was

inevitable that its leading practitioners should come to have an intense knowledge of, and concern for, their local community. They absorbed some of the ideas of '*Gemeinschaft*' so widespread in the later nineteenth century and attempted to apply them to the streets of East London or to the tenement blocks of New York City. They aimed to plough some of their social and cultural privilege back into a poor neighbourhood to help it become an organised, self conscious, self helping community. In doing so, they influenced the planners and builders of the new council estates and public housing of interwar and post war Britain and America, as to the need to provide for democratic community life. The community centre and the neighbourhood association were developments from the settlement ideal. (Rose 1995, p.2)

Community associations developed a distinct identity based on mutual aid principles and a strong emphasis on volunteering, but maintained many links with settlements both locally and nationally.

The disruption of war

For settlements in Germany and Japan, conditions became very difficult in the 1930s. In Germany, as later in Austria and other occupied countries, the National Socialists closed settlements and their federations. Many settlement workers, especially those who were of Jewish origin and/or Social Democrats, were forced to flee. Several benefited from international settlement contacts to escape from persecution, especially with the United States. In Japan, the Fascists introduced the 'Tonari-Gumi' system which forced people to inform on neighbours who disagreed with the war: if they did not agree to inform on others, not only they themselves but all members of their local 'Tonari-Gumi' were punished. The nature of social work itself changed during Fascism to promote the war, and settlements were seen as obstacles.

During the Second World War, the commitment of settlements to democracy, peace and social justice at all levels of society equipped them to take on the challenges and bring practical help to people in need. Where settlements were able to continue to work during the war they increased their efforts to meet the growing demand for help. Many settlements, for example, in London during the 'Blitz', played a crucial role in supporting the local communities, both those who stayed during the air-raids and the families who were evacuated. In the United States in the 1940s, with women replacing men in the workplace, settlements were in the forefront in setting up publicly funded day-care centres.

Settlements in postwar society

The immediate postwar period saw new challenges of many kinds, such as displacement and emergency relief, reconstruction, unemployment and difficulties in re-adaptation to civilian life. The United States and the United Kingdom were instrumental in re-starting German settlements as part of the wider programme of re-education for democracy in Berlin and the Western zones of occupation. Their main aim, well into the 1950s, was to meet the emergency needs of the population, almost one-quarter of whom were refugees and displaced persons (Oestreich 1965). In Japan the memory of 'Tonari-Gumi' and other grass-roots oppression kept people away from community activities even after the war, but some settlements did start work again, with an emphasis on meeting special postwar needs such as those of orphans.

The postwar years saw the foundation of new community organisations in several other countries. In France, the number of social centres grew from 50 in 1945 to 150 only seven years later, most of which can be attributed to the role of the *Caisses d'Allocations Familiales* as funders of social work. A theme which had already emerged before the war now became central in the work of social centres: user participation and representation on decision-making bodies. Great advances were made in this, and user participation fast became one of the distinguishing features of French social centres (Lestavel (undated) B). In the United Kingdom the Community Association Movement, which had begun with settlement involvement and gathered strength in the 1930s, in particular on the new housing estates, resulted in the foundation of their own national federation. A host of community associations and centres were formed on estates nationwide, run by volunteers and with few or no staff, and contributed to the fast growth of the federation, which joined IFS in 1954 (Clarke 1990). Following an informal meeting of settlement workers in Paris in 1947, the IFS was formally reconstituted in 1949, with the secretariat organised by the French Federation.

In many western countries the war years had led to a recognition of a public responsibility towards all sections of society which expressed itself in increased activity by the state in the social, health and education fields. Some countries introduced universal protection, as in the United Kingdom where both the author of the welfare state, William Beveridge, and the first postwar prime minister, Clement Attlee, had longstanding links with the settlement movement. Having campaigned for a greater role for the state, many settlements now became threatened by redundancy of their services, a perception strengthened by the growing affluence of large parts of society. A common reaction in the 1950s was to put more stress on cultural, recreational and sports facilities for the neighbourhood, especially in the large new housing estates in or near the outskirts of industrial cities. In an attempt to create a sense of community in the anonymous and increasingly unattractive estates, neighbourhood centres sprang up in many areas as a meeting place for the local population and as a base for outreach support work.

The greater involvement by the state, both financially and through regulations, also further increased the institutionalisation and professionalisation of settlement work. In the United States the ever greater professionalisation of social work brought changes in the composition of staff, with men for the first time ever outnumbering women as settlement headworkers in the 1950s (Trolander 1987, p.50). Multiple factors, including new work practices and funding difficulties, led to the end of many settlement residences. Urban neighbourhoods were disrupted through demographic changes and public housing programmes, and while some settlements were relocated and others lost their specific neighbourhood focus, the national federation and many members were involved actively in urban renewal projects and in promoting neighbourhood involvement. Other important national activities at that time were in the fields of economic planning, employment, housing and juvenile delinquency. Beginning in the late 1950s United States settlements became involved in community organisation, including tenant organisation and the creation of low-income and affordable housing.

In Canada, after abortive attempts in the preceding decades, 1958 saw the first Canadian Conference of Settlements with representatives from Vancouver, Winnipeg, Montreal and Toronto, which was eventually to result in the foundation of the Canadian Association of Neighbourhood Services (CANS) five years later.

The challenges of the 1960s

The turbulent 1960s presented a radical challenge to settlements in many countries. In the United States the 'rediscovery' of poverty in neighbourhoods throughout the country, combined with the Civil Rights movement and set against the background of the Vietnam War, saw settlements develop an important role locally and nationally, with interracial and economic justice key priorities for the National Federation. Much progress was made in making the Federation and its members more responsive to its local populations, especially the needs of minority groups (Berry 1986, p.8). Under the 'Great Society' programme there was an emphasis on 'empowerment' and 'maximum feasible participation of the poor'. The Federation's Race Relations Project attracted much attention and resulted in an important report in 1967. United States settlements also saw important extensions of programmes, with often large amounts of public financing, especially during the War on Poverty. While this allowed more work in low-income neighbourhoods, it also introduced settlements to the issues and pitfalls of public–private partnership. Throughout this time, the influence of settlement work was spreading in important new ways through the National Federation's own training centre, housed initially at Hull House.

For the international movement the 1960s was a period of great activity, with the first concerted attempt to put IFS onto a more professional footing. Through the International Programme of the United States Federation, Pan-American links and exchanges were developed and in 1962 there was a workshop of some 50 neighbourhood centre workers from different countries in Rio de Janeiro. Also thanks to support from the United States Federation, IFS maintained a wide network of contacts in all parts of the world through an active role at the United Nations in New York. In 1966 IFS gained consultative status with UNICEF and participated in a UNICEF aid project for community centres in Africa.

Settlements in many countries faced crisis or stagnation in the period of high economic growth during the 1960s. In Japan, for example, where the Japanese Association of Settlements and Community Centres had been founded in 1961 in Yokosuka, the escalation of the struggle for better schooling for children, seen as the key to economic success, meant that preparatory lessons after school hours were given preference over settlement children's clubs.

The late 1960s and early 1970s saw a growing awareness of problems accompanying affluence alongside the persistence of poverty and discrimination for parts of the population, especially for the increasing numbers of migrant workers. The student revolt in 1968 had an impact on many settlements, exposing them to questions about their wider role and sensitizing them to new social issues. There was increasing emphasis on multicultural work with different population groups. In the United Kingdom there began to be a growing interest in different approaches like community organisation, community development, community work and community social work. In Germany the national federation gave increasing emphasis to community work with the whole population, rather than the poorest groups in the immediate neighbourhood of a particular house or residence. Here, as in the Netherlands, France and other countries, there was now an increasing emphasis on professional methods and close links developed again between the social sciences, social science institutions and university departments on the one hand, and social work practitioners on the other.

The diminishing role of the state

In the mid-1970s the trend towards state involvement in social services began to reverse as there were growing cuts in public reform programmes in the wake of the oil crisis. This led to significant shifts in the complex and changing relationships that had developed between settlements and statutory authorities at the local, regional and national levels. One area was funding, another was 'agency work', and yet others were influencing policy and strengthening citizen participation and the civil society. With the state redefining its role, settlements were constantly obliged to reassess their work priorities in these areas.

In the United Kingdom links developed with self-help organisations and citizens' initiatives, as well as the social action movement, in which some settlements and workers took a leading role. BASSAC increased its profile by leading important national initiatives like the Right to Read campaign against adult illiteracy, based on work at Cambridge House Settlement, and the Right to Fuel campaign against fuel poverty, based on work at Birmingham Settlement (see Chapter Three by Matthews and Kimmis). In the United States, the national federation was involved in a wide range of programmes, many with federal funding, on issues such as economic development for minority populations, teenage parenthood, training programmes for the elderly and teenagers, and juvenile justice. The international movement was now more openly concerned with community work and social change. The wider horizons and ambitions showed themselves in the organisation of the first International Conference outside Europe, in Vancouver in 1976 under the title 'Participation in Local Development'.

The consequences of dependence on government funding were becoming evident in many countries. In the Netherlands the emphasis had moved away from an ideological position to professionalisation, with community centres only receiving state grants if they employed professionally trained social, community and youth workers. This brought to a culmination a process driven by the:

> ...connection between the state subsidy and the difference in emphasis on the work of youth clubs and community centres. The latter concentrated, at least officially, on matters that the government considered to be important: mass youth unemployment and the campaign against antisocial behaviour at the end of the 1940s and the beginning of the 50s; community work to help integrate the inhabitants of the new housing estates round the cities at the end of the 50s and in the first half of the 60s; bringing the citizen closer to politics, in the context of politicisation, democratisation and decentralisation, in the 1970s. In spite of all this, a high level of continuity can be seen in the work. The target groups remained broadly speaking the same and there were no great changes in the activities either. (Nijenhuis 1987, p.38)

The early 1980s proved a difficult time for IFS and many of its member organisations, especially federations. Mass unemployment became a fact of life in western countries and settlement work became more focused on unemployment and related issues, especially for youth. In many countries settlements were involved in various national campaigns to counter the effects of the erosion of welfare provision, but the stance was in many ways mainly defensive and undermined by funding difficulties. Many federations were facing difficulties in recruiting or even retaining members, and suffered losses in fees and grant income.

Strengthening the international network

In 1984, the 'Centennial Celebrations' of Toynbee Hall were held in conjunction with an IFS seminar with some 230 participants from 13 countries. Membership of the International Federation had fallen to 10 federations and single centres in 10 countries: Austria, Canada, Finland, France, Germany, Israel, Lebanon, Netherlands, the United Kingdom and the United States. The 1988 Conference in Berlin on 'Settlements as Bridges Between Cultures', which brought together over 400 participants from 25 countries, was a key event in several respects: it led to new and renewed direct co-operation and exchanges between members; it helped re-establish the role that an international organisation like IFS could play; and it put the multicultural theme at the centre of IFS work for the coming years.

Much of this turnaround was thanks to a number of committed individuals at all levels of the organisation who were able to reactivate goodwill and commitment to settlement work among many others inside and outside of the movement.

After a difficult decade the early 1990s saw a recovery of dynamism also at national and local level, in many cases because of a rediscovery and new emphasis of the link between local action and public policy. In the United States, (UNCA) started a remarkable recovery with membership increasing from 36 in 1992 to 129 two years later. In the United Kingdom BASSAC engaged in a determined effort to strengthen the movement through increased co-operation among members and a programme of 'Tackling Poverty and Injustice'. Similar new departures took place in other countries, such as Finland, Sweden and Germany. In France the national federation consolidated its already strong position by taking a leading role in promoting the needs and interests of the 'social economy' at national and European level.

After remaining a small network of committed western organisations for most of its existence, IFS began a determined attempt to reach out to all community-based, multipurpose organisations, especially in new countries, and to build up a professional organisation with a full-time Secretariat funded largely through earned income. IFS also began to take a stronger approach to participation in the United Nations and other inter-governmental bodies as they increased their concern with global social issues. In particular IFS was keen to use the great political changes in Central and Eastern Europe to work together with emerging community organisations, in some cases building on previous historical links. The most visible steps in the ensuing grass-roots linking process organised by the IFS Eurogroup (which was formed in March 1991) were four East–West conferences between 1991 and 1994. Following requests by conference participants, IFS also organised a first East–East meeting in Prague in April 1994.

These meetings resulted in the recruitment of organisation members in Budapest, Debrecen, Kaunas, Oradea, Prague, Moscow and St Petersburg. Follow-up work included exchanges on themes like volunteer training, community development and youth work, and the establishment of new projects, such as a pioneering adult education training programme in Budapest. IFS helped to initiate a co-operation programme on 'Multi-ethnic Living at Local Level' between partnerships of local authorities and community organisations in Hungary, Spain and the United Kingdom, and IFS members in the Netherlands initiated a three-year programme, funded by the Dutch government, to establish community centres in Lithuania.

The 1992 the International Conference on 'Organising for Social Change' in Toronto underlined the significant extent of co-operation among members and gave new impetus to the outreach activities of IFS, especially in the southern hemisphere. The increase in the level of activities continued and in 1993 IFS also achieved Consultative Status with the Council of Europe. The IFS International Seminar and Council meeting in Curaçao in 1994, the first to be held outside Europe or North America, saw the culmination of the overhaul of the organisation, with approval of incorporation in the United States and clear policies on equal opportunities and on the scope and remit of the organisation.

Curaçao also saw the launch of the IFS Americas Coalition, and two years later, in 1996, IFS was represented in 18 countries in South America. The attempt to reach out to new countries and continents also resulted in new members in Bangladesh and India, and an IFS Asia Network was started at the 1996 IFS International Conference in Helsinki. This conference saw the adoption of the IFS Global Community Partnership Programme, a four-year plan to increase the cohesion of the movement, especially using information technology, to increase advocacy on behalf of members and their communities, and attract new members and develop settlement activities in places where they do not yet exist. At a time of increasing globalisation, there was a need for stronger international co-operation among community-based multipurpose organisations and the settlement movement established an effective framework for combining the local and global aspects of working to strengthen communities in our society.

Outlook

At the beginning of this century, a settlement was described in a Toynbee Hall Report as

> ...an association of persons with different opinions and different tastes: its unity is that of variety; its methods are spiritual rather than material; it aims at permeation rather than conversion; and its trust is in friends linked to friends rather than in organisation. (quoted Barnett 1909, p.159)

This description is borne out by the history of individual settlements and it also applies to developments within the international movement and IFS. For well over a century now, the international movement has developed largely on the basis of personal encounters and contacts between settlement workers, volunteers and members from different countries, and with only minimal organisational infrastructure. Membership is open to single settlements and community centres, regional or national federations and individual people. Most of the funding continues to come from membership fees and donations by charitable trusts and individuals, and the core activities are practical exchanges of information and mutual support among members and towards newly emerging community organisations. This informality makes the movement's history and impact difficult to document, but it has also provided, and continues to provide, significant dynamism and strength.

There is another factor in the nature of settlement work which makes it difficult to appreciate the full extent and significance of the settlement movement. Guy Clutton-Brock, the former Head of

Oxford House in London, who died in early 1995, expressed it in the following way:

> Possessiveness in the work of a settlement, as in any form of friendship, is a difficult temptation to resist. But it must at all costs be resisted or else one of the main aims of our undertaking will be lost to sight. It is true of those who undertake social endeavour through a settlement, as again it is, in a sense, of a friend, that their ultimate objective must be to make superfluous the work they have initiated. (Oxford House Report 1944)

This should also serve as a reminder that, when looking back over the history and impact of the international settlement movement, the sense of achievement has to be put within the wider framework of the ultimate goals of settlement work. Barnett put it most starkly: 'Settlements exist simply to enable rich and poor to understand one another. Their success will be proved when they are unnecessary' (Barnett 1909, p.161). The work of IFS and its member organisations shows the dignity and value of trying to bridge social divisions and improve the human condition, but it also illustrates the way in which the need for this work, although ever-changing in its manifestations, has persisted and is continuing to persist.

Bibliography

Barnett, H. O. (1909) 'The Beginning of Toynbee Hall', in S. A. and H. Barnett, *Towards Social Reform*. London Longmans Green and Co.

Barnett, S. A. (1895) 'University Settlements' in *Nineteenth Century, December 1895*.

Barnett, S. A. (1909) 'Settlements or Missions', in Barnett, H. O. and S. A. *Towards Social Reform*. London: Longmans Green and Co.

Barnett, S. A. (1909) 'Retrospect of Toynbee Hall', in Barnett, H. O. and S. A. *Towards Social Reform*. London: Longmans Green and Co.

Clarke, R. (ed.) (1990) *Enterprising Neighbours. The Development of the Community Association Movement in Britain*. London: National Federation of Community Organisations.

Ely, P. and Mundy, B. (1980) *Review of the British Association of Settlements and Social Action Centres*. Canterbury: Christchurch College.

Kennedy, A. J. (1986) 'The Settlement Heritage'. In H. Nijenhuis (ed.), *Hundred Years of Settlements and Neighbourhood Centres in North America and Europe*. Utrecht: GAMA.

Kretschmer-Dorninger, T. (1987) 'History of the Vienna Settlements'. In H. Nijenhuis (ed.), *Hundred Years of Settlements*. Utrecht: GAMA.

Lestavel, J. (undated, A) 'Aux Origines des Centres Sociaux'. Paris: Fédération des Centres Sociaux.

Lestavel, J. (undated, B) 'La Participation des Usagers aux Origines des Centres Sociaux'. Paris: Fédération des Centres Sociaux.

Nijenhuis, H. (ed.) (1987) *Hundred Years of Settlements and Neighbourhood Centres in North America and Europe*. Utrecht: GAMA.

Oestreich, G. (1965) *Nachbarschaftsheime Gestern, Heute – und Morgen?* Munich and Basel.

Oelschlägel, D. (1994) 'Das Jüdische Volksheim in Berlin, 1916–1926', *Rundbrief* No. 1.

Oxford House (1944) *Report for 1943–44 on Oxford House in Bethnal Green*. London: Oxford House.

Rose, M. E. (1995) *Neighbourhood as Springboard: The Urban Community and the Settlement House Movement in Britain and the USA, c. 1890–1990*, Manchester: University of Manchester Working Papers in Economic and Social History.

Trolander, J. A. (1987) 'From settlement houses to neighbourhood centres: A history of the settlement house movement in the United States'. In Nijenhuis, H. (ed.), *Hundred Years of Settlements*.

5

One hundred years of the Birmingham Settlement

Jon Glasby

In 1999 the Birmingham Settlement is a thriving, community-based voluntary agency responsible for 24 different projects, 120 members of staff, 250 volunteers and an annual budget of nearly £2.5 million. In addition to its local presence and input it also works across the city, nationally and sometimes even internationally, to support those in poverty, develop effective ways of overcoming social disadvantage, and help people help themselves. In the process, it has been involved in a series of collaborative projects, working with local people and the public, voluntary and private sectors to develop new services to meet previously unidentified needs. On several occasions projects such as these have gone on to become autonomous agencies after having received support from the settlement until they are able to function independently. Despite its size and success the Birmingham Settlement has not always enjoyed the funding which it currently receives nor the profile it now enjoys. It has grown from relatively humble origins to become one of the largest settlements in Britain and one of the most significant social agencies in Birmingham. Founded on 29 September 1899, the Birmingham Settlement has recently celebrated its 100th birthday (Glasby 1999).

Birmingham and Summer Lane

Now Britain's second city, Birmingham was once a small rural hamlet surrounded by a number of larger communities, many of which have since been incorporated and now form part of its inner city. Blessed by its central location, its access to riverways and proximity to the raw materials of the Black Country, Birmingham began to expand in size from the Middle Ages onwards, developing initially into a busy market town and later into a major industrial centre. Renowned for its skilled craftsmen, thriving trade and prosperous manufacturing, the town began to attract rural migrants seeking employment and its population increased dramatically, rising from 24,000 in 1751 to 71,000 in 1801 and topping the 400,000 mark by the early 1880s (Gardiner and Wenborn 1995; Sutcliffe and Smith 1974). In recognition of its rapid expansion, Birmingham was designated as a borough in 1838 and, in 1889, a city.

Despite its prosperity, Birmingham's emergence as a major city brought a number of significant social problems. In the sphere of housing, the rapidly expanding population placed additional pressure on an already inadequate housing stock, with many local people having no choice but to reside in the substandard 'back-to-back' dwellings which soon came to dominate most of Birmingham's inner city. Although these properties were cheap to rent, they were also poorly constructed and badly ventilated, damp, insanitary and overcrowded. That such properties contributed to the ill health so prevalent in these areas is demonstrated clearly by contemporary health statistics, with infant mortality and overall death rates much higher in the inner city than in the more affluent suburbs (Briggs 1952; Vince 1902, 1923). Both the housing and the health problem were exacerbated by the exclusion of the very poor from what welfare services existed, and by the widespread material deprivation which many workers faced as a result of low pay, sickness, injury, variations in trade and unemployment.

During the twentieth century many of these issues have been resolved or at least ameliorated by economic growth and an expansion in statutory welfare provision. However, such changes often benefited certain sections of society more than others, leaving some of Birmingham's poorest areas just as impoverished relative to the society around them as they ever were. This is particularly true of the Summer Lane area in which the Birmingham Settlement has been based throughout its 100-year history. Once just a dirt track through open pasture to the north-east of the city centre, Summer Lane was transformed into a residential area in the early nineteenth century with the construction of large numbers of back-to-backs to house some of the city's poorest workers. Throughout its history, Summer Lane has remained one of the most deprived areas of Birmingham, renowned for its grinding poverty, its squalor, and the regular fights which used to take place in its many public houses. Like many such areas, however, this reputation is one which is created largely by outside observers, who tend to focus on the numerous social problems which do exist, rather than on the strengths and determination of the people who grapple against the odds to survive on low incomes.

Origins of the Birmingham Settlement

In many ways, the settlement movement which began in the last quarter of the nineteenth century was the product of the same processes of urbanisation and industrialisation which prompted the rapid growth of urban centres such as Birmingham. Conditions and developments in cities throughout the country were similar to those described above, with large sections of society facing chronic poverty, ill health and poor housing conditions.

Although most of the early British settlements were based in London, an increasing number came to be founded in provincial cities such as Liverpool, Manchester and Bristol. (For an outline of some of the key settlements see Beveridge and Wells 1949, pp.123–134.) In Birmingham, the idea of a settlement was first proposed at a meeting of the local branch of the National Union of Women Workers (NUWW), an umbrella organisation established to co-ordinate the activities of the various voluntary agencies working with women and children. After hearing of the work of settlements elsewhere in the country, a number of NUWW members decided to establish a similar organisation in Birmingham, renting a property in the Summer Lane area of the city and securing the appointment of a 'warden' from an older settlement in Southwark. Whereas many of the early British settlements were dominated by men, the Birmingham settlement was staffed initially by female residents and worked primarily with women and children. In recognition of this it was originally known as the Birmingham Women's Settlement, although in 1919 it changed its name to the Birmingham Settlement to reflect its work with both sexes. Despite this, the female-orientated nature of its early years continues to influence the settlement, with a number of key projects focusing specifically on the needs of women (see, for example, Davis *et al.* 1999) and women outnumbering men in positions of authority throughout most of its history.

Early years: 1899–1919

When the settlement first opened its doors it quickly began to involve itself in a diverse range of projects and initiatives. From the onset it sought to work in collaboration with the Crippled Children's Union, meeting the health and educational needs of disabled children, organising play hours and enabling disabled girls to earn a living from the production of woven goods at a special weaving school. Soon it was also running a Provident Society (a penny bank to encourage local people to save small sums on a regular basis) and operating a rent collection scheme to manage local properties on similar lines to the methods pioneered in London by the housing reformer, Octavia Hill. During the course of this work, the settlement provided its savers and its tenants with regular visits, part social and part financial, which not only helped to raise its profile locally, but also provided its workers with considerable knowledge of local conditions. Around the same time, it also started to organise children's and adult's clubs and worked with other agencies to provide financial support for those in need.

As the settlement became increasingly well established in the area, it began to see the need for new projects to support its neighbours.

From 1904 it worked with children leaving school and starting employment, wherever possible helping these young people to enter skilled professions rather than dead-end jobs, and ensuring they had access to leisure facilities in their spare time. Shortly afterwards, it became involved in a collaborative venture to provide medical services for local people, running a Medical Care Centre and a School for Mothers which sought to meet the health needs of children identified at school as requiring assistance, and provide a free infant welfare clinic. Both projects were particularly relevant in an area renowned for its poor health, insanitary housing and escalating infant mortality rate. Further health-related initiatives included the training of temperance workers and the opening of a temperance pub to combat the excessive alcohol consumption for which Summer Lane was renowned. At the same time, new initiatives sought to provide free legal advice for those unable to afford a solicitor, run classes to teach practical skills such as housewifery and sewing, provide safe child care at the settlement's kindergarten and offer placements for social work students from the nearby University of Birmingham.

From 1914, the settlement's attention was focused increasingly on the temporary problems caused by the First World War. Within ten days of the outbreak of war Summer Lane found itself in something of a crisis, owing to the large number of reservists who were suddenly called up. In response, the settlement worked with other agencies to provide emergency support for those whose sons and husbands had left the area with such short notice, and later sought to provide food and warm clothing for those unable to afford it themselves. During this period it also worked to teach Workers' Educational Association members home nursing and first aid and train local women as Welfare Supervisors in munitions factories. Once the initial crisis was weathered, the settlement was able to return to some of its pre-war work, campaigning for greater regulation of the sale of alcohol and providing a library for its neighbours.

Between the wars: 1919–1939

In the interwar period, many of the settlement's projects continued to develop and expand. This was particularly true of the Provident Society which on the eve of the Second World War was collecting in excess of £2,000 a year from some 1000 subscribers. Also popular were the settlement's recreational projects, and by 1939 it was running around 30 clubs for men, women, boys and girls, with well-established holidays, camping, sporting events, music and drama. After a brief closure during the First World War, the settlement's free legal service began to function again in the 1920s and attracted increasing numbers of people from across the city, while the library became a much-used resource for both children and adults.

In the immediate postwar period, the settlement was involved in a number of initiatives to ease the transition from a war-time to a peace-time economy, providing financial assistance to ex-servicemen and the unemployed and using its premises for a number of 'unemployment schools' as troops were demobilised. Once this transition had been achieved the settlement was able to look further afield, developing more long-term projects to meet previously unidentified needs. In the early 1920s, for example, it organised a housing exhibition to display affordable furniture, and was also involved in the creation of Copec, a housing association which was later to make a significant contribution to solving Birmingham's housing problems. Also at this time it was responsible for a series of educational projects, training local workers as club leaders, organising overseas visits for a number of service users, and running courses to teach trainee teachers, clergymen and social workers about life in the inner city. Perhaps the most practical of all its interwar contributions was the construction of a new mortuary on Summer Lane. Prior to this, most people would keep the coffin of a deceased family member in the only downstairs room (which also served as a kitchen and dining room) for relatives and neighbours to pay their last respects. On occasion, settlement workers would report how the children they visited actually ate their meals directly off the coffin, using it as a table.

In addition to the emergence of new projects such as these, the interwar period was also significant for the creation of a new council estate on the edge of the city in an area known as Kingstanding. Believed to be one of the largest estates in Europe (Chinn 1997), Kingstanding was constructed to relieve pressure on housing in the central areas, and many Summer Laners were rehoused there in anticipation of slum clearance in the inner city. With few social amenities, many of the new Kingstanding residents sought to travel back to the settlement to access its facilities but could not afford to do so on a regular basis. In response the settlement decided to establish an outpost in Kingstanding, describing this as a second 'branch' of the settlement and equipping it with its own warden, residents and executive committee. Opening in 1931, the Kingstanding settlement functioned until the early 1970s, when a series of financial problems prompted closure and amalgamation with Summer Lane. During this time it was engaged in similar work to Summer Lane, supporting local people from its community base and pioneering new methods of responding to unmet needs.

The middle years: 1939–1950

With the outbreak of war in 1939 both branches of the settlement suspended much of their previous work in order to concentrate on providing emergency support. On many occasions they opened their premises to provide food and accommodation for families made homeless by air raids, and the settlement's shelters were frequently full of local people huddling together to escape the falling bombs. In addition to this crisis intervention, the settlement also ran two Citizens' Advice Bureaux (CABs) to provide practical advice around issues such as rehousing and rationing. Although the CABs were part of a city-wide network which sprang up following the outbreak of war, the settlement's resources enabled its own bureaux to open on weekends and at night; they were the only ones in the city to do so (Rimmer 1980).

As with previous disruptions to the daily work of the settlement, the Second World War soon gave way to a period of relative stability when the settlement was able to turn its attention to developing new projects. Towards the end of the war it began to re-establish a series of educational classes, training people in public speaking, physical training, needlework, art and a diverse range of other topics. Also during the war, both branches had been involved in organising meetings and discussion groups for local care workers, some of who were later to build on these contacts to make a significant contribution to the local area. A classic example was the creation in 1951 of Birmingham's first Family Service Unit, which was the product of discussions held at the Summer Lane Luncheon Club for health visitors, clergy and social workers. Other new initiatives in this period included a temporary hostel for homeless women and children and the inauguration of an innovative visiting service for isolated older people, which was later to have profound implications for the future work and direction of the settlement.

All change: 1950–1979

In many ways this period was one of transition in which the settlement was forced to reappraise its role in light of significant changes in the local community. During this time the Summer Lane back-to-backs were demolished as part of a radical redevelopment of Birmingham's inner city and replaced with large numbers of tower blocks (Birmingham City Council 1989; Chinn 1999). While these new properties were much less overcrowded and insanitary than those they replaced, they have since been criticised for design faults, for the cost and difficulty of maintenance, for breaking up previously tightly-knit communities and for concentrating on physical regeneration at the expense of underlying social issues (Birmingham Settlement 1986; Chinn 1999; Glasby 1999). In addition to the tower blocks, the whole area was redesigned on the basis of residential, industrial and recreational zones, and the district was renamed Newtown in a competition to find names which would make the redeveloped areas sound more attractive places to live. Once based in the heart of a major residential area, the settlement suddenly found itself in one of the new industrial zones, isolated from its previous friends and neighbours and located at some distance from the main housing areas. To make matters worse, the expansion of state welfare provision was threatening some of the settlement's more traditional projects, while changes in funding priorities meant there was relatively little money available for work in the local community.

Faced with such dramatic changes, the settlement had little option but to refocus its work and redirect its energy. One of the main results of this process was a reduction in locally focused youth and recreational projects and a growth of experimental initiatives to meet newly emerging needs. While some of these initiatives failed to make a significant impact, others became regionally and nationally renowned for their innovative and pioneering work. This was particularly the case in four main areas.

First, the settlement developed new Legal Advice and Money Advice Centres to provide legal support for those on low incomes and to support people in debt. Whereas the former soon became an independent project run by the solicitors themselves, the latter has remained a central feature of the settlement, pioneering the concept of money advice and leading to a range of related projects. As its expertise grew, the settlement found itself providing a range of training courses and conducting a series of research studies into the problem of debt, later emerging at the forefront of the national campaign against fuel poverty (the Right to Fuel).

Second, the settlement was involved in developing a range of community care services for older people and people with learning difficulties, building on its initial visiting service and pioneering a series of day care, meals-on-wheels and transport projects for those unable to access mainstream community facilities. Third was a significant contribution in the area of literacy, developing a voluntary tutor scheme to support adults with reading difficulties, providing one-to-one support to young people excluded from school, pioneering a preventative literacy project and taking part in the national Right to Read campaign.

Finally, the settlement was also responsible for the formation of the National Association for the Childless (NAC), Britain's oldest established organisation supporting those with difficulties in conceiving children. Initially part of the settlement, NAC later became an autonomous body and now operates under the name of iSSUE.

As its position began to stabilise, the settlement was also able to turn some of its attention back to local issues, building on previous themes and traditions from its history. Always closely linked to the University of Birmingham and to the training of social workers, the settlement continued to receive students on placement throughout this period, and in 1971 established a student unit to train a much larger group of workers through a system of group supervision. This was facilitated by the secondment of a social worker from the city council, allowing the settlement to build on previous visiting projects such as the Provident Society or the rent collection scheme to work on a one-to-one basis with local families. Simultaneously the settlement was able to continue some of its club work and recreational heritage through new initiatives to make leisure and training opportunities available for young people in full-time employment, and to provide play and holiday projects for local children. Perhaps the most significant projects of all were the Community Flats (which were established as outposts to retain the settlement's traditional community presence) and the Residency. The latter was a new scheme which used the settlement's residential facilities to encourage children in local authority care and settlement workers and students to live and learn together in a communal setting.

The recent past: 1979–1999

Since the transition of the 1960s and 1970s, the settlement has been able to develop a degree of financial stability and expand in size. One particular area of growth has related to the emergence of unemployment as a major social issue following the economic problems of the 1970s and 1980s. The settlement responded with a range of employment-related projects including job search and support programmes, many of which also offer access to vocational and pre-vocational training. Although these employment projects cater for a range of people, the settlement has developed particular expertise in working with women and members of ethnic minorities, supporting them in overcoming the barriers which stand in the way of their securing paid employment. A second major area of expansion has been in the field of money advice, with the development of projects to support people in debt as they seek to re-establish their independence. These have included schemes to advise on energy efficiency, to provide welfare rights advice, to enable local people and businesses to save and borrow at favourable interest rates, and to offer support to individuals and small businesses in debt through the country's first-ever national debt and business debt telephone helplines. In continuing to work in an inner city area such as Newtown, the settlement has also been able to access local and central government funding made available for large-scale regeneration schemes such as City Challenge, the Single Regeneration Budget and Urban Aid. As part of this process, the Settlement has been involved in a series of environmental and community capacity building projects, working to improve the physical infrastructure of the area, the condition of the local housing stock and people's abilities to participate in decision-making about their own neighbourhoods and lives.

In addition to these areas of expansion, the settlement has built on previous initiatives and projects. After developing expertise in the provision of services to older people, for example, it became involved in the 1980s with a series of schemes designed to support middle-aged people adapting to the lifestyle changes brought about by the ageing process. Continuing to work with trainee social workers, it developed Practice Learning and Practice Development Centres to provide placements in a range of voluntary sector agencies and to promote anti-discriminatory practice. Building on its recreational heritage, it rented rooms to two local drama companies and established its own recording studio and record label for local people to access. Finally, the settlement has also sustained its commitment to understanding social problems and using this expertise to educate others. In the late 1980s this led to the creation of a specialist research unit, and in 1994 to a formal research partnership between the settlement, the University of Birmingham and a number of other voluntary sector organisations. In many ways these ongoing links with the University are a classic example of some of the continuities and changes evident throughout the settlement's history, building on links established in the early 1900s but manifesting themselves in a new and different context in the late 1990s.

Conclusion – looking to the future

After 100 years of working with poverty issues in Birmingham's inner city, the settlement occupies a unique viewpoint. Looking back at a century of history, it is also conscious of the need to use this knowledge and experience to understand the present and move forward into the future. Its centenary celebrations have therefore been both 'backward-looking' and 'forward-looking', with staff, supporters and service users proud of the settlement's heritage and past achievements, but equally aware of the many challenges which the future may hold. From 1899 to 1999, the settlement has been able to respond to the needs of its neighbours, working alongside them, empowering the people it comes into contact with, using its expertise to educate and train others and developing new projects to meet previously unidentified needs. If these themes and ways of working can be maintained as the settlement moves forward, there seems no reason why it cannot continue for another 100 years and beyond. In many ways, the start is just the beginning.

POSTSCRIPT

To mark the centenary of the Birmingham Settlement a detailed history of its work was commissioned. Written by Jon Glasby and entitled Poverty and Opportunity: 100 years of the Birmingham Settlement *(ISBN 1-85858-151-6), it is published by Brewin Books.*

References

Beveridge, W. and Wells, A. (eds) (1949) *The Evidence for Voluntary Action.* London: George Allen and Unwin.

Birmingham City Council (1989) *Developing Birmingham 1889 to 1989: 100 Years of City Planning.* Birmingham: Birmingham City Council.

Birmingham Settlement (1986) *Birmingham Settlement: Annual Report, 1985–1986.* Unpublished annual report, Birmingham Settlement.

Briggs, A. (1952) *History of Birmingham. Volume II: Borough and City 1865–1938.* London: Oxford University Press.

Chinn, C, (1997) 'On the royal road to fame: Kingstanding'. In C. Chinn, *Our Brum.* Birmingham: Birmingham Post and Mail.

Chinn, C. (1999) *Homes for People: Council Housing and Urban Renewal in Birmingham, 1849–1999.* Studley: Brewin Books.

Davis, A., Betteridge, J., Burton, P. and Marsh, S. (1999) *Overcoming Barriers to Women's Economic Independence.* Birmingham: Enquiry into Action (ENACT).

Gardiner, J. and Wenborn, N. (eds) (1995) *The History Today Companion to British History.* London: Collins and Brown.

Glasby, J. (1999) *Poverty and Opportunity: 100 Years of the Birmingham Settlement.* Studley: Brewin Books.

Rimmer, J. (1980) *Troubles Shared: The Story of a Settlement, 1899–1979.* Birmingham: Phlogiston Publishing.

Sutcliffe, A. and Smith, R. (1974) *Birmingham 1939–1970.* London: Oxford University Press.

Vince, C. (1902) *History of the Corporation of Birmingham. Volume III, 1885–1899.* Birmingham: Cornish Brothers.

Vince, C. (1923) *History of the Corporation of Birmingham. Volume IV, 1900–1915.* Birmingham: Cornish Brothers.

6

Raising the past

Toynbee today

Martin Walker

Many remnants of nineteenth-century East London can be found around Toynbee Hall, in the triangle of half forgotten inner city wedged between Shoreditch and Aldgate. This area of markets, narrow alleyways, cultural diversity and poverty occupies a quarter of a square mile. As it is only now being extensively redeveloped, reflections of earlier communities linger within the architecture and street furniture. The Whitechapel Art Gallery and the Bishopsgate Institute, for example, have a decorative panache which contrasts starkly with the glass and steel buildings slowly encroaching on the surrounding area. Other older buildings also draw one back to the past and the acute poverty which characterised the locality. Among these is the 'Soup Kitchen For The Jewish Poor' which still announces its original purpose but has more recently been transformed into luxury apartments.

Despite the outward changes Tower Hamlets, the London Borough in which Toynbee Hall is located, remains one of the poorest local authorities in Britain. The sixth most deprived overall, it contains some of Britain's worst housing stock, and in 1991 ranked first regarding the percentage of children living in unsuitable accommodation. It has 11 per cent overcrowding compared with an Inner

London average of 5.6 per cent and shares with Monklands in Scotland the lowest wealth value score. Tower Hamlets also has the highest mortality rates associated with a number of illnesses – cancer, heart disease, strokes and TB. The Bangladeshi population which displaced the Jewish families from the Brick Lane area often live in accommodation little changed from that encountered prior to 1939. Their presence gives the locality many of the features of a Bangladeshi town. Although this is new, in many other respects the Brick Lane area has been relatively untouched by the massive redevelopment that has taken place since the demise of the London Docks. The Broadgate development that replaced the ramshackle Liverpool Street station on the City side of Toynbee has also not yet intruded, as undoubtedly it will, as the financial heart of the capital expands to the east.

Changing climate of charity

By the 1970s many local charities and organisations, including settlements, were receiving a high proportion of their funding from local authorities. With the cutbacks in public spending which commenced in the 1980s, these charities were forced to move away from secure grant aid and into contract service agreements. Rather than the local authority or central government providing block grants and sometimes unmonitored funding to voluntary sector organisations, many were now paid to provide specific services. Inevitably this approach often impeded the establishment of innovative projects which fell outside the provider–user equation. This change was particularly damaging for Toynbee Hall, because it had for over a 100 years survived as an institution which sought to foster such innovative social projects.

One contemporary Toynbee initiative which illustrates how this inability to obtain primary capital funding hampers innovation was the *clothes recycling project*. The idea was to open a warehouse as a market selling low-priced, quality secondhand clothes. As conceived, this project needed grant funding to cover the initial costs of collection, rent and professional management. Toynbee envisaged expanding their existing charity shop to create this project but when they failed to secure funding they were left with a loss-making facility which also failed to serve the needs of the local poor.

Reductions in local authority funding also meant charities became increasingly reliant upon corporate sponsorship as well as 'for profit' contracts. Some went to the wall as they fought, while most, like Toynbee, after initial resistance had by the mid-1980s succumbed to the 'inevitable'. Those agencies delivering a measurable product or service were in the best position to take advantage of these changes. Unfortunately Toynbee's 'commodities', like the nature of its service provision, had often been charitably vague and it therefore appeared philosophically antagonistic to 'book balancing' types of social intervention. This growing privatisation of charities and voluntary organisations was by 1983 certainly evident to members of the Toynbee Council. As Lord Henniker, Deputy Chair of the Council at that time, pointed out, this meant that as local authority funding dried up, so would the creation of innovative social projects. He argued:

> It is a sad paradox that at a moment when innovation and new thinking about the provision of social services and help for the deprived is more than ever necessary it is ebbing. Why? Because as charities have to carry experiments for a longer period, the costs of these experiments increase year by year, and there is no relief from statutory sources in sight. There is another factor – when statutory money was in generous supply, so, too, were would-be social innovators. Now they are far fewer, because whereas once they could start on a financial shoe-string, inflation and the uncertainty of the future have made this impossible; the innovators are discouraged because they see no sufficient help in sight, and the charities which are put to it to keep their established and proven clients afloat, are not, as before, out looking to anything like the same extent for innovations. (quoted Briggs and Macartney 1984, p.179–80)

Involuntary drift 1986–1993

Throughout the 1960s and 1970s, the social action traditions of Toynbee fitted the mood of the times. This approach, however, combined with a lack of assertive management, led to overspending, which was made worse by the Council's decision to build 'workshops' to commemorate the centenary of the settlement. The resultant debt, by the mid-to late 1980s, forced the Toynbee Council to do a number of things which, by default rather than design, radically changed the nature of the organisation. They sought to achieve solvency while being determined not to succumb to 'market forces'.

John Profumo and other members of the Council held that the work of the settlement should be based upon liberal humanitarian values and a desire to create equitable social change. As such they appeared unsympathetic to the harsh, market-orientated approach of the Thatcherite years. The Council, however, found themselves in conflict with more than just an economic philosophy. Inequality became acceptable, even desirable, during the 1980s and, like competition, it was considered inevitable. This new climate of individualism, coupled with the absence of sustainable revenue, began to undermine and reshape the historical ideals upon which Toynbee Hall was founded.

In early 1987 John Profumo, President of Toynbee Hall, told the Council it was becoming increasingly difficult to raise money for a charity with an overdraft of £430,000 and growing. At this time the Council was a free-standing committee which appointed its own members and was in no way directly accountable to either employees or users. By tradition it overwhelmingly comprised men with finance, legal or political backgrounds, plus, as time moved on, a few local residents. There was no input from the staff except via the warden and deputy warden, and no apparent democratic process operating within the various departments.

Below the Council, many of the ordinary members of Toynbee Hall – the core of which had in the past been made up of residents – were involved in the Toynbee Association. The Association, like a members' club, had no power of decision-making. In April 1987 the

Council called an emergency general meeting (EGM) of the Association and the declining financial situation was made public. This 'public' acknowledgement of Toynbee's circumstances made the settlement immediately vulnerable to criticism from community organisations which had for some time been seeking a foothold within it. At the meeting it was suggested that members of the Association should have more power and more influence. Younger members in particular expressed the view that 'the Council kept everything very close'.

The meeting was a stressful event. For many Council members, the growing debt and the previously ungovernably liberal regime of Donald Chesworth, who had been warden since 1977, led them to countenance less democracy rather than more and a tougher, more centralised and autocratic approach to management.

John Profumo outlined the conflict at the heart of the financial difficulties at a Council meeting after the EGM. Toynbee, he argued, had to secure a long-term, sustainable income because voluntary fundraising and statutory subsidies would no longer provide sufficient means for survival. Therefore they would have to become more professional and more cost-centred. Profumo was of the opinion that the only way of securing long-term, sustainable income was by 'the appropriate development of the site on which Toynbee stood'. There was, he maintained, no alternative but to put the Hall's assets to work; indeed, it was 'Toynbee's responsibility under the Charity Commission' to do so.

Selling off or renting property to recoup debts and create a sustainable return was an option which appealed to many organisations at this time as the financial crisis began to hit the voluntary sector. In some cases it looked like short-term panic, in others, good housekeeping. At Toynbee the debate regarding this option was to continue over the next couple of years. Suggestions for developing the site ranged from complete sale or leasing of all the buildings except the administration block, to a selective renting of parts of the property linked to a privately financed building programme.

Following their discussions the Council decided upon a plan which would see a section of the Toynbee Hall complex privately developed as offices and residences for the elderly, while other parts would be purpose-built for the finance provider. For Toynbee, if re-organisation resulted in the profitable use of under-utilised space, then the deal looked a good option. Estimates suggested the proposed development would eventually yield an annual return of between £150,000 and £200,000.

Council members could not have known they were planning into a property slump, or predicted that difficulties in reaching an agreement concerning the development with a local company would lead to the scheme being abandoned after four years of fruitless negotiations. Such ungovernable problems are, however, not unusual when charities move into the market and become subject to its vicissitudes.

The ultimate failure in 1995 of the property development plan forced Toynbee into much deeper compromises with the social care market. However, because the Council adopted this course with reluctance, and against their better judgement, the market approach never became a central tenet of its philosophy. Indeed, Toynbee it continued to retain, in many respects, a distaste for all that the market stood for, and exhibited a determination that market values would not secure a long-term presence.

The problems Toynbee encountered throughout the late 1980s and early 1990s went much deeper than the property development crisis and struggles with the local mainly Bangladeshi community organisations over 'accountability' and access. Rather these were surface manifestations of the underlying problem of a nineteenth-century institution trying to adapt itself for survival in a late twentieth century, market-orientated society. In this respect Toynbee was not alone, for many settlements and voluntary organisations were obliged to undergo a similar transition.

Making cuts in Toynbee's philosophy

Even if the private finance initiative had been successful and the bulk of Toynbee's short-term debt had been paid off, there would still have been a need to make cuts and rationalise. Because of Toynbee's idiosyncratic nature, particularly its historical dependence upon volunteers, the financial structures reflected its underlying philosophy. It was inevitable therefore that whatever strategies the Council adopted to reduce the growing debt, these would have a profound impact. In the end the measures employed to achieve financial stability swept away nearly all the founding principles which had sustained the settlement for over 100 years.

The changes in philosophical approach were well illustrated by the way in which the Council felt forced to handle the question of student residence. Accommodation had been used traditionally by postgraduate student volunteers who came to work in the community. Residents made up the bulk of the internal community, and besides living and eating together attended open seminars and meetings and worked on projects in the locality. From the beginning these residencies were free, or highly subsidised. They were an essential part of a voluntary contract which enabled students to give to the community. Indeed it was this principle of voluntaryism and the social contact between the residents and their 'neighbours' in the surrounding community that did so much to differentiate Toynbee from other charities and social service agencies.

Significantly, over time, but especially during the 1960s and 1970s, residents' rooms had become increasingly occupied by a diverse group of individuals, many of whom had little or no connection with Toynbee, nor any understanding of its philosophy. One of them had been allowed to accumulate over £12,000 arrears. By 1987, in order to recoup arrears and reduce the overall debt, the Council decided to charge an economic rent for their rooms.

John Profumo, always at pains to defend the founding principles of the settlement, predicted conflicts would emerge from this new style of residency. He suspected rightly that by renting vacant rooms to undergraduate students attending London universities Toynbee would become just a 'hall of residence' filled with people with little interest in voluntary work. This inevitably happened and today the campus lacks all the features essential for a working residential community. Few, if any, of the resident students now know anything of Toynbee Hall's history or purpose. Other traditions also disappeared during this period of austerity and restructuring. Over the years Toynbee had come to employ a retinue of kitchen and catering staff. It was decided that approximately £45,000 could be saved annually by ending evening and weekend meals, which with breakfast had been the core of the communal gatherings for residents and staff. Instead residents were provided with self-catering facilities. This, alongside the decision to charge an economic rent and no longer require participation in voluntary community work, was perhaps the most serious blow to Toynbee's historical vision of an active, structured, socially engaged community.

These decisions were not shaped solely by financial considerations. Some felt a landlord could no longer select tenants on the basis of their political or philosophical beliefs, nor could they impose what others might deem to be chores. Similarly, regarding communal meals, certain staff argued that 'in this day and age' you could not reasonably expect residents or workers to eat at set times. That such views prevailed is an indication of how far Toynbee had, by this time, drifted away from its original objectives and purpose.

The absence of a warden

The decision in 1992 not to replace the departing warden, due to financial difficulties, perhaps more than anything else symbolised the end of the structure put in place by the Barnetts. For no longer did Toynbee have an individual responsible for organising residents, directing the work, and building links with both the universities and neighbourhood.

The last long-serving resident warden was Donald Chesworth. He devoted considerable effort to fostering the internal community and building links with both established and more recently arrived communities living in the locality. Chesworth was an energetic organiser and campaigner, but also a man reluctant to address issues of management and administration.

When Chesworth retired in 1987, Alan Lee Williams was appointed warden. His family came from East London and after serving as a Labour MP in the 1960s he had become secretary of the English Speaking Union. His approach was quite different from that of Chesworth. From the beginning, with the support of the Council he began to scale down the range of activities and focus on developing Toynbee's role as a centre for policy research. Williams, unlike his predecessor, was not 'a man of the people' and although in residency, quickly became isolated from the resident community and some of the staff. An able administrator, his strengths lay in organising and networking at an academic level. He arrived just as the Council resolved to tackle the debt which by then stood at £750,000. This could only be eradicated by wholesale rationalisation. Williams's stay was short and unhappy, for like most messengers of austerity he encountered hostility and misunderstanding on all sides. Nor did Williams obtain much support from Toynbee Council which was itself split, some members having misgivings about a rationalisation which, although necessary, seemed so at odds with the spirit and tradition of the organisation.

Williams resigned in 1991, having almost completed the rationalisation which was asked of him, but having achieved little in terms of building a coherent research programme. He worked hard to attract American academics and others and at resurrecting the links with the universities. The slow and intricate work of creating a base for research in the community was only partially completed by the time he left. Sadly he seems to have been judged by Toynbee's inner community largely on the basis of the rationalisation programme he implemented. One which he recalls in horror, required him on one day alone to terminate the employment of 11 staff.

Williams was not replaced; instead, the Council appointed Alan Prescott, then finance officer, as chief executive, a post previously equivalent to the role of deputy warden. He came from a local authority social services background and possessed a keen under-standing of how those organisations operate. Warden in everything but name, the Council even subsequently appointed a deputy warden to assist him. His primary task was to eliminate the debt which became increasingly intractable as the property deal floundered: Toynbee was in 1992 losing over £100,000 per annum.

Prescott's approach to the development of Toynbee was different from that of his two predecessors. His vision was based on a commitment to voluntarism, socialism and communitarianism. Despite being hindered by scarce resources and debt, he turned out to be an able administrator who worked well with community groups.

The absence of a warden between 1992 and 1998, had significant consequences. For the previous 100 years, the warden had provided intellectual direction and social guidance, helping to co-ordinate the work of different departments, while protecting their individual interests. The warden had also linked the departments with the wider academic work of the settlement by providing academic and pastoral care for the postgraduate residents. Without a warden, and with the chief executive working almost full-time on reducing the debt, Toynbee's departments were increasingly forced to husband their own resources. The most serious consequence of this was that they inevitably became 'cost centres', separate to the extent that competi-tion over funding occasionally arose between them. While this approach might, for example, have been beneficial for the Children's Department, the Asian Studies Department generally fared less well.

By the middle of the 1990s an odd dichotomy existed within Toynbee Hall. In spirit some key personnel still clung to the original ideals. In practice, however, the organisation had been forced into many of the corners which market economics constructs for modern charities.

The modern legacy

Today Toynbee Hall exists within an extensive complex of buildings and undertakes a variety of functions. The core building which survived bombing in the Second World War, is now listed and carefully maintained. There are some lectures, principally the annual Barnett Lecture, conferences and evening meetings in the old building. The theatre block opened in the 1930s is now let out to an organisation which fosters and helps community arts projects. It also contains a modern restaurant and offers a programme of films throughout the summer, and the theatre provides a venue for multi-cultural productions. This area is clearly developing an identity of its own, and has begun to assume the atmosphere of a community-based arts centre.

The overall complex provides meeting rooms, lecture rooms and offices for a large number of community organisations, including Tower Hamlets Homeless Families Campaign; East London Small Businesses; Toynbee Housing Association; National Association Against Racism; various asylum campaigning groups; At Ease, (a group which helps members of the armed services and their families with problems); and Tower Hamlets Education and Business Partnership. It also provides space for youth clubs, Bangladeshi and Jewish cultural activities, art classes twice a week, and, in a purpose-built and recently refurbished unit, facilities for mothers and toddlers. The training workshops built during the centenary year have been occupied, since Toynbee Training moved to larger premises, by a selection of commercial and charitable organisations, and in one of them Toynbee runs its own charity clothing shop. Throughout the complex there are rooms and flats let to students, visitors and the elderly, while at the heart lie a number of departments which, despite cuts, have remained surprisingly intact.

Toynbee Training

Throughout the nineteenth century charities provided training for employment in many poor areas. Toynbee Hall has always been involved in adult and workers' education, but has only relatively recently begun to provide government-initiated employment training. The government schemes organised for the unemployed over the last 20 years presented the host organisation with two difficulties. First, they offered little control over content, quality, philosophy or duration of courses. Second, government determination to cut public spending on welfare benefits and training seriously restricted the options available to those who undertake them. Many who have enrolled on such schemes often see themselves as being press-ganged into them and exploited for negligible wages. Despite reservations Toynbee Training, as this chapter is written, still provides programmes franchised by the government-financed local Training and Enterprise Council (TEC). In addition, Toynbee Training is also financed by City Challenge and the Spitalfields Market Community Trust, and has recently sought European Community funding, all of which allow some freedom to develop independent training programmes. The work undertaken by Toynbee Training invariably involves vocational training with a work experience component but has little in common with the education for citizenship and personhood which was the hallmark of the early years. There is little involvement of the local community in the management and monitoring of this training, and a complete absence of the libertarian ideals which underwrote the 'learning and skill exchanges' initiated in the 1970s. Toynbee Training also shares little with the progressive 'informal education' programmes and 'Saturday University' ideas which individuals and organisations elsewhere have discussed.

The Asian Studies Department

In the early 1980s Donald Chesworth recruited Bangladeshi staff to work in Toynbee's Education Department, principally to teach English and familiarise immigrants with British institutions. A few years later, to develop this work it was decided to rename this sector the Asian Studies Department. This department has expanded in line with the growth of the local Bangladeshi population. Increasingly, however, the Asian Studies Department has become something of an anomaly, existing within Toynbee but to a degree disconnected from its management structure. It now has around 200 pensioners on its books. On average 30 to 40 of these attend the settlement every Monday. Special sessions on housing or health, attract even more.

The department also offers help and advice on matters as diverse as health, immigration, the repair of domestic appliances, letter reading, banking, as well as assistance in dealing with land and tax problems which members experience in Bangladesh. Workers also provide news of what is happening 'back' in Bangladesh and in similar communities elsewhere. These gatherings also have a wider educational role in helping participants learn more about the UK. Like its white counterpart (Senior Care and Leisure) the Asian Studies Department organises day trips and parties for pensioners. Over the last few years, the department has been recording the oral history of the first generation of people from Bangladesh to arrive in the neighbourhood. Other projects undertaken include courses in English as a Foreign Language; sessions designed especially for Bangladeshi mothers and children; after-school booster classes in maths and English for 9- and 10-year olds; and self-defence for children and young people.

Much of Toynbee's work is funded by long-established charitable bodies which tend to favour the more traditional programmes. The Asian Studies Department has found it difficult to raise money independently within its own impoverished community.

Senior Care and Leisure

The Senior Care and Leisure Department works with the local non-Bangladeshi elderly, including a declining number of Jewish people who remain in the neighbourhood. As well as advice, support and practical help, the unit provides meals, hairdressing facilities and transport to and from Toynbee. There are also classes in painting, tailoring and yoga. There is no longer any substantial voluntary student input into these services.

The Children's Department

The problems created by the partial disintegration of Toynbee during the late 1980s and early 1990s are demonstrated by the way in which the Children's Department has grown and developed. Headed by Robert Le Vaillant, it has reaped the benefits of good management, creative foresight, energetic independent fundraising and, most important of all, a popular charitable cause. The virtual autonomy of the Children's Department has given rise to conflicts which partially reflect historical tensions between charity and social reform. For some, the work is too 'charity' orientated, too parochial, and insufficiently concerned with generating programmes and policies which address the causes of poverty. It now organises the Stepney Children's Fund and the Children's Country Holiday Fund (CCHF). The former undertakes outreach work with juveniles, organises a variety of clubs and grant-aids work in local primary schools, as well as supporting Guide and Scout groups throughout the Borough. The Children's Department has remained committed to involving graduate volunteers in its work, using them to help run the children's holidays, outreach and befriending programmes.

Toynbee Hall today

Toynbee Hall has never been a 'community organisation'. The governing bodies have traditionally determined their own membership, while none of the departments have been directly accountable or managed by their users. Founded by a small group of middle-class social reformers, it was for many years the closest thing to a university to be found in East London. With an independent notion of its own direction, the organisation has in the past struggled to be a resource for original social reform, a provider of social services and a laboratory for social and educational experiments. It grew largely from one radical idea: that education provided by volunteer graduates and others would empower the poor and ultimately alleviate their apparent spiritual and certain material poverty. Outside of that one idea, Toynbee Hall has rarely had a clearly articulated ideology, moral or social agenda; rather it has acted as a clearing-house for new ideas and social projects which have loosely conformed to the original principles and ethos.

The last 20 years have possibly been the most difficult and precarious for Toynbee Hall, not simply because of problems over funding or the expectations of the local community, but principally because the prevailing social ethos has never been more antipathetic to the founding philosophy of the settlement movement. Nevertheless it has survived, and it still has many friends and visitors committed to it and interested in both its past and present.

It is interesting to look at what still exists of the ideas which motivated the founders, and perhaps even more intriguing to ask whether any organisation has an obligation to its history? Is it, for example, significant that Toynbee Hall is no longer a voluntarist organisation attracting postgraduate students anxious to contribute to a process of social reform in the East End of London? If historical continuity is not important, then perhaps we should review all organisations by their current performance and ability to adapt to the contemporary environment? Many of the organisational problems over the last two decades, however, seem to have grown from a loss of Toynbee's sense of uniqueness and identity, linked to a reluctance on the part of the Council to articulate either those losses or the new identity which has come to pass.

Briggs and Macartney concluded their centenary history with a reflection upon the choices then facing Toynbee, noting that:

> As Toynbee Hall looks into its own future ... it has to take stock not only of what it has achieved but of what it has not been able to do. Moreover, it has to consider not only society as it is today but society as it is likely to become or might become. There is no one single option. The conditions of the time suggest that the time is ripe for a new set of initiatives, concerned with how best to deal with heavy unemployment, financial pressure on statutory social services, discontent with the fiscal system; continuing environmental problems, beginning with housing; and on the positive side, the desire to be of service, not least on the part of many university graduates ... The fact that the statutory social services are under constant governmental scrutiny with a view to cutting costs at a time when what they were devised to secure is not being secured not only provokes resistance but forces a reassessment both of need and of 'machinery'. Attention is inevitably focused on the position of the Volunteer. (1984, p.179)

Toynbee still continues its everyday work of providing a resource for the poor and the underprivileged in a small part of East London. However, it has been unsuccessful, over the last 15 years, in bringing about change on a local or a national level. Increasingly it has been unable to live up to its history and its vanguard role in the formation of the welfare state and inner-city social services. In this, Toynbee manifests an increasing powerlessness which is common to so many institutions committed to progressive social change in contemporary society. It has also been increasingly unsuccessful in drawing post-graduate students into the East End to work voluntarily on projects of social reform and education.

Toynbee was once renowned for its initiation of innovative services and facilities; however, in a world of increasing complexity and with highly developed structures of regulation and competitive professionalism, the needs of what superficially appear to be the 'new poor' are perhaps not as obvious as they once were. Apart from the material poverty that has always existed in East London, there now seems to be a poverty linked to an absence of community and growing alienation. It is a poverty that encourages despondency while discouraging activism. The area now lacks the campaigning political and community groups that can give people hope in the battle to change conditions. The new poverty, in part, therefore embodies a poverty of belief in any alternative.

Some projects are apparently timeless, like the unattached youth work undertaken by Bob Le Vaillant at Toynbee, a strange, twilight work, the nature of which has probably changed little since the times of Booth and Barnardo. Similarly the work with women affected by violence, along with the reading of official letters and forms for elderly immigrants, differs little in style from what might have been encountered a century ago. Even the art classes, which have staggered on, continue as if in a time-warp. Likewise the legal advice evenings which developed from the Poor Man's Lawyer set up in 1889 seem not to have faltered through two world wars, and still attract a disparate collection of litigants and defendants (Leat 1998).

It would, inevitably, be possible to chop and prune these projects, give them the gloss of the marketplace and bring Toynbee up to speed with the often glib vernacular of the modern social care market. But first, perhaps, the old philosophy and vision which has survived should be resurrected and thoroughly re-examined. The contemporary Toynbee has undeniably lost certain central features. There is no longer an inner community of like-minded people with a common ideology or 'religious' focus. The emphasis on voluntarism has gone, the reforming zeal and the transforming philosophy which must accompany it have all but withered away, but, most spectacularly, the immense projects of social investigation driven by a mix of curiosity and altruism have disappeared. It seems as though Toynbee, like so many other organisations and individuals, has largely stopped being surprised or curious about poverty.

Like similar projects it has either to recall its history and the ideas which inspired it, or develop new and different approaches and strategies. Whatever it does in the future Toynbee will if it wants to have a reforming impact, have to listen, discuss, research and understand the poverty and powerlessness which still occur on its doorstep. New projects should be directed towards addressing real need within the community – need that often has first to be acknowledged and quantified.

It may have to be conceded that Toynbee cannot again be the influential instrument of social change that it once was. However, as spending cuts on social services and welfare continue under successive governments and social networks increasingly fall apart, it is clear that institutions founded on the principles and ideals which underpinned the settlement movement still have a significant role to play. At the end of 1998 an improvement in the financial position allowed for the appointment of a new warden. He is Luke Geoghegan, who was previously a social services manager. The choice may reflect a decision to redefine the role of Toynbee and recast it more clearly as a service-provider organisation. One therefore wonders if this marks the final abandonment by the Council of any desire for it to serve once again as a political, social, academic, intellectual and social laboratory.

Bibliography

Briggs, A. and Macartney, A. (1984) *Toynbee Hall: The First Hundred Years*. London: Routledge and Kegan Paul.

Leat, D. (1998) *The Rise and Role of the Poor Man's Lawyer*. London: Toynbee Hall Press.

7

Settlements and adult education

Mark K. Smith

Ask about settlements and adult education provision, and the most likely response will be in terms of the classes and structured programmes on offer. But settlements are often not what they seem. As Samuel Barnett once wrote of Toynbee Hall:

> [It] seems to be a centre of education, a mission, a polytechnic, another example of philanthropic machinery; it is really a club and the various activities have their root and their life in the individuality of its members. (Barnett 1898, p.20)

In this chapter I want to look to the life of settlements and social action centres – and make sense of them not just as providers of educational courses and programmes for adults, but also as centres of social pedagogy, animation and association. The 'life' of the association – the friendship and community involved, and the commitment to learning for all – is the central characteristic of the 'settlement approach'.

The chapter is based on an analysis of the activities of a number of agencies within the field. Material has been gained from recent settlement reports and publications, a general review of the literature, and conversations with workers over a significant period of time. My focus is on the work of British settlements, but I have also attended to the considerable contribution of North American experience to the development of adult education in settlements. I have not sought to quantify the work, but as Sarah Banks suggests elsewhere in this collection, the overall balance of residential settlement (but not necessarily educational and social action centre) activity is probably towards children and young people.

Adult education

Just how we define 'adult education' is a matter of some debate. Courtney (1989, pp.17–23) suggests we can approach the notion from five basic and overlapping perspectives. Each of these has some resonance with the work of settlements and social action centres. Adult education can be seen as:

- *the work of certain institutions and organizations.* What we know as adult education has been shaped by the activities of key organizations. Adult education is simply what organizations such as the Workers Educational Association (WEA) or university continuing education departments do.

- *a special kind of relationship.* Adult education can be contrasted with the sort of learning that we engage in as part of everyday living. Adult education can then be seen as, for example, the process of managing the external conditions that facilitate in adults the internal change called learning (see Brookfield 1986, p.46). In other words, it is a relationship that involves a conscious effort to learn something.

- *a profession or scientific discipline.* Here the focus has been on two attributes of professions: an emphasis on training or preparation, and the notion of a specialized body of knowledge underpinning training and preparation. According to this view 'the way in which adults are encouraged to learn and aided in that learning is the single most significant ingredient of adult education as a profession' (Courtney 1989, p.20).

- *stemming from a historical identification with spontaneous social movements.* Adult education can be approached as a quality emerging through the developing activities of unionism, political parties and social movements such as the women's movement and anti-colonial movements (see Lovett 1988).

- *distinct from other kinds of education by its goals and functions.* This is arguably the most common way of demarcating adult education from other forms of education. For example, Darkenwald and Merriam (1982, p.9) argue that it is concerned not with preparing people for life, but rather with helping people to live more successfully. If there is an overarching function, it is 'to assist adults to increase competence, or negotiate transitions, in their social roles (worker, parent, retiree, etc.), to help them gain greater fulfilment in their personal lives, and to assist them in solving personal and community problems' (*op. cit.*). Approached via an interest in goals, 'adult' education could involve work with children so that they may become adult. As Lindeman (1926, p.4) put it: 'This new venture is called *adult education* not because it is confined to adults but because adulthood, maturity, defines its limits'.

This leaves us with questions around the various meanings given to 'adult'. We might approach this notion, for example, as a biological (post-puberty), legal, psychological state; or as a form of behaviour (adulthood as being in touch with one's capacities whatever the context); or as a set of social roles. Different societies and cultures will have contrasting understandings. 'Adult' can be set against 'child'. In between adult and child (or more accurately, overlapping) there may be an idea of 'youth'. At base adults are older than children and with this comes a set of expectations. They are not necessarily mature. 'But they are supposed to be mature, and it is on this necessary supposition that their adulthood justifiably rests' (Paterson 1979, p.13).

Most current texts seem to approach adult education via the adult status of students, and a concern with education (creating enlivening environments for learning). Adult education is work with adults, to promote learning. Or as Merriam and Brockett put it, adult education is: 'activities intentionally designed for the purpose of bringing about learning among those whose age, social roles, or self-perception define them as adults' (1996, p.8). We will follow this definition in our exploration here.

The nature of adult education in settlements

From their inception residential settlements looked to an appealing mix of courses, discussions and social engagement. Not surprisingly, given their orientation, this and their associational nature mirrored the experience of adult schools – the forerunners of educational settlements (Rowntree and Binns 1903). Both had 'wide ideals' as educational and social centres and, like Toynbee Hall, many looked to education for life, not for a living (Pimlott 1935, pp.142–143). Furthermore, G. M. Trevelyan's description of process at the Working Men's College, London as 'friends educating each other' (quoted in Yeaxlee 1925, p.157) could be applied equally to the aspirations of many early settlers. Contemporary practice still bears the imprint of these concerns.

EXPERIENCE

First, 'experience' remains central to the way settlement and social action workers generally describe their educational approach. To some extent this may well have come through the influence of American educators. Certainly Jane Addams looked to it. She sought to 'work out a method and an ideal adapted to the immediate situation' (Addams 1910, p.436) and to educate 'through use of the current event' (Addams 1930, pp.380–413). In this she was influenced by her friend John Dewey and his belief that the 'business' of education could be defined as 'an emancipation and enlargement of experience' (Dewey 1933, p.340). This is alive today in the common way of describing practice as 'learning from experience'. Workers frequently allude to Kolb's (1984) famous circle of experience, reflection, abstraction and application (Smith 1994, pp.29–31). With this often comes an interest in opening up and widening experience, deepening understanding and encouraging people not to be unnecessarily constrained by what has gone before.

INFORMALITY

Second, there is a consistent interest in the informal. Much of the learning involved with settlement and centre programmes is deliberate and purposeful 'in that the adults concerned are seeking to acquire knowledge and skills' (Brookfield 1983, p.15). However this may not involve closely specified goals.

> Learning may be apparently haphazard and therefore unsuccessful at times. A tenants group faced with a massive increase in rents may spend much time engaged in unprofitable and inappropriate enquiries as they are initially unable to specify the terminal skills and knowledge they require to achieve their broad objective. (*ibid.*)

In this respect, a lot of the educational work of settlements can be described as informal. Some of the time work has a clear objective – perhaps around the development of reading. At other times work 'goes with the flow'. Outside the provision of courses lies a wide range of educational activity that is not curriculum-based. The direction it takes depends on the conversations that people have (Jeffs and Smith 1999). In this there is the chance, for example, to connect with the questions, issues and feelings that are important to people, rather than what workers think might be significant. There is some evidence that Addams, again, approached the settlement as a process: 'a stage for social interaction that presented a unique opportunity to link Dewey's educational theory and James's pragmatism to transform traditional ideas of social service' (Carson 1990, p.107).

THE RANGE OF SETTINGS

Third, the work of educators associated with settlements can take place anywhere. While settlement buildings offer the chance both for more formal teaching and the sorts of social setting that make for conversation, those committed to community development and social action are likely to undertake much of their work elsewhere. They are not dependent on classrooms or specialized settings, but are able to make use of everyday settings to build an atmosphere or grab an opportunity, so that they may engage with others and teach. Thus a considerable amount of work sponsored by settlements and social action centres takes place in social areas and beyond the building, in people's homes, local shopping areas, and in cafés.

A CONCERN WITH COMMUNITY AND THE WHOLE PERSON

Fourth, there is a concern to build the sorts of communities and relationships in which people can be happy and fulfilled. It is possible to find quite a lot of talk of working with the 'whole person', and of seeking to enhance 'community'. Certain values appear and reappear. These include commitments to: work for the well-being of all; respect for the unique value and dignity of each human being; dialogue; equality and justice; and democracy and the active involvement of people in the issues that affect their lives (see Jeffs in this collection).

LA VIE ASSOCIATIVE

Last, there remains a considerable emphasis on animating group and club life – *la vie associative*. In many respects 'the club' came to represent settlement life. As Robert Woods used to argue, the settlements' true mission lay in fostering 'every helpful form of association, from neighbourhood improvement groups to labour unions, that would strengthen their tendencies toward co-operation and mutual tolerance' (quoted in Carson 1990, p.118; also Carson in this collection). It was also a force with those with a more philanthropic orientation:

> To woman the enjoyment of University life brought home a knowledge of the infinite power and force that lie in the idea of association... [of] fellowship with those associated with us in study, but differing from us in experience, in the object of their work, and in the destinies that await them... If this fellowship were of value in a life of study, would it not be of infinite service in social work, in the efforts directed towards making society a better society, and especially in that particular effort of Settlement work – to raise the standards of social work among the poor

(Ethel Hubbard, Principal of Bedford College, London, quoted in Vicinus 1985, p.221)

The political and educative power of association has been a long-standing strand in adult education thinking and practice. For example, one of the pioneers of the Mechanics Institutes and, incidentally, one of the first English writers to discuss social education, James Hole (1860) explored the 'educative tendency' of associations. The landmark *1919 Report* on adult education looked to the educative power of social movements and voluntary associations. The Committee saw the value of 'the imponderable influences which spring from association in study' and the significance of 'the informal educations which come from sharing in a common life' (Ministry of Reconstruction 1956, p.76). More recently Konrad Elsdon and his colleagues demonstrated empirically the educative potential of voluntary groups. They comment on:

> ... the great range of learning, change and satisfaction over and above those which are deliberate, inherent in the organization's objectives, and expected by their members. The one which was given priority almost universally, and reported as being of greater importance than the content objective of the organization, is quite simply growth in confidence, and its ramifications and secondary effects of self-discovery, freedom in forging relationships and undertaking tasks, belief in oneself and in one's potential as a human being and an agent, and ability to learn and change both in the context of the organization's objectives *and* in others. (Elsdon 1995, p.47)

Groups, of whatever nature, can become, in Knowles' words, 'laboratories of democracy' – places where people can have the experience of learning to live co-operatively. 'Attitudes and opinions', he wrote, 'are formed primarily in the study groups, work groups and play groups with which adults affiliate voluntarily'. He went on, 'These groups are the foundation stones of our democracy. Their goals largely determine the goals of our society' (Knowles 1950: p.9).

In some respects, this tradition of thinking has been more fully formed in relation to adult education in France. *La vie associative* is, according to Toynbee (1985, p.33), a difficult term to translate into English – the 'life of the associations' or the 'associative life' are inadequate translations.

> One cannot reduce adult education to a series of regular activities consisting of modules which have now become ritualized in the form of courses. The very participation in the life of an association, being conscious of what one is doing there (such as the running of a centre) is, in itself, a form of education. And the life of the association sometimes constitutes a springboard for taking on other responsibilities at a local or national level. (Ormessano, quoted in Toynbee 1985, p.10)

One of the striking features of current work in settlements and social action centres is the continuing emphasis on the club, group and association – and this runs through the various areas of work they are involved in. Indeed, at least two of the old educational settlements – Percival Guildhouse and Bristol Folk House – have strengthened their associational nature. Following the removal of local authority money for wardens, the latter, for example, has been run by a co-operative, formed of tutors and students (Bristol Folk House 1998).

Current practice

The five elements outlined above can be found in different ways in many of the education programmes, action research and developmental projects hosted by British settlements and social action centres. It may have been fortunate that Barnett's vision of Toynbee Hall as a university college was never realized, as 'the result would have been the loss of an invaluable spontaneity and capacity for experiment' (Pimlott 1935, p.144). Significantly, that spirit is still abroad today. An inspection report dealing with Blackfriars Education Centre could be applied to many others: 'The centre lays greater emphasis on personal and social development than on course completion and accreditation' (Further Education Funding Council (FEFC) 1998, p.4). Similarly, Bede House attempts to design its education work around accessibility, flexibility, qualifications at people's own pace, localness, informality, and help with a particular difficulty (Annual Report 1996/7, p.7). Settlements have had to respond to the growing concern with product and accreditation within education – but there has been an attempt to safeguard a concern with process and experience.

To explore these elements I have organized the work happening in British settlements initially into four categories. The categories are:

- *liberal and basic education.* This includes basic education and literacy work, and what might be described as liberal education.

- *vocational and professional training.* Here the main focus has been on social work, community and youth work, and care training.

- *social pedagogy and casework.* Significant elements of the work are similar to what is described in Germany as social pedagogy – this includes work around health, ageing, and with those with learning difficulties. It is also possible to find examples of more educationally oriented casework.

- *animation.* This looks to an interest in promoting and enhancing people's participation in communities and their appreciation of different cultural forms.

Liberal and basic education

For many policymakers, basic education, liberal education and vocational programmes constitute 'adult education' in organizations like settlements. This is not surprising, given both the narrowness with which 'adult education' is often defined, and the contribution that settlements, and initially especially Toynbee Hall, made. The latter, for example, began by providing a wide range of evening and extension classes, and debates and discussion; as well as facilitating a significant number of cultural clubs and associations. Part of Barnett's initial vision placed the settlement as the core of an East London 'working man's university', but it was not to be. However, the work was of lasting significance, for example, through the development of tutorial classes and the History School (under the direction of R. E. S. Hart in 1898) and the collaboration with Albert Mansbridge (a former student of Toynbee Hall) to establish and sustain the WEA (founded in 1903).

The contribution of settlements to the development of liberal, vocational and basic education is still significant. The 'rediscovery' of the need for literacy education in the 1970s was a direct consequence of work being undertaken by settlements and social action centres; and today the more associational and informal approach to liberal and vocational education in many agencies attracts students not well represented in further education.

BASIC EDUCATION AND LITERACY PROGRAMMES

From their inception settlements and adult schools have looked to the teaching of reading, writing and arithmetic. Some, like Barnett, saw this as a temporary phenomenon – as public provision developed, there would be less need. Others, particularly in educational settlements, viewed basic education as a central element of their work. Following the Second World War, 'the conventional wisdom ... was that state-provided education had eliminated illiteracy from Britain' (Rochester 1989, p.35) – and little emphasis was given to basic education within settlements. Early in 1963 Cambridge House recruited a small number of volunteers to give tuition to young people on probation orders who had difficulties with reading and writing. In so doing they unearthed a significant demand from adults for provision to learn to read and write. A number of settlements (particularly in London and Liverpool) joined Cambridge House in pioneering tuition schemes. Blackfriars Settlement, for example, soon had a scheme under a full-time organizer funded by Inner London Education Authority (ILEA) – but this was later expanded considerably in association with other organizations such as Cambridge House (Barrett 1985, p.61). A moral panic concerning adult literacy began to develop, with the British Association of Settlements Right to Read Campaign in 1973 helping the 'bandwagon' to roll (Levine 1986, p.151). The result was a series of major policy initiatives around adult literacy – the impact of which is still felt today.

Many settlements have some form of basic education provision – often with a significant number of participants. Bede Education Centre, for example, had 300 students in 1996/7. Their project aimed to provide flexible learning opportunities for people over 16 who need to develop skills in an informal setting; to enable people to improve their levels of literacy, numeracy, English for speakers of other languages, and computing skills; and to offer a supportive atmosphere, small class sizes, good access to a wide range of external accreditation and crèche support. They were also involved in some interesting approaches to learning – for example, one group organized a maths conference and worked on a maths magazine. A number of schemes use the Basic Skills Agency (BSA) quality mark for literacy and numeracy. Several agencies also have computer facilities and programmes linked to their basic education work. However, these can also be free-standing. For example, Barton Hill Settlement has a computer room with 25 to 40 courses per year. There were 400 users in 1996/7. The computer room also had separate membership (with some 200 people joining).

One of the significant aspects of programmes may well be the extent to which the localness and informality of provision attract people not normally drawn to formal educational institutions. An inspection of Blackfriars Education Centre concluded that 'the centre widens participation. It recruits many students who would not usually enrol in further education' (FEFC 1998, p.1). This included people with learning difficulties, mental health problems, refugees and students with many different mother tongues. The same report identified some weaknesses, including teaching that did not encourage students to work on their own or to take account of the range of ability. There was some comment that records showed low rates of attendance, retention and achievement on many courses. This is an inevitable consequence of the more informal approach; the narrow indicators used by inspections (centres like Blackfriars are not only concerned with qualification and accreditation but also with exploring wider issues); and the focus on groups that do not normally come into further education provision.

LIBERAL PROGRAMMES

Just what constitutes liberal education is a matter of debate – it being often defined by what it is not – it is not 'vocational'. The terms are 'imprecise, emotional and ideological' (Tight 1996, p.30): the same experience of learning could be vocational for one person and non-vocational for another. However, Harold Wiltshire (1956) has set out some of the defining elements that proponents of liberal education call upon. These have been summarized by John Wallis. Liberal education involves:

1. A commitment to a particular curriculum – to studies that concern us as men or women, not as technicians, functionaries or examinees.

2. A concern for social studies and those aspects of other areas that look to people as social beings. It is learning as a means of understanding the great issues of life.

3. A particular student attitude (non-vocational) that deplores examinations and awards.

4. The combination of democratic notions about equality of educational opportunity with an optimism about the educability of adults that results in a resistance to student selection.

5. The adoption of the 'Socratic Method' as a characteristic form – with the use of small tutorial groups and guided discussion. (Wallis 1996, p.ix)

As we have already seen, settlements like Toynbee Hall have helped to breathe life into this particular vision of education. The development of tutorial groups, the interest in education as a means of understanding the great issues of life, and the concern for the social, have each been a prominent feature of work. In the current political context with its narrow functional and vocational emphasis, settlements and social action centres have had to fight hard to keep alive a more liberal curriculum. Some have simply given up the chase for elusive funding, others are still able to offer a fascinating range of provision. Examples of work in 1996/7 included:

- a women's history week with an exhibition and workshops at Oxford House

- a local history programme at Time and Talents. This involved a themed range of subjects, walks and talks, e.g. around the docks. This has now formed into a local history group

- environmental education, conservation and adventure education at Mansfield House's 54-acre farm at Lambourne End. This included various family projects

- wartime aviation in Warwickshire; Shakespeare: from page to stage; writing workshops; Freud's Oedipus and Literature; and Latin workshops at The Percival Guildhouse (1998/9)

- family history; wine appreciation; the trees of Britain; French conversation at Bristol Folk House (1998/9).

Some of the older educational settlements, with their long-standing involvement with older university extramural departments and the WEA commitment, have been able to sustain a liberal curriculum. The Percival Guildhouse, for example, has built up 'a strong and distinctive ethos which has influenced both the lives of its members [currently some 800] and of its community' (Stewart *et al.* 1992, p.6). However, a review of the programmes does show a number of contrasts with the activities of the early settlers and activists within the educational settlement movement. There is noticeably less emphasis on political education and upon the exploration of social issues. With the rise of television and other media forms, classic forms such as the debate and the talk have become far less common.

Vocational and professional training

Three areas of training predominate within settlements and social action centres: work skills training; volunteer development; and social work/community and youth work training.

WORK SKILLS

While there was some resistance to trade instruction in some settlements, it became a key feature of many (for example, see Addams 1910, p.439). With the development of polytechnics and evening institutes in the early 1900s in London, many settlements moved away from vocational and commercial programmes. However, the focus of settlements and social action centres on the needs of different groups within their neighbourhoods has brought about a continuing concern with the vocational. Some, like Cambridge House and Talbot, are involved in New Deal provision with local further education colleges. Current examples of programmes include the provision of:

- computer rooms and courses – for example, at Barton Hill, Bede House and Alpha Grove

- training in clothing technology (pattern cutting and textile technology to City and Guilds standard) run by the African Women's Welfare Association at Alpha Grove

- programmes of vocational rehabilitation for people who use mental health services (around 30 people each week) at Blackfriars Work Centre. This involved developing work-related skills such as time-keeping, concentration, etc. Members produce products and services, e.g. undertaking office work.

VOLUNTEER TRAINING

The current interest in volunteer development is hardly surprising, given the origins of the settlement movement. Early wardens gave a considerable amount of their time to nurturing and directing the education and work of the settlers. Alongside the chance to learn about the realities of poverty, settlement residents were offered the chance 'simultaneously to *be* and to *do*: to represent in his or her person the 'highest life of his day'… and to share that life in active and concrete ways with the less fortunate' (Carson 1990, p.8). While there was a considerable movement away from the practice of 'residence' in the 1960s, there has been a turn to the development of local volunteers. In recent years this work has been significantly augmented by a BASSAC initiative run with local agencies involving National Lottery money. Examples of work include:

- The Link Project at NU-TRAC which recruits, trains and supports a team of volunteers to work with users 'providing them with encouragement, support and information during their involvement with the organization' (NU-TRAC 1995/6, p.6). The core training programme for volunteers deals with areas such as commitment, communication, equal opportunities, boundaries and supervision and support.

- The Volunteer Training Programme at the Markfield Project which involves the use of flexible learning packages for those wishing to work in a social care setting; on-going training for crèche and child-minding projects; and training for local authorities on formulating policies and for teams around 'putting integration into practice'. Work is undertaken in partnership with users, parents and carers, and this involves co-training on relevant events.

- Burley Lodge is working to give unemployed people in the local community a chance to get involved in voluntary work in local youth projects. Training has included a series of issue-based workshops plus support and supervision.

- The Salmon Youth Centre is currently working with residents and with local people to develop their abilities as youth workers and informal educators. This has taken the form of specially designed courses, individual supervision and support, and involvement in national programmes.

A number of these programmes can also lead to some form of qualification. For example, long term volunteers at Alpha Grove who mostly work on placement with community elders or with children are involved in an NVQ in Community Care; and some community volunteers at the Salmon Youth Centre are completing a Foundation Programme in Informal Education.

SOCIAL WORK TRAINING

Many early residents were able to use their time in settlements as a way of accessing social work. Women's settlements in particular provided an opportunity for more structured forms of experience and training. 'The leaders of women's settlements were determined to turn philanthropy into a paid profession' (Vicinus 1985, p.227). A number of women's settlements offered one-year training courses linked to the Charity Organizations Society's School of Sociology (Harris 1989) and there is some evidence of women choosing to go to particular settlements because of the programme of study that they offered (Vicinus 1985, p.227). Settlements did open up a vocation for women – although not on the scale of the American pioneers.

> Whatever may have been the class limitations of this generation of women, working during the years 1880–1920, they were extraordinarily successful in laying the foundations for effective social welfare. While the men theorized, the women proved it could work. (Vicinus 1985, p.246)

The scale of the work was significant. The Women's University Settlement (Blackfriars) had 31 resident and 61 non-resident workers at the start of 1895 and was soon organizing training and developing programmes. It hosted the first social work training course in the United Kingdom (with the Charity Organizations Society). Later, in 1903, settlement students joined the newly formed School of Sociology (incorporated in 1912 into the London School of Economics) (Barrett 1985, p.4). More recently it hosted a student unit for the training of social workers (established there in the late 1960s and renamed the Practice Learning Centre in the 1980s). It organized a range of placements in other agencies – but closed in 1996/7 when Central Council for Education and Training in Social Work (CCETSW) funding was withdrawn. A Practice Teaching

Programme had also been developed (and is now situated at South Bank University). Several other settlements also had units or were involved in consortium – for example, Virginia House Settlement in Plymouth – but with changes in CCETSW policy these have now ceased.

A number of settlements and centres still provide placements for students on social work, community and youth and informal education programmes. For example, Charterhouse in Southwark has students on placement on child care courses in their play group, and the women's centre there has trainee therapists and social workers. Caseworkers at Evelyn 190 Centre are on placement from New Directions, a preparatory course for social workers.

Social pedagogy and casework

For many of those involved in the first wave of settlement activity, 'social work' was a far more inclusive activity than is the case today. It entailed social investigation, social education (perhaps in the form of youth work and club work), and social casework. The latter was defined by Mary Richmond as processes which develop personality through adjustments consciously effected, individual by individual, between men and women and their social environment (Richmond 1922, pp.98–9). In North America the work was classically conceived as involving social casework, community organization and groupwork. However, casework and, later, case management came to dominate training and practice within social work. The concern with social reform evident in the earlier part of the century rather slipped away in the 1920s in favour of a more individualized treatment or containment orientation. However, within a number of settlements, more educationally or pedagogically-inclined forms of practice have continued to develop (and fall within our definition of adult education). Relatively under-theorized, perhaps the closest association is with the German tradition of social pedagogy – and this can be seen in some of the concerns of Jane Addams.

Addams looked initially to extend 'college-type of culture' (Addams 1910, p.436) to immigrants, for example, through lecture programmes and the hanging of reproduction masterpieces on the settlement walls. Such an Arnoldian vision was gradually set aside in favour of *socialized education* and a concern for democracy (Kett 1994, p.181). 'It was the function of the settlements to bring into the circle of knowledge and fuller life, men and women who might otherwise be left outside' (Addams 1930, p.404). This runs very close to early conceptions of social pedagogy (see Lorenz 1994).

The problem for Addams and others was that socialized education involved social control.

> The proposition that education ought to be used, not for the 'mere' dissemination of knowledge, but to 'adjust' men 'in healthful relations to nature and their fellow men' easily led to the conception of education as 'life adjustment' which subsequently became so popular. (Lasch 1966, pp.13–14)

There is a problem of 'adjustment' moving along conservative rather than progressive lines, that 'culture was irrelevant, or damaging, to the children of immigrants rather than to immigrants themselves' (Kett 1994, p.298). Similar concerns could be expressed about the direction of work within British settlements at the same time. Settlers, like missionaries, might place an emphasis on 'conversion' – encouraging people to change without necessarily appreciating the cultures of which they are a part. Samuel Barnett wanted to combat this, placing an emphasis on 'friendship rather than charity' and upon 'sharing with neighbours', but the suspicion of patronage remained.

In Germany the notion of social pedagogy has become associated with social work – particularly since the end of the Second World War. The fear that the educational socialization apparently implied within social pedagogy could be directed to the needs of the nation at the cost of individuals and of significant groups hung heavy during post-war reconstruction. Moves towards more individual, problem-based work seemed a safer option than the mass and group work of the then recent past. Thus, as the German social welfare system evolved, social pedagogy came to be seen as the 'third' area of welfare beside the family and school. It can be represented today as:

a perspective, including social action which aims to promote human welfare through child-rearing and education practices; and to prevent or ease social problems by providing people with the means to manage their own lives, and make changes in their circumstances. (Cannan *et al.* 1992 pp.73–74)

Conceived in this way, it includes a wide range of practice including youth projects, crèches and nurseries, day-care centres, work with offenders and some areas of church work. The linkage with social problems and crisis work situates social pedagogy alongside social work. Social work in Germany is currently divided into two major branches: *Sozialarbeit* (casework) and *Sozial Pädagogik*. The former is a 'general social work service to families and other selected groups' (Cannan *et al.* 1992, p.73).

Currently we can see a substantial amount of work that can be described as social pedagogy. For example:

- Health education: At Bede House there have been recent workshops on primary health and female genital mutilation. 'One objective', they claim, 'is to foster an environment of increased self reliance' (Bede 1997/8, p. 4). Charterhouse hosts a health project specifically concerned with the needs of the local Asian population.

- Social skills training: NU-TRAC runs programmes in areas like parenting skills; assertion; self advocacy; and basic listening skills. These are run for two hours per week for eight weeks at NU-TRAC (funded by a local further education college and the WEA).

- Developmental opportunities for those with disabilities and learning difficulties: The Markfield Project provides integrated services for people and families both with and without disabilities, and a drop-in for adults with learning difficulties, with opportunities for around 30 adults to access social and educational activities. They are also currently pioneering work on raising awareness of the needs of siblings – the brothers and sisters of disabled children. The

Bede Café Training Project provides a range of educational and training opportunities for people with learning difficulties in the 'realistic integrated world of a café open to the public'. Skills for employment and a concern to enable trainees to participate more independently in the activities and opportunities of society lay at the centre of their activities. Only Connect at Cambridge House and Talbot brings together a range of services for people with learning difficulties including arts-based development workshops, 19-Plus (a group promoting independent living), an integrated play group, and after-school clubs. The 'People to People' project works with people with learning difficulties to help them celebrate, explore and develop themselves by offering social education groups, events and activities, and counselling services.

• Family learning projects and support for carers: Barton Hill has a number of activities focusing on the needs of families. At Katherine Low there is a programme of groupwork providing support for mental health carers, and for carers of adults with learning difficulties.

Perhaps the strongest elements in the work reviewed in this area concerned the development of practice around the needs of people with learning difficulties, and around women's health and well-being.

Animation

Animation in France and Italy is linked to the activities of community workers, arts workers and others, for example:

• using theatre and play as means of self-expression with community groups, children and people with special learning needs (sometimes called creative-expressive animation)

- working with people and groups so that they participate in and manage the communities in which they live (sometimes called socio-cultural animation)

- developing opportunities for pre-school and school-children, such as adventure playgrounds, toy libraries, outdoor activity centres, and organized sports activities (sometimes called leisure-time animation).

A fairly standard way of approaching animation in a European context is via 'community development'. The following definition is taken from a Report of the European Cultural Foundation in 1973:

> Animation is that stimulus to the mental, physical, and emotional life of people in a given area which moves them to undertake a wider range of experiences through which they find a higher degree of self-realization, self expression, and awareness of belonging to a community which they can influence. (quoted by Simpson 1989, p.54)

Some animators (animateurs) are less keen on an emphasis on stimulation, motivation and inspiration as it can lead to doing things *to* people, rather than working *with* them. Animators in this sense look to breathe life into situations rather than people. They help to build environments and relationships in which people can grow and have a care for each other. This idea runs quite closely to the concerns of experiential educators such as David Boud and Nod Miller. They talk of 'animating learning'. They use 'animation' because of the word's connotations: to give life to, to quicken, to vivify, to inspire. They see the function of animators to be that of 'acting with learners, or with others, in situations where learning is an aspect of what is occurring, to assist them to work with their experience' (Boud and Miller 1997, p.7).

While the notion of animation is not common among settlements and social action centres (other than with some arts workers), the practice is. Settlements have long been associated with innovations in creative-expressive work (see Gilchrist elsewhere in this collection).

One or two, like the Albany, have specialized in arts work; some others, like Virginia House, house autonomous arts centres or groups.

Current examples of practice include:

- The annual Somali Festival associated with Oxford House. This includes an exhibition, art workshops, a poetry and book show, concert and folklore dance, and special interest days. The aim is to help the Somali refugee community celebrate its culture and to encourage public understanding of that culture. Oxford House was host to a number of arts organizations from the 1970s on – such as Outwrite and the Half Moon Young People's Theatre. It had an artist in residence for a time (Bradley 1984).

- Craft groups at the Coppleston Centre which 'meet in a friendly atmosphere … to explore techniques of patchwork and quilting, fabric painting, embroidery, soft furnishing and herbs and scents… Outings are an integral part of the group's education to gain more experience of arts and crafts'. (Coppleston Centre 1997/8). The centre also has a 'Looking at Books' Group which follows termly themes, for example air, water and earth in 1997/8 (the latter involved reading Hardy's *The Woodlanders* and a range of poems on flowers, fruit, vegetables, animals, insects and trees).

- The community darkroom and photographic club at Barton Hill.

- The arts and craft group at Time and Talents. Recent projects have involved the making of a large ceramic mosaic and a stained glass mural depicting life on the River Thames.

Similarly, many settlements and social action centres have strong programmes of sociocultural animation (more usually described today as community development or social action). As can be seen elsewhere in this collection, there has been a long-standing concern with neighbourhood, democratic advance and working for social justice particularly within North American traditions of practice.

However, with a growing focus on social action in the 1970s there were some significant developments in practice. To some extent work associated with settlements held onto a significant educational strand while practice in some other agencies shifted to more of a concern with social planning and economic development. In part this may have been due to the emphasis on association within the settlement movement. Recent and current examples of practice include:

- working with local people to develop credit unions (Community Links, Bradford and Beswick)

- developing community-based groupwork such as pensioners' action groups (Blackfriars)

- developing local community groups on estates, e.g. playgroups, parent and toddler groups, gardening group, and newsletter groups (Community Links)

- establishing a fresh food co-operative (Bradford and Beswick)

- working with local people to campaign for more imaginative services for those with disabilities or learning difficulties (Coppleston Centre).

Finally, there is a very strong interest in leisure-time animation – and again we find the same emphasis on association. A significant amount of work is undertaken with children and young people in the form of play schemes, adventure playgrounds, youth clubs and projects and various enthusiast and special interest groups (see Chapter Eight). A number of settlements specialize in developing leisure opportunities for older people. A good example here can be found in Time and Talents' older people's social programme. The chief objective is to provide 'interesting, informative, creative and educational afternoons for the Over-50s' (1997, p.7). The 1998 programme included a visit to Westminster Flower Show, a tour of the Swedish church in Rotherhithe, and visits to the Museum of Childhood and Shakespeare's Globe Theatre. At Fern Street we find pensioner clubs, a lunch club and a social centre for older people, and at Bath Place a women's fellowship, coffee bar and community garden.

In conclusion

Echoes of the early concerns of settlers can still be found in much of the adult education practice within settlements and social action centres today. The work undertaken does not make the same use of courses, debates and lectures as did the pioneers, but there is still significant innovation and attempts to keep alive more liberal and informal practice. Here it is perhaps worth noting some specific issues associated with this.

1. In the current narrowly vocational and product-oriented context, many settlements and centres struggle to gain funding for their work. Furthermore, they sometimes have to work hard to convince people of the worth of educational programmes and activities that are not linked to some form of accreditation.

2. The struggle to attract funding and support has not been helped by a general lack of attention to the development of theory in the area. Dominant definitions of, and practices around, curriculum, competence and process have not met with a sustained critique nor encouraged the creation of countervailing theory within settlements and social action centres. In part this is a problem of the broader field and of training – but surprisingly little has emerged since the pioneering work of Jane Mace (1979) and others associated with the literacy projects of the 1970s. The re-emergence of the notion of informal education, and renewed interest in some quarters in the practices of social pedagogy and animation, allow for some hope in this area.

3. There is a further problem within the British settlement and social action movement of a relative neglect of association. In many respects, it remains the symbolic form of the agencies involved in this review. However, it has tended to be expressed

through a focus on community development and neighbourhood renewal, on organizing around 'enthusiasms' (Bishop and Hoggett 1986) and on the demand and need for social settings for informal education. The educative power of association in itself, and the contribution to democracy it holds, has not been worked through in most settlements and centres. To some extent, there is a need to reconnect more fully with the concerns of early pioneers.

4. Last, and connected with the above, a review of the practice of settlements and social action centres still leaves questions as to how strongly many workers identify with the educational traditions that have informed their practice. In the conversations of workers, and in their reports, one can find plenty of reference to learning from experience and the like – but the extent to which they take on the identity of educator or teacher in their community development activities, for example, varies considerably.

In the field of organised adult education, the activities of settlements and social action centres can go unnoticed. They are undertaking some innovative work, and most look to more progressive purposes than do the bulk of agencies in the area. The interest in association, the emphasis on animation and the attention given to the informal hold within them considerable potential for those seeking to develop more democratic and enlivening educational practice. In part it is these fractions which can and do enable the settlements to make a unique contribution in an area of practice where conformity is being imposed with ever greater rigour by external funders.

Their history teaches the importance of integration in drawing together people and disciplines. In an era when governments are seeking once more to separate the vocational, the productive, from the simply 'enjoyable', history reminds us not only of the folly of such artificial divisions but of the gains and benefits which flow from ignoring them.

Bibliography

Addams, J. (1910) *Twenty Years at Hull-House with Autobiographical Notes.* New York: Macmillan.

Addams, J. (1930) *The Second Twenty Years at Hull-House, September 1909 to September 1929 with a Record of a Growing World Consciousness.* New York: Macmillan.

Arnold, M. (1869) *Culture and Anarchy.* Cambridge: Cambridge University Press. (1970 edn)

Barnett, S. A. (1898) 'University settlements'. In W. Reason (ed) *University and Social Settlements.* London: Methuen.

Barrett, G. (1985) *Blackfriars Settlement. A Short History 1887–1987.* London: Blackfriars Settlement.

Bede House (1997) *Annual Report.* London: Bede House.

Bede House (1998) *Annual Report.* London: Bede House.

Bishop, J. and Hoggett, P. (1986) *Organizing Around Enthusiasms: Mutual Aid in Leisure.* London: Comedia.

Boud, D. and Miller, N. (1997) *Working with Experience. Animating Learning.* London: Routledge.

Bradley, I. (1984) *Oxford House in Bethnal Green. 100 Years of Work in the Community. A Short History.* London: Oxford House.

Briggs, A. and Macartney, A. (1984) *Toynbee Hall. The First Hundred Years.* London: Routledge and Kegan Paul.

Bristol Folk House (1998) *The Bristol Folk House.* http://www.bristol.digitalcity.org/org/hfe/folkhouse/history.htm.

Brookfield, S. (1983) *Adult Learners, Adult Education and the Community.* Milton Keynes: Open University Press.

Brookfield, S. (1986) *Understanding and Facilitating Adult Learning.* Milton Keynes: Open University Press. ·

Cannan, C., Berry, L. and Lyons, K. (1992) *Social Work and Europe.* London: Macmillan.

Cannan, C. and Warren, C. (eds) (1997) *Social Action with Children and Families. A Community Development Approach to Child and Family Welfare.* London: Routledge.

Carson, M. (1990) *Settlement Folk. Social Thought and the American Settlement Movement, 1885–1930.* Chicago: University of Chicago Press.

Coppleston Centre (1998) *Annual Report.* London: Coppleston Centre

Courtney, S. (1989) 'Defining adult and continuing education'. In S. B. Merriam and P. M. Cunningham (eds) *Handbook of Adult and Continuing Education.* San Francisco: Jossey-Bass.

Darkenwald, G. G. and Merriam, S. B. (1982) *Adult Education. Foundations of Practice.* New York: Harper and Row.

Dewey, J. (1933) *How We Think.* New York: D. C. Heath.

Elsdon, K. T. with J. Reynolds and S. Stewart (1995) *Voluntary Organizations. Citizenship, Learning and Change.* Leicester: National Institute of Adult Continuing Education.

Elsdon, K. T. with Stewart, S., and Reynolds, J. (1993) *Adult Learning in Voluntary Organizations. Volume 3: Case Studies 16–30.* Nottingham: University of Nottingham Department of Adult Education.

Further Education Funding Council (1998) *Blackfriars Education Centre. Inspection of FEFC-funded Provision in External Institutions.* Coventry: Further Education Funding Council.

Hall, W. A. (1985) *The Adult School Movement in the Twentieth Century.* Nottingham: University of Nottingham, Department of Adult Education.

Harris, J. (1989) 'The Webbs, the Charity Organization Society and the Ratan Tata Foundation: Social policy from the perspective of 1912'. In M. Bulmer, J. Lewis and D. Piachaud (eds) *The Goals of Social Policy.* London: Unwin Hyman.

Hole, J. (1860) *'Light, More Light': On the Present State of Education Amongst the Working Classes of Leeds.* London: Longman, Green, Longman and Roberts.

Jeffs, T. and Smith, M. K. (1999) *Informal Education. Conversation, Democracy and Learning.* Ticknall: Education Now.

Kett, J. K. (1994) *The Pursuit of Knowledge under Difficulties. From Self-improvement to Adult Education in America, 1750–1990.* Stanford, CA.: Stanford University Press.

Knowles, M. (1950) *Informal Adult Education.* New York: Association Press.

Kolb, D. (1984) *Experiential Learning.* Englewood Cliffs: Prentice Hall.

Lasch, C. (1966) *The New Radicalism in America 1889–1963.* London: Chatto and Windus.

Levine, K. (1986) *The Social Context of Literacy.* London: Routledge and Kegan

Lindeman, E. C. (1926) *The Meaning of Adult Education* (1989 edn). Norman: University of Oklahoma.

Lorenz, W. (1994) *Social Work in a Changing Europe.* London: Routledge.

Lovett, T. (ed.) (1988) *Radical Approaches to Adult Education: A Reader.* Beckenham: Croom Helm.

Mace, J. (1979) *Working with Words: Literacy Beyond School.* London: Readers and Writers.

Martin, G. Currie (1924) *The Adult School Movement. Its Origin and Development.* London: National Adult School Union.

Merriam, S. B. and Brockett, R. G. (1996) *The Profession and Practice of Adult Education.* San Francisco: Jossey-Bass.

Ministry of Reconstruction (1919; 1956) *Report of the Adult Education Committee of the Ministry of Reconstruction.* London: HMSO. (Republished as R. D. Waller (ed.) *A Design for Democracy.* London: Max Parrish.

NU-TRAC (1996) *Annual Report.* Northampton: NU-TRAC

Paterson, R. W. K. (1979) *Values, Education and the Adult.* London: Routledge and Kegan Paul.

Pimlott, J. A. R. (1935) *Toynbee Hall. Fifty Years of Social Progress 1884–1934.* London: Dent.

Richmond, M. (1922) *What is Social Case Work? An Introductory Description.* New York: Russell Sage Foundation.

Rochester, C. (1989) *Cambridge House. The First Hundred Years.* London: Cambridge House and Talbot.

Rowntree, J. W. and Binns, H. B. (1903) *A History of the Adult School Movement.* London: Headley Brothers.

Simpson, J. A. (1989) 'Sociocultural animation'. In C. J. Titmus (ed) *Lifelong Education for Adults. An International Handbook.* Oxford: Pergamon Press.

Smith, M. K. (1994) *Local Education: Community, Conversation, Praxis.* Buckingham: Open University Press.

Stewart, S., Reynolds, J. and Elsdon, K. T. (1992) *Adult Learning in Voluntary Organizations. Volume 2: Case Studies 3–15.* Nottingham: University of Nottingham Department of Adult Education.

Tight, M. (1996) *Key Concepts in Adult Education and Training.* London: Routledge.

Time and Talents (1997) *Annual Report.* London: Time and Talents.

Toynbee, W. S. (1985) *Adult Education and the Voluntary Associations in France.* Nottingham: University of Nottingham Department of Adult Education.

Vicinus, M. (1985) *Independent Women. Work and Community for Single Women 1850–1920.* London: Virago.

Wallis, J. (ed) (1996) *Liberal Adult Education: The end of an era?* Nottingham: Continuing Education Press, University of Nottingham.

Wiltshire, H. (1956) 'The great tradition in university adult education'. *Adult Education,* XXIX: 2. Also reprinted in A. Rogers (ed) (1976) *The Spirit and the Form.* Nottingham: Department of Adult Education, University of Nottingham.

Yeaxlee, B. (1925) *Spiritual Values in Adult Education. A Study of a Neglected Aspect.* Volumes 1 and 2. London: Oxford University Press.

Plus Annual Reports from various settlements and centres (see below).

Acknowledgement

My thanks to all the settlements and social action centres that provided material for me and answered my questions: Alpha Grove Community Trust, Isle of Dogs; Barton Hill Settlement, Bristol; Bath Place, Leamington Spa; Bede House Association, Bermondsey; Beswick and Bradford Community Project, Leeds; Blackfriars Settlement; Bristol Folk House; Cambridge House and Talbot, Camberwell; Charterhouse in Southwark; Community Links, Newham; The Coppleston Centre, Southwark; Dame Colet House, Stepney; Evelyn 190 Centre, Deptford; Fern Street Settlement, Bow; The Katherine Low Settlement, Battersea; Manchester (University) Settlement; Mansfield House, Plaistow; The Markfield Project, Tottenham; Nu-Track, Northampton; Oxford House,

Bethnal Green; The Peckham Settlement; The Percival Guildhouse, Rugby; The Salmon Youth Centre, Bermondsey; Time and Talents Association, Rotherhithe; Virginia House Settlement, Plymouth.

Internet resource

Further material and links to some of the agencies mentioned in this chapter can be found in 'keywords' on *the education homepage* – http: //www.infed.org/biblio.

8

'Something to give and much to learn'

Settlements and youth work

Tony Jeffs

Early settlements invested heavily in work with young people. Unfortunately, according to Davis, many did so to the extent that they never progressed beyond being 'elaborate boys' clubs' (1984, p.25). The focus on work with young people remained pronounced and a 1951 British Association of Residential Settlements survey reported that 43 out of 155 full-time staff were 'engaged in youth work' (British Association of Residential Settlements 1951, p.15). Initially the emphasis reflected the demographic profiles of the surrounding neighbourhoods. In the 1880s around 45 per cent of the British population were aged 19 or less, compared with less than 20 per cent today. In poor inner-city areas high rates of birth, death and immigration rates invariably ensured that the proportion was far higher than the national average. Organisations such as the Bermondsey Settlement seeking to become a local 'centre of social life' (Lidgett 1936, p.117) were therefore obliged to actively address the needs of young people.

The demographics of the American localities that attracted the attentions of the early settlers were similar. Immigration to the United

States, which paradoxically was being sponsored by youth workers in Britain, added an extra dimension, ensuring that inner-city areas teemed with young people, many of whom struggled to survive in an alien environment.

Demographic imperatives aside, other factors fostered an active engagement in youth work. First, as social and religious missionaries, settlers rightly perceived winning the rising generation as a quick route towards the achievement of their long-term objectives. As Addams explains:

> ... the wonderful and inexplicable instinct for justice which resides in the hearts of men, [– which] is never so irresistible as when the heart is young. We may cultivate this most precious possession, or we may disregard it. We may listen to the young voices rising clear above the roar of industrialism and the prudent councils of commerce, or we may become hypnotized by the sudden new emphasis placed upon wealth and power, and forget the supremacy of spiritual forces... It is as if we ignored a wistful, over-confident creature who walked through our city streets calling out, 'I am the spirit of Youth! With me, all things are possible!' (Addams 1914, p.161)

A second justification for the emphasis was that within these neighbourhoods young people, rightly or wrongly, were commonly viewed as posing a disproportionate threat to good order. Unruly youth were deemed a public nuisance which Barnett discovered many vocal members of the surrounding community wanted 'dealt with' (Barnett 1918: see also Pearson 1983). Therefore settlements that failed, like contemporary youth and community projects, to deliver effective boys' work risked sacrificing their credibility.

Third, the 'new psychology' of G. Stanley Hall and myriad followers unambiguously warned settlers that adolescence, the interval betwixt child- and adulthood when he held character to be indelibly formed, was a period of unprecedented risk and danger. An interlude when unsupervised boys too easily descended into savagery (Ross 1972: Schlossman 1973). Nowhere was this more likely to happen than in poor inner-city neighbourhoods where raucous street life, pubs, gambling and music halls constantly tempted the unwary (Slaughter 1911). Therefore, Addams explained, if workers were to protect young people it was their duty to 'know the modern city in its weakness and wickedness and then seek to rectify and purify it' (1914, p.14). Or as Veltman (1989, p.1) urged, they must go to where the 'dangers of temptation and vice to the young' were most acute.

Finally, the welfare needs of the young self-evidently demanded attention. For example, homelessness was rife, with London alone, during this period, having approximately 30,000 youngsters sleeping rough, in casual wards and unregistered lodging houses (Rose 1988, p.136). While as workers knew, many living at home were scarcely any better off due to overcrowding and low family incomes. Therefore settlement clubs supplied meals; ran education classes and clothing stores; set up savings clubs; provided medical help and shelter; administered emigration support programmes; and offered careers advice which often involved securing employment with responsible and trustworthy employers.

What is youth work?

Youth work in Britain and America was well established prior to the advent of settlements. Pioneers such as Robert Raikes, instigator of the Sunday School Movement, and Hannah More laid the foundations of contemporary youth work a century earlier. Subsequently the YMCA, the first international youth organisation, was launched in 1845, followed quickly by the early uniformed groups, and Boys' and Girls' Clubs. Individuals closely involved in the first settlements often played a pivotal role in these initiatives. Octavia Hill, a close friend and mentor of Henrietta Barnett, was typical of such activists. In setting up some of the earliest clubs and playgrounds she drew into her endeavours individuals such as Henrietta, who via their involvement became convinced of the need for such provision.

The links between youth workers and the founders of the first settlements were complex. In some instances it was the coming together of those already involved in youth organisations that predicated the establishment of settlements. Representatives of the YWCA and Girls' Friendly Society (GFS) were among a small coterie of women's groups that launched the Ladies' Union of Workers among Women and Girls. This expanded rapidly until by the 1880s branches were operating in most urban areas. Many of these actively promoted the establishment of settlements that in turn sponsored youth work (Rimmer 1980).

Modern youth work arrived along with industrialisation. Most early clubs and organisations were sectarian. Consequently agencies usually perceived themselves to be in competition one with the other. Beyond seeking converts they generally sought to counter the dis-welfares of industrialisation and urbanisation. From the onset all struggled to thrive alongside a more self-assured and generously funded formal education sector. Always overshadowed and under-resourced, youth work has been obliged constantly to tack and alter course as client needs altered and the formal sector encroached upon its realms of expertise (Jeffs 2000). Focus and content may have shifted over time, yet youth work has retained certain identifying characteristics:

- A commitment to managing the deviant behaviour of young people. This function has granted an enduring *raison d'être* for intervention on the grounds that managing anti-social behaviour simultaneously serves the interests of both young people and the 'community'. Incidentally such preventative and diversionary programmes always attract more generous funding than other forms of youth work.

- A welfare element designed to address some basic needs. Accordingly clubs provided such services as basic education, health care, libraries, clothing and training for employment. Apart from easing the burdens of poverty, workers found these services boosted membership. Over time expanding state welfare and growing affluence drastically reduced the demand for such interventions. For example, club libraries and clothing stores rarely operated post-1920 (Spence 2001). However, fresh needs were identified, thereby ensuring the continuation of welfare programmes. Birmingham Settlement, for example, in response to the sudden growth in unemployment among young males during the early 1920s set up an Unemployment School staffed by two teachers (Rimmer 1980). Contemporary welfarist initiatives have focused on counselling, health education, advice giving and out-of-school care.

- It is an age-specific service. Upper and lower boundaries have shifted in both directions; however, the focus remains on young people. Consequently it has assembled a discrete history (Davies 1999; Jeffs 1979) and claimed professional status on the basis of being able to work with young people in semi- and unstructured settings.

- The voluntary principle distinguishes youth work from most services provided for this age group. Young people freely enter into relationships with workers and retain the autonomy to terminate them. This has profound implications for how workers operate and can create unique opportunities for learning through dialogue. The voluntary principle also requires workers either to go to where the young people are (outreach or detached work) or provide programmes capable of enticing them to a club or centre.

- Finally, youth work is distinguishable from leisure provision and commercial entertainment by its underlying educational purpose. This also disconnects youth work from interventions designed primarily to convert young people to a religious or political creed (Jeffs 2000: Smith 1988).

Settlements take up the challenge

Initially young people proved deceptively easy to entice into settlement clubs. As one worker reports, on the opening day he 'saw one lad leaning against the railings. He invited him in, and from that time it has never been necessary to seek new members. The news soon spread from mouth to mouth among the poor lads, and the Club was overfilled very shortly' (Cambridge Medical Mission Settlement – undated). Basil Henriques was similarly overrun on his first club night at the Bernard Baron Settlement. In a letter he recounts:

> The Club is open! I had a terrible time, the first day. No gas – but a long row of candles, and then worst of all, no games, as the ones ordered never arrived until too late. However, I was able to borrow some from Victoria Club, and at about 8, I opened the doors to let in nearly 50 boys! Imagine the muddle – semi-darkness, all those new faces, no one with the least idea what the Club is; me trying to keep order, trying everything at once. In the end I turned out 20 boys either on the excuse that they were too old or too young, or because they belonged to some other club, or had not been especially sent to me. The boys, thank goodness, soon made themselves at home and we continued on until 9.45. I started straight off with prayers on closing, they very seriously said the Shema together, and then I started an extemporary prayer. This made them roar with laughter! Most disconcerting, and I finished as quickly as I possibly could. (Bernard Baron St George's Jewish Settlement 1964, p.7)

Apparently all that was needed to secure an abundant supply of patrons was to provide a diet of play, games, activities, outings, snacks and, in the wintertime, shelter. Especially if this mix was available after school and during holiday periods they risked being overrun with takers and were obliged to ration access (Ashworth (undated); Barrett 1985; Trevelyan 1920).

Acquiring members may have been relatively simple; however, controlling them and retaining their affiliation was not. Club work was exhausting, frequently dispiriting. Among paid or unpaid staff alike turnover was high. Workers were often shocked by the 'dirt and neglect and wretchedness' (early worker quoted by Vicinus 1985, p.238). Even those well prepared for the encounter sometimes felt overawed by the enormity of the task before them. One advised:

> Have plenty going on: it's hands that break up furniture. Have, if possible, plenty of room: it's crowding that spoils discipline. Let them box in your presence for three months: it's the only thing they can do or care to do. Have a few papers in another room for the quietest, and after six months get a bagatelle board, but don't be surprised if they mark this advance in civilization by prodding holes in the ceiling. (Ashworth (undated), p.15)

Hensley Henson, the first boys' club warden at Oxford House, who survived barely a year, concluded volunteer workers were unreliable and frequently not up to the task. Therefore club work, Henson held, should be delegated to paid staff. Even the most dedicated might be driven to despair. Margaret McMillan used the metaphor of a 'deep ford' to convey to the uninitiated the personal sacrifice wrung from workers:

> Very deep and steep it is, the soft black yielding mass under the black waters of poverty. At every step one goes down and down. At first it looked as if service would be joy. But it was not so. Real service is, in the beginning, and to the end, courage in going down and not turning back… First in darkness and poverty and pain – yes, even in disgrace, for the pioneer cannot always equip himself well. He may have to bear reproach – just reproach – to despise the shame. The ford has not a good bottom – it has no bottom at all – the waters rise and rise. (McMillan 1927, p.121)

Finding individuals willing to immerse themselves in this work was difficult. Consequently settlements often opted to recruit paid workers. Although the YMCA, YWCA and other pioneering youth agencies, including the Metropolitan Association for Befriending Young Servants and Maude Stanley's Girls' Club Union employed staff, settlements were still among the first in Britain and the United States to do so on an extensive scale. Scarcity of volunteers and the arduous nature of the work were not the sole reasons for the drift to professionalisation. Few without independent means could contribute more than a limited number of hours a week in an era when working days were long and holidays short, and this gave rise to problems of continuity and reliability. As Kingman and Sidman (1935, p.9) explain, all parties realised rapidly that the dearth of those anxious and able to devote sufficient time meant club work could only flourish if ways were found to employ those 'just as willing, just as anxious to serve ... but had not the means'. They stressed that this policy had additional benefits. Not least, it created a 'career ladder' for aspiring members and volunteers.

How the settlement movement offered someone from a poor background this opportunity for service can be illustrated via reference to the career of J. H. Whitehouse, who began working life as a clerk with Cadbury's at Bournville. George Cadbury soon recognized his talents and encouraged the junior clerk to open a youth club for apprentices and local children. This work, alongside his involvement in Ruskin's Guild of St George, helped Whitehouse secure in 1905 the post of secretary to Toynbee Hall. While at Toynbee he founded the influential National League of Workers with Boys prior to becoming warden of Ancoats Settlement (Manchester) three years later. In 1910 he entered the House of Commons as Liberal MP for a local constituency. Interestingly, Baden-Powell asked Whitehouse to organize his new 'scouting scheme' through the National League now based at Ancoats. However, with everything agreed, Pearson, Powell's avaricious publisher, vetoed the plans and Baden-Powell was obliged to strike out on his own (Jeal 1989). Yet still the settlement connection flourished, with Baden-Powell recruiting Vane from Toynbee Hall as the first London Commissioner.

Patterns of youth work varied among settlements. However, core activities and foci are identifiable. As with adult provision, 'clubs' were central to the work. The club or troop and unit (in the case of uniformed groups) operated under the umbrella of the settlement but usually enjoyed quasi-independence. Settlement youth clubs were intended to be places where, as one early worker argued, members acquired 'a respect for and knowledge of self-government' (Coleman quoted in Crocker 1992, p.29). Clubs were rarely mere timetabling devices or means to allocate staff responsibilities, although they bestowed on individuals a discrete role and sense of belonging, more importantly the club ideal embodied a commitment to higher principles. Clubs furnished opportunities for developing friendships, stimulating group activity and allowing space for members to plan for themselves under the watchful eye of mature 'leaders'. They offered the experience of a safe, protected community which succeeded or faltered as a consequence of the young people's own efforts. As Samuel Barnett explained in the Toynbee Record clubs, 'encourage associated action, they promote sociability, and they offer a field in which ideas may be planted' (quoted H. O. Barnett, 1918, p.463). Havens where, Barnett insisted, the boy was to be treated as an equal able to 'run his own show', pay his own way, lead his own life, respect himself, hold up his head in his community' (account of Barnett's views given by Lea and quoted in H. O. Barnett, p.465).

The club tradition was not, as Lea claims in the talk quoted above, the brainchild of early settlers. However, they enthusiastically embraced and extended it. Clubs in many respects often grew 'into the single most important branch of work' (Barrett 1985, p.7). Henrietta Barnett, prior to moving to Whitechapel in 1873, was active in girls' club work. This continued and she developed a series of initiatives incorporated in the Toynbee Hall programme. The range of work undertaken during this initial period was impressive, embracing a nightly club for girls; an 'at home evening'; the Band of White and Gold Club which organised educational classes appropriate for young women; St Jude's Guild, a club for senior girls; and a Daisy Guild specifically for young female servants. Henrietta also helped administer a parish branch of the Metropolitan Association for Befriending Young Servants (founded in 1878 by her friend Jane Nassau Senior) with almost 2500 members.

Boys' work was not sidelined. Samuel Barnett formed the first official Army Cadet Corps in 1885 commanded by H. W. Nevinson, the war correspondent, women's suffrage campaigner, journalist and father of the war artist Christopher Nevinson. The Corps sought to offer:

...interesting occupation for the evening hours of London working boys, especially for those of an enterprising and active character, and the inculcation of habits of order, discipline, cleanliness, punctuality and good conduct, thus developing self-respect at an age (13 to 18) when most susceptible to good or evil influences, and when character is forming. (Quoted Darley 1990, p.245)

Besides uniformed groups, settlement youth work usually included an extensive array of clubs and activities. Most ran junior and after-school clubs; sports clubs, with football, cricket, swimming and boxing especially popular; libraries; cultural activities such as recitation classes, theatrical productions, music – bands were commonplace; intellectual activities including debating societies, visits to museums and galleries, guest speakers and classes; and, perhaps the most popular of all, annual camps. Meticulously planned, replete with quartermasters, these often took place on sites or in the grounds of houses donated or lent to the settlement by wealthy patrons. For most participants they were the only holiday of the year and although 'low cost', participation generally demanded thrift and sacrifice.

A special contribution

Settlement youth work always operated alongside alternative providers. Uniformed organisations, boys' and girls' clubs and Christian missions all competed for the allegiance of their clientele. Replication was inevitable, yet to an impressive degree settlements succeeded in carving out a unique *modus operandi*. Certainly this was the case pre-1939 but their capacity to occupy a discrete niche faded after then.

So what features coagulated to give settlement youth work a distinctive slant? First, it was a component within an integrated or extended programme. Unlike mainstream units that operated within the confines of regulations delineating upper and lower membership ages, settlements eschewed such restrictions. As one account of their contribution explained, they strove to be 'centres for the whole family' wherein 'a place and a welcome can be found at any age' (Self 1945, p.244). Thus the 'club' was not a free standing entity but a segment of a greater whole. A 'club', troop or group might aim to meet age-specific needs or target a cohort but it was always assumed that participants were members of something bigger – the settlement. Moreover, irrespective of the entry point, there were other groups and activities simultaneously offering members a welcome.

Second, it consciously set out to bridge class and other social boundaries by drawing individuals from disparate backgrounds into close contact, as Samuel Barnett explained, the broader endeavour being 'to make men friends, to unite all classes in common aims' (quoted Nettleship 1982, p.577). Day trips for Bermondsey boys to Cambridge cloisters, incorporating college tours, boating, afternoon tea and cricket may seem quaint, even naïve, but they boasted a higher rationale than mere entertainment. Unlike trips to the Dome or karting, such ventures had a substantive educational function. Surely few participants, at either end, did not in retrospect come to contemplate the configuration of their own and other's life chances and the social inequalities which infused British society. More mundanely, settlements fostered within the club setting a constant interplay between individuals from diverse backgrounds – something absent from much contemporary youth work, which tends to assume that like is best served by like and thereby reinforces a laager mentally among staff and clients – a mentality which limits the ambitions, curtails the horizons and narrows the range of social interaction of all parties. At its best youth work in this environment was predicated on an assumption that it was only worthwhile if 'change' was a two-way process, beneficial for both worker and member.

Third, youth work was embedded within a wider social movement, one devoted to publicising the plight of the poor; quantifying social problems via action research; creating social movements to campaign for and implement reforms; and stimulating the emergence of self-help and co-operative movements among the dispossessed. Youth work therefore was more likely to be imbued with a wider, deeper purpose than mere conversion or the control of 'hooligan' behaviour. In particular, settlements tended to insert an overtly political dimension that had hitherto been absent from youth work. For it took place in the context of institutions where, according to one commentator, 'staff were living socialism' (Self 1945, p.246). And if not affiliates of that ideology, then most settlers were at least seeking to offer 'a practical demonstration of cooperative living' (Crocker 1992, p.26).

Fourth, they injected an intellectual dimension into a tradition that focused disproportionately, especially in relation to young men, on harnessing and inculcating a love of sport. Settlements in the early years attracted into club work 'fervent and brilliant' young men and women (MacKenzie and MacKenzie 1977, p.342), individuals who brought with them a rich spread of cultural and social interests which they hoped to communicate to club members. These aspirations were enshrined in the ethos of the settlements. Manchester's ambition to create 'a centre of aesthetic culture' (Picht 1914, p.117) was mirrored in a close association with the Municipal and Whitworth art galleries and local museums as well as its own reading circle and Elizabethan Society aimed at reviving the 'dramatic spirit' (Rose and Woods 1995, p.34). Hull House had programmes calibrated to promote sympathetic appreciation of folk and ethnic cultures among young members (Addams 1930). This pattern was reflected in the high proportion of respondents to Picht's 1914 survey, who listed among their activities libraries, lecture programmes, drama, art classes and various cultural activities for all age groups.

Fifth, although club work with young women pre-dated the arrival of settlements and indeed provided them with guidelines regarding effective practice, they made a distinctive contribution to this area. Within months of the foundation of Oxford House and Toynbee Hall women were planning independent settlements. These came to specialise in work with families, children and adolescent girls. Vincus (1985) notes that women's settlements had an inimitable style, ethos and even appearance, for whereas the early male establish-

ments were modelled on the Oxbridge Colleges of the settlers' adolescence, women's settlements 'looked like urban homes' and the
income was far more likely to be spent on furthering 'the social
services, not for the buildings' (*ibid.*, p.216). Charitable work granted
middle-class women the freedom to enter areas they were otherwise
debarred from; settlements allowed many more to live for days or
years in such localities. Whereas the male variant sought to entice
young professionals to experience 'life' in these districts, it was never
expected that this encounter would lead them to abandon their career
aspirations. Indeed, such an outcome would defeat the object as it
was hoped they would move on to acquire positions of influence,
transporting with them a heightened understanding of the causes of
poverty, and sympathy for the poor. Few, if any, women until
relatively recently expected to follow such a trajectory. Consequently
most leaders of the women's settlements 'were determined to turn
philanthropy into a paid profession' (*ibid.*, p.227). Almost instanta-
neously they were offering young women training in social and
community work, linked to prestigious universities such as Chicago
and London. It was from such programmes linked to settlements, as
well as the movement itself, that key figures such as Pearl Jephcott,
Josephine Macalister Brew and Margaret Simmey emerged to shape
girls' work and youth work post-1930.

Finally, settlements became focal points for innovative practice.
Autonomy from the state and, in many instances, organised religion
bestowed on many linked with them unprecedented opportunities
for experimentation. Pioneers often enjoyed the personal freedom
bestowed by a private income and this also allowed the space to 'take
risks'. These factors, for example, allowed special-needs groups
deemed 'unproductive' by state bodies to be catered for, and initiatives such as play work, which offered little in the way of measurable
outputs, to be developed (Trevelyan 1920). They also bestowed an
autonomy from 'short-termism' that allowed workers the option to
wait for the emergence of a 'social interest [which] can be led into
educational channels' (Lasker 1930, p.52).

Within the settlement movement youth work had its critics. One strand posited unequivocally that it was counterproductive. Youth work as a form of intervention being rejected on the grounds that 'the segregation of adolescents all at the same stage of development, when they should be freely learning from every possible degree of maturity, is one of the worst crimes committed against growing boys and girls' (Innes, Pearse and Crocker 1943, p.223). Others from a diametrically different tradition questioned the methodology.

Roland Phillips spent his university vacations at Oxford House and enjoyed the work; however, subsequent encounters with the Boy Scouts persuaded him that settlement clubs were predominately organisations via which adults 'could "run things" for the benefit of boys', whereas a Scout Troop properly established 'was a "gang" run by boys to develop themselves and needing adult help only incidentally' (Barber 1960, p.22). Phillips opted to devote his life to scouting, and paradoxically gave up his West End flat to become again an Oxford House resident and work full-time as Scout Commissioner for East London. Killed in action in 1916, Phillips left the Scouts a property in Stepney that in 1920 became Roland House, their own settlement. This was a remarkable and unique experiment. It was designed to offer Scouts from Britain and overseas, few of whom had enjoyed a privileged background or university education, the opportunity to live in a settlement and undertake social service in Stepney (East London). It was unique in that it was managed by a youth organization and designed, in the words of one warden, 'to enable members to devote their leisure to the service of boys whose circumstances make every step of your work uphill' (quoted in Barber 1960, p.115: see also Nevill 1960).

Undoubtedly by 1914 settlement youth initiatives had achieved much. Baden-Powell, for example, in his *Yarns for Boy Scouts* (1909) quotes approvingly Gorst's statement that they had succeeded in training and civilising some of the most difficult boys in every city where they operated, while Henrietta Barnett (1918a, pp.50–51) justifiably boasted that they had led the way in drawing (for the first time) into philanthropic endeavours significant numbers of young men, among them some of the most 'brilliant' of their generation.

A fading presence

A perceived rise in delinquency levels during the 1914–18 war prompted for the first time direct government intervention in youth work. Local authorities were obligated to establish Juvenile Organisation Committees comprising representatives of the Local Education Committee, voluntary organisations and interested persons. Overall the response was rather half-hearted as Committees had limited access to funding under Section 86 of the 1921 Education Act, and most voluntary agencies were more attuned to competing against each other than collaborating. Leaving aside such matters, their appearance and longevity nevertheless signalled the onset of a process that eventually fashioned an irreversible shift in the balance of power. The youth service that emerged amalgamated the voluntary and statutory in a loose federation. However, the latter gradually secured dominance, initially via control of the lion's share of funding, and subsequently by manipulation of the inspection and contracting mechanisms. Many voluntary youth agencies and providers disappeared during the course of the next 80 years. Some survived, a few thrived, and new 'players' emerged. With the exception of barely more than a handful of religious and uniformed organisations, only the biddable, willing to adapt to an agenda dictated by statutory funding regimes, thrived (Jeffs and Smith 1999). The new voluntary organisations that have materialised since 1945 have been generally handcrafted to respond to the 'needs' of young people as interpreted by central and, to a lesser extent, local government.

As previously noted, providers were pushed aside by a state that catered increasingly for the welfare and educational needs of young people. Similarly the raising of school-leaving ages and constant expansion of post-school education led inevitably to youth provision being relocated in formal education settings. Such changes marginalized voluntary youth providers, including settlements (Davis 1984, p.77), and encouraged those who remained to focus on excluded and sub-cultural groups of young people who, for whatever reasons, are external to or disaffected from the formal education sector (Jeffs 2000). This is a trend reflected in the spiralling of attention devoted to those from minority ethnic and cultural groups, to the homeless and those at risk, and overall to the provision of outreach and detached work. As the popularity of 'youth clubs' declined and, in some cases, the demography of the locality changed in a way that denied them a viable client group, so some settlements opted to curtail or abandon mainstream work, concluding that 'youth clubs were not fashionable, or ultimately, viable' (Glasby 1999, p.187: Rochester 1989).

Settlements, like others, had to adjust to this reconfiguration. Indeed, as they were independent units unprotected by a national organisation capable of co-ordinating a collective response, settlements were obliged to do so more than most. Oxford House, for example, one of the key progenitors of settlement youth work, by the mid-1950s decided to reduce the youth worker's salary, it being no longer possible to sustain either a 'club or membership' (Ashworth (undated), p.49). The decision was rescinded with the influx of government funding subsequent upon publication of the *Albemarle Report* (HMSO 1960). Others who had once been major providers, such as Edinburgh University Settlement, withdrew quietly, not to return. Even the Scout Settlement closed. Those remaining increasingly undertook work according to a blueprint imposed upon them by the funding agencies. Within a couple of decades they, like most other voluntary agencies, were operating in ways scarcely distinguishable from mainstream local authority clubs and units (Burgess 1996; Barrett 1987; Rose and Woods 1995; Armstrong 1992; see also Chapter Six by Martin Walker). Provision was often of a high standard but it was no longer distinctive by virtue of being affiliated to a settlement.

Noticeably key elements evaporated as the century progressed. Iremonger, Head of Oxford House, noted even prior to the onset of the Great War that 'Settlement fever at Oxford … has passed' (Picht

1914, p.224). Today it is non-existent. The ties that once bound most settlements to the old universities and public schools and endowed them with a stream of enthusiastic club workers faded long ago. This model, according to one history, 'disappeared in the 1950s and 1960s when fewer people had the time, interest and finance to be able to do full time and especially residential work without pay' (Rendel and Kyle 1989, p.36). Tenuous links survive; for instance, girls from Cheltenham Ladies' College remain involved in aspects of the work of St Hilda's East, and intermittent contact between Charterhouse and the settlement in Southwark, founded by old boys, lingers. Wardens overwhelmingly now have backgrounds similar to those of other community and youth workers; few are now identified by their college or university affiliation. Also the residential element has largely disappeared. Those such as the Salmon Centre (once the Cambridge University Medical Mission Settlement), where residents are involved in the daily life of the settlement, are atypical.

The cumulative impact of these changes has been to denude the uniqueness of the settlement contribution to youth work. In particular, what have vanished are those elements designed to erode class barriers; foster an abiding sense of social responsibility among the young and privileged, and from their ranks sire lifetime advocates for the poor; sponsor innovative practice; and bestow upon youth work an intellectual dimension – indeed, the very attributes that in 1911 inspired the young Basil Henriques, then an undergraduate, to devote his life to youth work:

> Alec Paterson introduced me to the Clubs of the Oxford and Bermondsey Mission, where he made me feel I had something to give and much to learn. There I saw Christianity really lived in a wonderful fellowship of dockers and undergraduates, which showed such a spirit of happiness and friendship, of service and loyalty, that I felt a challenge. Could Judaism produce such fellowship among Jews? (Bernard Baron St George's Jewish Settlement 1964, p.4)

Conclusion: rediscovering the past

Current funding criteria applied to youth work are based on a deficit model of education. Overwhelmingly product-orientated, they consequently abandon the focus on the group in favour of an obsession with individual outcomes. The client group is perceived as lacking transferable skills (the attributes employers judge desirable), a willingness to engage in civil society, and a sense of responsibility. Underpinning funding directives is a conviction that all young people are inadequate but some are dangerously so. Measurement and monitoring therefore becomes essential to identify the scale of the individual deficit and to enable the selection, on the basis of 'sound data', of those to be targeted. To varying degrees all need a diet of guidance, control and mentoring, but some require a great deal. Much as Victorians of a particular bent perceived leisure to be a menace, so contemporary Gradgrinds perceive it as a lost opportunity for learning. Extended school days, compulsory homework, as well as after-school and holiday coaching programmes, are all judged self-evidently valuable in so far as they erode the capacity of young people to enjoy and administer their 'free time'. The space to forge friendships and enjoy association within the context of a highly competitive educational system is becoming ever more restricted (Scott 2000). Opportunities to relate to the spiritual, aesthetic and creative shrink by the day for many young people. Whereas early settlers saw employment and long working hours as the impediment to a rich and full life, for the young today the problems spread from a narrow, vocationally-orientated education system.

These shifts have to be set alongside a continuation of trends within housing and employment that are fostering acute social divisions in relation to locality. The social mixing of young people across class boundaries, whether in the context of an educational institution or leisure and social setting, is unlikely to be any more extensive today, in many areas, than it was century ago. In other words, although certain challenges that taxed the ingenuity of early settlers in relation to young people have evaporated or at least contracted, many remain tantalisingly intractable.

We cannot, and indeed should not, seek to reconstruct the original settlement model. However, we must extract from the 'settlement approach' those elements that did so much to craft and sustain an alternative creative tradition within youth work and, having once identified them, endeavour to develop and build upon them. Youth work based upon concepts of friendship, free association, cultural and spiritual growth, may sound quaint to some ears, but it has so much more to offer than current versions spawned by an overarching fear of the underclass and diminishing rates of productivity. It is a form of practice founded upon a conviction that those engaging with young people do indeed, like Henriques, 'have something to give' but above all have 'much to learn'.

Bibliography

Addams, J. (1914) *The Spirit of Youth and the City Streets*. New York: Macmillan.

Addams, J. (1930) *Twenty Years at Hull House*. New York: Macmillan.

Armstrong, K. (1992) *Homespun: A Story of Spennymoor and its Famous Settlement*. North Shields: Northern Voices.

Ashworth, M. (undated) *The Oxford House in Bethnal Green: 100 Years of Work in the Community*. London: Oxford House.

Baden-Powell, R. (1909) *Yarns for Boy Scouts*. London: Pearson.

Barber, D. H. (1960) *The House on the Green*. London: Roland House Scout Settlement.

Barnett, H. (1909) 'Town Children in the Country'. In S. and H. Barnett (eds) *Towards Social Reform*. London: T. Fisher.

Barnett, H. O. (1918) *Canon Barnett: His Life, Work and Friends, Vol. 1*. Boston: Houghton Mifflin.

Barnett, H. O. (1918a) *Canon Barnett: His Life, Work and Friends, Vol. 2*. Boston: Houghton Mifflin.

Barrett, G. (1987) *Blackfriars Settlement: A Short History 1887–1987*. London: Blackfriars Settlement.

Bernard Baron St George's Jewish Settlement (1964) *Fiftieth Anniversary Review 1914–1964*. London: Bernard Baron Settlement.

British Association of Residential Settlements (1951) *Residential Settlements: A Survey*. London: British Association of Residential Settlements.

Burgess, D. (1996) *My Life as a Youth Leader*. Drayton, Hants: T and A Publishing.

Cambridge Medical Mission Settlement (undated) *Miracles of Grace in Bermondsey*. London: Cambridge Medical Mission Settlement.

Cole, G. D. H. (1945) 'Mutual aid movements'. In A. F. C. Bourdillon (ed) *Voluntary Social Services*. London: Methuen.

Cormack, U. M. (1945) 'Developments in case-work'. In A. F. C. Bourdillon (ed) *Voluntary Social Services*. London: Methuen.

Crocker, R. H. (1992) *Social Work and Social Order: The Settlement Movement in Two Industrial Cities, 1889–1930*. Urbana: University of Illinois Press.

Davies, B. (1999) *From Voluntaryism to Welfare State: A History of the Youth Service, Vol. 1*. Leicester: Youth Work Press.

Davis, A F (1984) *Spearheads for Reform: The Social Settlements and the Progressive Movement 1890–1914*. New Brunswick, NJ: Rutgers University Press.

Darley, G. (1990) *Octavia Hill: A Life*. London: Constable.

Glasby, J. (1999) *Poverty and Opportunity: 100 Years of the Birmingham Settlement*. Studley: Brewin Books.

HMSO (1960) *The Youth Service in England and Wales (Albemarle Report)*. London: HMSO.

Hurley, A. (2000) 'Grey Lodge Settlement, Dundee'. *Young People Now (134)*.

Innes, H., Pearse, H. and Crocker, L. H. (1943) *The Peckham Experiment*. London: Allen and Unwin.

Jeal, T. (1989) *Baden-Powell*. London: Hutchinson.

Jeffs, A. J. (1979) *Young People and the Youth Service*. London: Routledge and Kegan Paul.

Jeffs, T. (2000) 'First lessons: historical perspectives on informal education'. In L. D. Richardson and M. Wolfe (eds) *Informal Education: Principles and Practice*. London: Routledge.

Jeffs, T. and Smith, M. K. (1999) 'Resourcing youth work: dirty hands and tainted Money'. In S. Banks (ed.) *Ethical Issues in Youth Work*. London: Routledge.

Jones, H. (1994) *Duty and Citizenship: The Correspondence and Papers of Violet Markham*. London: Historians' Press.

Kingman, J. M. and Sidman, E. (1935) *A Manual of Settlement Boys' Work*. New York: National Federation of Settlements.

Lasker, B. (1930) 'The new youth'. *Neighborhood: A Settlement Quarterly* (3) pp.48–53.

Lidgett, S. (1936) *My Guided Life*. London: Methuen.

MacKenzie, N. and MacKenzie J. (1977) *The First Fabians*. London: Weidenfield and Nicolson.

McLeod, H. (1974) *Class and Religion in the Late Victorian City*. London: Croom Helm.

McMillan, M. (1927) *The Life of Rachel McMillan*. London: Dent.

Nettleship, L. E. (1982) 'William Fremantle, Samuel Barnett and the Broad Church Origins of Toynbee Hall'. *Journal of Ecclesiastical History*, October 1982.

Nevill, P. B. (1960) *My Scouting Story*. London: Roland House Scout Settlement.

Pearson, G. (1983) *Hooligan: A History of Respectable Fears*. London: Macmillan.

Picht, W. (1914) *Toynbee Hall and the English Settlements*. London: G. Bell and Sons.

Rendel, M. and Kyle, E. (1989) *St Hilda's East: A Century of Community Service*. London: St Hilda's East.

Rimmer, J. (1980) *Troubles Shared: The Story of a Settlement 1899–1979*. Birmingham: Phlogiston Publishing.

Rochester, C. (1989) *Cambridge House: The First Hundred Years. London: Cambridge House Settlement*.

Rose, L. (1988) *'Rogues and Vagabonds': Vagrant Underworld in Britain, 1815–1985*. London: Routledge.

Rose, M. E. and Woods, A. (1995) *Everything Went on at the Round House: A Hundred Years of the Manchester University Settlement*. Manchester: University of Manchester.

Ross, D. (1972) *G. Stanley Hall: The Psychologist as Prophet*. Chicago: University of Chicago Press.

Schlossman, S. L. (1973) 'G. Stanley Hall and the Boys' Club: Conservative applications of recapitulation theory'. *Journal of the History of the Behavioral Sciences*, 9 (April).

Scott, C. (2000) 'Going home with the chaps: Young urbanites and space'. *Youth and Policy* (69).

Self, P. J. O. (1945) 'Voluntary organisations in Bethnal Green'. In A. F. C. Bourdillon (ed.) *Voluntary Social Services: Their Place in the Modern State*. London: Methuen.

Slaughter J. W. (1911) *The Adolescent*. London: Swan Sonnenschein.

Smith, M. (1988) *Developing Youth Work*. Milton Keynes: Open University Press.

Spence, J. (2001) 'Impact of the First World War on the development of youth work'. In R. Gilchrist, T. Jeffs and J. Spence (eds) *Essays on the History of Community and Youth Work*. Leicester: Youth Work Press.

Trevelyan, J. (1920) *Evening Play Centres for Children*. London: Methuen.

Veltman, J. (1989) *Oxford and St George's: A History of 75 Years*. London: Oxford and St Georges Old Boys and Girls Club.

Vicinus, M. (1985) *Independent Women: Work and Community for Single Women 1850–1920*. London: Virago.

9

Settlements and the arts

Ruth Gilchrist

From the outset the arts lay at the heart of the settlement movement. They were viewed as a way of expressing the core philosophy which sought to bring different social classes together to learn each from the other. Inspired by Ruskin's ideas of the relationship of art to a social and moral framework, key settlement thinkers such as the Barnetts and Addams were convinced that the use of 'high' arts would improve the local population and offer an alternative to the music halls, public houses and penny arcades where working-class people gathered in significant numbers in areas adjacent to the settlements. The arts were perceived as a way of educating people, lifting expectations, promoting conversation, stimulating debate, teaching new skills, building community and improving social conditions. However, the settlers knew, like William Morris, that art alone could not cure social ills, although few of them echoed his call for social revolution. Lord Rosebery, a leading Liberal, captured this consensus that art could contribute towards social reform when opening the Whitechapel Art Gallery in 1901, arguing that 'Art and art galleries would not solve the social question, but people accustomed to look at beautiful things would acquire a dislike for ugliness which is nearly the same as love of the beautiful' (Pimlott 1935, p.171).

Access to and understanding of the benefits bestowed by the arts was seen as something that university men and women could bring to the East End of London and elsewhere. The founders employed the arts as a 'bridge' between the 'university cultured' and their new neighbours. However, the arts venerated by those from universities were imbued with cultural values which required certain skills or 'cultural capital' to understand and unlock. As Garnham and Williams explain:

> Specific competences are required, that is to say knowledge of the codes specific to a given art form, competences that are not innate but can only be acquired either through inculcation in the setting of the family through experience of a range of artistic objects and practices and/or through formal inculcation in school. (quoted in Lewis 1990, p.8)

Settlers overwhelmingly acquired such competences from family and education – as is to be expected of their class. Perhaps inevitably, they focused on what they could teach and what they valued, but also on those arts they deemed most likely to improve the mind and morals of the poor. The traffic was not one way – sometimes these young men and women besides seeking to share their culture and knowledge displayed a wish to learn about and preserve elements of the social and cultural life of those they now lived among. This can be seen in, for example, the Hull House Labor Museum initiative, which was created initially to bridge the gap between young and old immigrants, and sought to do so by reviving traditional crafts from the homeland, promoting cultural understanding and, incidentally, creating employment. At their best the settlements in their various localities worked as a link between cultures and offered limited access to the arts as well as opportunities to understand, enjoy and build upon encounters which grew from artistic actions.

Employing the arts

As already noted, for some settlers art was always part of a wider cause – namely a route to reform. For this reason many leading members of the Arts and Crafts movement in the early years were drawn into active involvement in the settlement movement, where they were able to recruit like-minded souls. They were part of a group of activists born out of the need for an alternative to the harshness of industrialism and the division of labour which Ruskin and Morris believed divided men. Their concern was not only for the quality of the end-product but also for how it was made and the quality of life of the craftsmen involved in its manufacture. Arts and Crafts as a style concentrated on simple, honest lines, textures and decoration. Adherents always sought harmony between the architect, designer and the craftsman; truth to the materials of the region; greater accessibility to good design; and the promotion of individual 'joy in labour'. These were the key elements of their philosophy, which led them to seek a community of craftspeople and to tie production to a social and moral purpose (Cumming and Kaplan 1991; Naylor 1992).

C. R. Ashbee, an early resident of Toynbee Hall, took these ideals further than most. Like Ruskin he maintained that good craftsmanship can only spring from a good and healthy life. In 1902 Ashbee took around 50 members and their families from the Guild of Handicraft that he had set up 14 years earlier in Whitechapel to the Cotswold village of Chipping Campden in search of the simple life. Here they were to continue the educational and social experiment which had grown out of the settlement movement. Indeed, they actively sought to translate these principles into a form which would be applicable to a rural setting. Their aims were the

> ...improvement of conditions for the local population; conservation and revival of local craftsmanship; reconstruction of local education: all these urgent village problems, together with such enthralling possibilities as infiltration of the Rural District Council, were to preoccupy Ashbee and the more enlightened of the Guildsmen in the coming year (MacCarthy 1981, p.88).

Ruskin and Morris had advocated that art should be an integral part of society and not an add-on extra for those with money and time to spare. They believed passionately that art should belong to the people. Barnett shared this view and, like them, argued that painting,

along with music and literature, was one of the great means of communication through which ideas could be spread and enthusiasm for
the progress of humanity engendered. Art consequently was to be
harnessed to promote the social causes close to his heart (Pimlott
1935, p.173). In America Ellen Starr also looked to Ruskin and
Morris as an inspiration in respect of her artistic activities at Hull
House. There she pursued the goals of social justice and the democra-
tisation of art through overseeing the early picture exhibitions,
teaching the history of art and building up arts and crafts studios
(Carson 1990, p.82). Performance arts were also encouraged for the
same reasons. In addition, amateur theatrical productions were
organised by settlements. Hull House and Greenwich House, in
particular, saw these as not only providing people with an artistic
outlet but also as a way of helping immigrants to learn English (Davis
1967, p.49).

From its earliest years the settlement movement sought to balance
two aims in relation to the arts. First, the need to bring art to the
people through local exhibitions, classes and theatre productions.
Second, to develop and build upon this while giving due recognition
to the 'arts and crafts' of those residing in the local neighbourhoods.
This was undertaken through the support of workshops, education
programmes and activities. Carson points out that the emphasis in US
settlements shifted after 1900 from the visual to the performing arts
of dance, drama and music, a move which reflected a belief that the
latter were more central to 'education for life' (Carson 1990, p.116).
Divisions of opinion certainly occurred. Addams (1910, 1914) saw
the pulling power of public recreation such as the five-cent theatre
and film and recognised how they brought together all classes of the
community. However, she was not happy regarding their content
while realistically recognising that 'high' art did not necessarily
reflect the experiences of the common people in a way popular entertainment did. She thought dramatic art was an important means of
moral education while popular theatre was a debased form of it which
had to be countered.

As the twentieth century progressed, settlements continued to use the arts to support social action and research. In October 1938, for example, Bensham Grove settlement in Gateshead hosted a weekend school based around an exhibition of work by non-professional painters, among whom the main contributors were the Ashington Group. This collection of amateur artists had grown from a Workers Educational Association art appreciation class run by Robert Lyon in a YMCA hut in the depressed mining town of Ashington (Northumberland). It became a model for other settlement-based art groups to emulate, among them Bensham and Spennymoor. Their tutors shared Lyon's enthusiasm for encouraging local men and women to capture and share in their paintings the hardships and pleasures of their lives in a way that communicated these to a world beyond-one, which had long displayed an indifference towards their needs and suffering. What was significant about the Bensham Grove gathering was that it was organised by Mass-Observation, an organisation set up by Tom Harrison and Charles Madge to gather information about the habits, beliefs and customs of ordinary people. The aims of the weekend went further than mere information-gathering. They were cited as being planned '(1) to make contact with other working class painters wherever they might be; (2) to form other groups like the Ashington group; (3) to influence people; (4) to influence painters' (Corlett (undated), p.14). These ambitions were not met, perhaps because, as McManners and Wales (1997) suggest, the members of the Ashington Group did not seek to become professional artists. They came to art through a wish to learn and understand it rather than to be trained in it.

Raising the tone

It was held to be self-evident by the sponsors of the settlement movement that university graduates could add an extra dimension to the lives of East Enders by bringing a 'higher' culture to their neighbours – one which would lift their spirits and aspirations. Most settlers viewed working-class culture as deficient at best, and dangerous at worst, frequently linking it to poor moral standards.

They almost universally assumed a connection between 'good' culture and 'good' morality (Carson 1990, p.7). Thus picture exhibitions as well as some of the best arts and crafts designs, music and theatre productions were brought by the Barnetts to Whitechapel. Regarding the 1885 Picture Exhibition Barnett wrote 'This has been *the* event of the week. Day after day crowds have come. The spectators have learnt wonderfully. They study their catalogues, remember the pictures of the past years and compare their lessons...' That year 46,763 people were recorded as visiting the first of these and the following year this rose to 55,300. Indeed he noted that 'people came in such numbers that, at intervals, the iron gate at the end of the street passage had to be closed, to enable some of the crowd to leave the building before others were admitted' (Barnett 1921, p.156).

The picture exhibitions held in St Jude's schoolrooms were so popular that they led to the building of the Whitechapel Art Gallery. Undeniably they brought art to an area which had never previously had access to this resource. Indeed, in this respect it represented a revolutionary shift in location by moving art, as opposed to entertainment, out of the city centre and country house. The Whitechapel was built in a 'community', not a town centre, 'a few minutes from Toynbee Hall Public Library, in the midst of the slums'. In the first six weeks of opening it attracted over 200,000 visitors (Picht 1914, p.63). It also widened the definition of the arts by including in its programme of exhibitions work by local artists, posters and items designed to stimulate interest in local issues and developments. The latter included window boxes, plants grown in London parks, models of roof playgrounds and schoolyards, displays, and the plans for Hampstead Garden Suburb which were shown at the Country in Town Exhibition (1907). The underlying purpose of the organisers of this 1907 exhibition, who included Gertrude Jekyll and Joseph Rowntree, was to extol the benefits of cleaner air and greener streets and to spread this message to an often indifferent public. It was an event which directly linked art to social concerns. The hope of the organisers was 'that other parts of London, may develop similar or greater efforts, so we propose by an exhibition in Whitechapel Art Gallery to lead people to think and talk about the subject' (undated pamphlet, Toynbee Hall Library).

While Barnett may have seen the use of pictures as a way of preaching moral values, he also recognised the need for interpretation, and that merely exposing people to 'the best art' might not be enough. Therefore residents and others were used as guides to explain and draw attention to the exhibits. The success of this approach encouraged their use elsewhere, not only in art galleries such as Leeds, which quickly followed suit, but also Kew Gardens. This mode of teaching was also adopted in other settings. Besides encouraging people to visit exhibitions, the settlers from the beginning were commited to taking art out into the community. For example, at a time when art work on the walls of schoolrooms was seen as merely an unwanted distraction undermining the 'serious activity of learning', Barnett arranged for the work of Walter Crane to be used to decorate the schoolrooms of St Jude's which stood beside Toynbee Hall. Subsequently, encouraged by Barnett, Crane and others founded the Art for Schools Association. This was a major breakthrough; St Jude's showed that schools need not be the dull, high, blank-walled buildings, with no aesthetic merit or value, but might become exciting places in which to encounter the visual arts.

The point to stress was that the arts were integrated within the overall programme of Toynbee and other settlements linked to the youth clubs, leisure provision and adult education, all of which were encouraged to employ them in their work. It was envisaged that those who came through their doors and others who could only be reached by going out to the local community would, via the work of the settlements, encounter cultural experiences normally denied them.

Involving leading artists

The settlement approach was founded on a belief that 'only the best' would suffice. Therefore the support and active involvement of leading artists was sought. Figures from the Arts and Crafts movement, as already noted, were involved from the start. Many lent their paintings, pottery and other artefacts for exhibition, others their support and advice. William Morris and Frederick Watts designed decoration for St Jude's church. Burne-Jones advised on the setting up of the Whitechapel Art Gallery, while Harrison Townsend was the architect. Holman Hunt and Henry Irving were among those who opened various exhibitions at the Whitechapel, while Gertrude Jekyll served alongside Joseph Rowntree on the committee of the Country in Town Exhibition. Morris spoke many times at Toynbee Hall, as did Oscar Wilde. The housing reformer Raymond Unwin was actively involved and eventually, with encouragement from Henrietta Barnett, became the main architect of Hampstead Garden Suburb. Lutyens was also persuaded to design its central square.

Hull House adopted a similar approach early on, opening an art gallery and studio. Several residents were also members of the Chicago Arts and Crafts Society, one of whose founding members, Frank Lloyd Wright, gave a famous lecture at Hull House in 1901 entitled 'The Art and Craft of the Machine'. In this he argued that the machine could be used as another tool of the craftsman. It was a viewpoint which subsequently became a constant source of disagreement between him and his friend Ashbee.

As noted earlier art was also taken out of buildings and into the community. Ancoats Settlement in Manchester had a unique way of doing this. 'Down into the courts and alleys of darkest Manchester and Salford trundled the Ancoats Hall piano, roped like the Ark of the Covenant to its swaying milk float, surrounded by missionary musicians' (Stocks 1956, p.20). Here perhaps were the beginnings of street theatre as a vehicle for social change. The willingness to innovate was well captured by Spennymoor Settlement's mobile theatre group which in its desire to play the more inhospitable venues experimented with rubber scenery.

The movement was not merely one-way; according to Emmeline Pethick-Lawrence (1938), part of the revival of old English folk dances throughout the length and breadth of the country prior to

1914 flowed partially from the desire of settlers to preserve and learn from the 'best' of mass culture.

A belief in the value of taking art to communities has survived in new forms of practice. For example, in the 1960s the Albany Institute (Deptford) became the Albany Empire, concentrating on theatre. In the 1970s the emphasis shifted to live entertainment and as part of this developed as a venue for 'radical community arts and music scene', hosting 15 'Rock Against Racism' gigs before being gutted by fire in 1978 (Steele 1993). It is now rebuilt as the Albany – a community centre with, among other groups, three theatre companies that continue to sustain the long tradition of bringing theatre and the arts to the locality.

Oxford House, which in the early years, like Toynbee Hall, held picture exhibitions, continues its involvement with the arts in various ways. It supplies studio space to seven artists in exchange for them undertaking work with the community – an approach that can be seen as an updating of the historic commitment to service while providing an opportunity for local people to meet and learn at first hand from the artists whose work they view. Also, the art exhibitions in the coffee bar continue the idea of the work of local artists being brought to a wider audience via an informal setting. In recent years Oxford House has become a centre for the Somali arts work (see Chapter Seven). It is also developing a visual and performing art centre that will include new performance and rehearsal spaces, a recording studio, gallery, workshops and training rooms.

Another example of continuity is the current work of the Spennymoor Settlement. In 1930 Bill Farrell, a 'resting actor' and resident of Toynbee Hall, was funded by the Pilgrim Trust to set up a settlement in Spennymoor. It soon became a thriving settlement with arts at its heart. In 1937 and 1938 the German artist Tisa Hess stayed with Bill and Betty Farrell at the Spennymoor Settlement, the link having been made through the Artists International Association (AIA). She taught in the sketching club and learnt about the miners' lives by visiting their homes, and teaching them to draw and carve.

Neither foreigners nor women were allowed to go down the pit, but Hess managed a 'secret' visit. It was arranged as a reward for her work, and she had to sign a paper saying she would publish nothing of what she saw. In her diary she wrote:

> This Settlement was like a small 'pit university'. ...Volunteers helped by teaching art and drama and by giving lectures... It was a place glowing with an intense inner life, something quite outstanding in these drab and dreary surroundings (Armstrong 1992, p. 41).

Spennymoor Settlement today has plans to build a new workshop theatre with digital studio, gallery space and an archive, thereby re-establishing itself as a community arts centre.

Creating art with people

Through the settlements we can trace the continuation of Ruskin's experiment in art education which began at the Working Men's College in Red Lion Square, London in 1854, where he taught the elements of drawing. Sketching clubs were part of the adult education programme at most of the early settlements. In the North East four such groups were especially successful and well documented. These were at Spennymoor, Bensham Grove, Durham House and Rock House settlements. Under the combined influence of Lyon and Farrell this work spread to outlying centres such as Ashington. The success of these in turn rejuvenated the work of other local settlement houses.

In the 1930s the walls of Bensham Grove Settlement, Gateshead were covered in murals completed by members of the art appreciation classes. One room was decorated with a scene of the house and garden, in which distinguished visitors were depicted. Included amongst these were such luminaries as the philosopher and politician, Lord Morley, William Morris, Joseph Chamberlain and Fridtjof Nansen, the explorer and recipient of the Nobel Peace Prize. The class of 1937, the year book notes, carried out:

> ...an experiment in co-operative work (as distinct from individualistic work), to see if we could recapture some of the spirit which

gave rise in the past to traditional work, the character of which depends largely on the fact that it is the expression of community. (Annual Report 1937)

The end result was the decoration of the walls of the entrance to the settlement on the theme 'Welcome'. Not only the artists were involved in innovative work. In 1941 the Bensham Grove Settlement Players took the theatre out into the community and stimulated audience participation via a performance entitled 'I want to be an actor' (Annual Report 1937/38).

The approach of engaging with local people and the encouragement of hidden talent often had exciting results. The Art Students Club at Toynbee Hall was set up by Samuel Henry Hancock, a local postman, who on visiting the St Jude's art exhibition enquired if a sketching club could be arranged for working men such as himself. He was promptly asked to work with the residents to develop a group. A decade later it had a membership of 50. Hancock himself went on to exhibit at the Royal Academy and the group in slightly different form survives to this day (*Lloyds Weekly News* 3.2.07, cutting from Toynbee Hall Library). The Spennymoor sketching club likewise produced two notable working artists, Tom McGuinness and Norman Cornish. Importantly, it was not simply a place where 'classes' operated in isolation from one another. As Cornish has said, like other settlements it has a vibrant cultural life that encouraged participation and engagement beyond the narrow confines of an individuals' own enthusiasm.

> Most of us used to go down and draw the actors on the stage during rehearsals. In a strange way, all this homed in on us without realising it. All of these various influences from O'Casey to Bernard Shaw to Shakespeare rubbed off on me – a kind of university education. (Armstrong 1992, p.4)

This commitment to 'integration' is reflected in the current work of Time and Talents' settlement, Bermondsley. One of its arts projects involves people with learning disabilities, many of whom are returning to the community after spending the greater part of their lives in long-stay hospital accommodation. With the aid of artists within the community, people are encouraged through drama, dance, video, music and song to 'make sense of their lives' and 'participate in a range of activities that enables them to be recognised and celebrated as active and contributing members' of their community (Annual Report 1998, p.5). The reminiscence and memories group provides the opportunity for members to draw from their own experiences of life to create a 'fictional' story about one family's life in Bermondsley. The first instalment of this is 'Last Chance', the story of Alice, who in 1945 faces the return of her husband from military service and explains the changes that to the family which have taken place during his absence.

Nurturing and recognising craftsmanship within the community

From a Ruskin reading class at Toynbee Hall came the Arts and Crafts' most radical experiment in art education, the Guild and School of Handicraft. Described by Crawford (1998) as probably the most outstanding example of bridging the divide between art, work and education, it went on to have world-wide influence. But it started from the enthusiasm of the working men involved in the classes taught by the architect and resident C. R. Ashbee.

From Toynbee, Ashbee took the lessons of community and 'cultural philanthropy' into the world of work. When the workshops closed for the night there were 'sing-songs and amateur dramatics; in the summer there were country excursions; there was even a Guild football team. These activities were a piece with the art exhibitions, lectures and social clubs which were organised at Toynbee Hall' (Crawford 1998, p.4).

The history of the Guild and School is well documented, and we learn how members in the early years were encouraged to acquire their skills through trial and error, not merely instruction. Ashbee himself describes the process as follows:

> It is in the learning of how to do things and do them well that many fresh design motives are evolved. So it comes about that when a little group of men learn to pull together in a workshop, to

trust each other, to play into each other's hand, and understand each other's limitations, their combination becomes creative, and the character that they develop in themselves takes expression in the work of their fingers. Humanity and craftsmanship are essential. (Ashbee, quoted Naylor 1992, p.252)

By 1900 the Guild was employing about 50 men, all from the East End of London. From a reading class grew a real experiment in allowing the arts and crafts to offer a more satisfying experience of work. It is an approach that could be, but is not, applied to current government training schemes whose purpose seems to be largely about containment and the provision of 'a competitive workforce'.

Settlement houses often sought to enable those involved to 'develop new skills by offering classes in bookbinding, metalwork, woodwork and pottery. After training with Cobden-Sanderson, Ellen Gates Starr established a hand bindery at Hull House in 1898' (Cumming and Kaplan 1991, pp.154–5). This was linked to a desire to preserve dying arts or skills so that they could be used and absorbed into contemporary culture. While the hand-bindery business failed due to the exorbitant cost of the product, the skills nevertheless survived to be passed on. Starr believed that 'industrialism had brought about a separation of cultural and vocational interests' (Davis 1967, p. 49). For over a century she and others saw settlements as a vehicle for countering this trend which still exists. Historically settlements did not attempt to make art popular by removing the difficulty from it. They thought communities deserved the best that art could offer, not merely the most accessible, and believed that if the ideas were shared then they must be debated and explained. Today there is still a role to be played by settlements and others in bringing the 'expert' and the amateur together to look at the problems that affect people's lives.

Part of the reason for using the arts, in the late nineteenth and the early twentieth centuries, was the concern for 'the welfare of the worker and in particular with redirecting the leisure hours that reformers feared would otherwise be spent in drinking and gambling'

(Cumming and Kaplan 1991, p.22). Alternative skills in the handi-crafts were also encouraged:

> Crafts programmes at settlement houses such as Jane Addams's Hull House in Chicago provided an escape from the tedium of factory work. In addition, settlement houses offered immigrants a chance to affirm and express their native heritage. With classes and salesrooms the South End House and Denison House in Boston helped immigrant women to refine their manual skills and market their embroideries and laces. (*ibid.*, p.154)

There is still an argument for preserving the techniques of arts and crafts derived from different cultures. However, as well as keeping them alive attention needs to be given to developing and encouraging experiment and where possible employment opportunities. Oxford House and Praxis's current work with Somali and Bangladeshi immigrants is a perfect example of how this historic tradition has been sustained. It builds on the talents people bring with them while encouraging the development of new skills. Many of the Somalis were (and remain) prominent artists within their country of origin which has a culture rich in oral and visual artistic traditions as the Somali language has only recently been written down. This culture is not merely sustained and enriched but is being taken into the wider community in the best traditions of the settlement movement, thus enhancing self-confidence and eroding barriers.

Building and strengthening community

In the life of the settlements the arts played an important role in bringing people from the community together for mutual learning through festivals and plays, sing-songs and musical productions. The internal community of residents used the arts for social and intellectual ends, but they also developed more informal ways in which people could learn from each other and improve their skills and interests. This, plus communal meals and living, helped to relieve tensions and to build a positive working environment by involving people in the creation of their own entertainment and community. Drama was used extensively in this context. Most settlements had drama groups 'and not without good reason, since few activities transcend so imperiously the difference of age and sex and class' (Stocks 1956, p.73). At Ancoats, the Shakespeare production was so successful that Ellen Terry visited it to give a reading to the cast. However, it was when the settlement moved to the Round House that, according to Stocks, drama came into its own.

At a fundraising supper in aid of a new theatre at Mansfield House, Bernard Shaw (1930) spoke of how vital this settlement's approach to theatre was, as it was 'not run on commercial lines [but] simply a case of getting the poor people around them and educating them'. As a consequence Shaw agreed to grant the rights to perform his plays to them and other educational groups at a reduced rate.

The Toynbee Pantomime was much more a form of entertainment for the players than a serious drama production – a manifestation of communal life. But later productions at Toynbee by the 'People's Free Theatre for Poetic Drama' (founded in 1910) had a much more serious aim: that of establishing free theatre as an aspect of education (Pimlott 1935, p.175). Its production of *Electra* at Toynbee Hall in 1910 was so successful that people had to be turned away, but according to Pimlott the long-term impact of this initiative was probably not substantial. From these early philanthropic ventures designed to bring theatre to the masses we can, however, trace the beginnings of the subsequent Little Theatre Movement and the People's Theatre projects of the inter-war years (Samuel *et al.* 1985). In this respect they have left a substantial legacy.

The role of architecture in enhancing neighbourhoods

Canon Barnett was of the opinion that art belonged to the people and they deserved the best. His pamphlet 'The Ideal City' concluded 'We have to preach the coming of the Ideal City; to open the eyes of citizens to see what is possible; to show them "lying here" amid the hills and by the river, a city where there shall be nothing to offend, everything to help' (Barnett 1893, p.65).

Henrietta Barnett incorporated and developed these ideas in relation to her Hampstead Garden Suburb project, which was to be a 'harmonious community of all classes and generations'(Cumming and Kaplan 1991). The architecture and design of the suburb aimed to embody this concept and she employed Raymond Unwin, the housing reformer and architect of Letchworth Garden City, to carry it out. In 1911 he wrote to her regarding its fame in America:

> The Garden Suburb has at least led the way in showing how thousands of people of all classes of society, of all sorts of opinion, of all standards of income, can live in helpful neighbourliness; and that at the Institute people of every shade of thought can unite to exchange ideas, and by their care for literature, art, music, history, or nature obliterate class barriers. The scheme is founded on an ethical basis, and has as its aim the development of human understanding, whereby spiritual forces are given freedom. (Barnett 1921, p.716)

Henrietta also saw this use of art as a way of improving people's physical well-being. She insisted that it would be 'an essential condition of building that the dwellings of all classes be made attractive ... As are the cottage and the manor house of the English Village' (Miller and Gray 1992, p.45). In part what the settlement did was to imbue the New Town movement with a commitment to the arts. The postwar New Towns, under the guidance of Henry Morris who was heavily influenced by the settlement movement, initially aimed to blend the cultural and the administrative. Morris envisaged a Further Education College like the Bauhaus in Germany, with a theatre, art gallery, concert hall and the town's main library all set around a central square or piazza. The tragedy was that the New Towns of the 1950s, 1960s and 1970s turned their back on this vision and the opportunity to 'associate education with the ordinary life and the practice of the Arts and with civic administration' (Morris quoted in Jeffs 1998 p.72). In ignoring the aspirations of the Barnetts they created some appalling legacies which we are still struggling to overcome.

Conclusion

Why were the arts so important to the settlement movement and what can we learn from their experiences?

First, by being involved in lots of activities people came across art – it was and remains an integral part of the life of the settlement, not an add-on extra. Consider, for example, Oxford House where, as Lewis suggests, it is because it 'does not call itself an arts centre and it links into local residents' groups and schools instead of the usual "arts networks", that it has managed to attract a wide range of users outside the middle-class world normally colonised by the Arts' (Lewis 1990, p.43). As we have become more specialised, those people who seek out art go to arts centres that are rarely in their own communities. Settlement workers realised gradually that people's craving for beautiful things could be satisfied by involving them in the creative process. Contemporary advocates of community arts such as Matarasso still speak the language of the settlement pioneers:

> It is in the act of creativity that empowerment lies, and through sharing creativity that understanding and inclusiveness are promoted... Again and again, it is the opportunity to get involved in – indeed to define – what matters that motivates people, transforming them from passive consumers of culture and social policy into engaged participants in arts projects and, by extension, in local democratic processes. (Matarasso 1997, p.85)

However, the modern exponents of community arts have largely rejected or simply overlooked a key component. They separate the arts and artists to a great extent. They encourage arts centres, specialised workers and a sense of difference. The settlements, in placing the arts alongside welfare work, community action and youth programmes, forged a sense of combined purpose. They forced the arts to address their role as agents for social change. Therefore with hindsight we can view the decision of Barnett to allow the Whitechapel Art Gallery to be built half a mile away from Toynbee Hall as a mistake. One which undermined the principle of integration.

Second, art, as we have seen, was involved in planning communities. Today there is little talk of new towns, just inner-city problems and restrictive housing policies. What is largely lacking is a concern with improving conditions for the poor and engaging with them alongside creative professionals to find solutions. As Barnett argued, architects and communities need to be brought together. Many of today's leading architects seem more concerned about making bold style statements, showing off their design skills while exhibiting little concern regarding their usefulness. In Ward's *Talking to Architects* Giancarlo De Carlo criticised them for 'the habit of taking the side of the powerful and leaving the weak to their fate' (Ward 1996, p.9). Some work with self-build and co-operatives, but most of the profession are failing to address the problems of dispersed communities and social isolation, or to display any interest in helping people to build their own communities through dialogue and workshops.

> Implementing social policy without reference to its cultural dimensions… has not always been our approach: in Britain's booming Victorian cities, the role of culture was widely appreciated not only as a civilising force, but in places like Bourneville and Port Sunlight as an essential component of a stable, cohesive community. The absence of such perspectives during the 1950s and 1960s – when it was possible to see slum clearance as merely an issue of housing and sanitation – had consequences which are still evident. (Matarasso 1997, p. 84)

This gap was never something the settlements viewed as inevitable or desirable. From the Country and Town Exhibition onwards the aim was always to place the arts at the heart of the community and civic life. To make the public sphere a place of beauty.

Third, the settlements set out to compensate for the narrow curriculum and philistine nature of schooling. In the settlements education through music, art, drama and handicrafts were tried out before most schools considered adding them to their curriculum. It is ironic that today we see the arts being squeezed out to make way for the core components of the National Curriculum and its preoccupation with literacy and numeracy targets, so that 'teachers are under such intense pressure to raise standards in the three Rs that only a brave headteacher will be prepared to sacrifice targets to widen pupils' aesthetic horizons' (Judd 1999). We can find examples today of settlements using arts in their overall programme and working from people's own interests, talents and visions. The graffiti arts project at Charterhouse came from the young people themselves. Workers encouraged their use of street-art 'graffiti' to decorate some of the walls of the settlement, building on the interests of young people but taking it further in acquiring skills and techniques to make a blank wall look colourful and welcoming and also, in the process, providing opportunities to build relationships and work together creatively. Another example is Edinburgh University Settlement's multi-arts project 'Origins', which uses 'drama, music, art and writing to create a performance developing the themes of nature, growth and human experience' (Annual Report 1998). Once completed it will reach a wide audience but it will also have involved many people in its creation and production and taught the value of learning through doing. There still remains today, as in the 1880s, a need to create ways in which people, old and young, can discover for themselves the value of the arts.

Finally, the two evils of commercialism and the division of labour are still very much in evidence today. We see this in technology, in computer programmes offering off-the-peg designs for posters and banners, and in machines with ready-made sounds for DJs to put together. The price put on art creates much more debate than its use or the joy it brings. The separation of the arts into 'high' and 'popular' continues to flourish. Art is used as a commodity to attract money into an area and, more recently, to perform the role of social services.

Each generation of artists and critics strives to find something new and more outrageous that will appeal to the art market, drive prices up, and keep them in a job. Art's defenders are driven to prove its worth through its impact on health, key skills, as therapy, while 'stars' such as Hirst and Emin make a killing and become more important than the work they produce. As community workers, community artists and social workers have become more specialised they have grown apart from each other, and to an extent from the people they once worked alongside. They are experts brought in for a short time to show people how things are done, rather than living alongside them and tackling the problems and solutions in the communities. Today there is much less enthusiasm given to social enquiry. 'We seem to have lost our curiosity about social conditions as though nothing can be done' (Simey 1999). Perhaps it is time therefore to recognise once again the strengths inherent in the settlement approach and to seek to re-apply their philosophy and adapt their methodologies to modern circumstances. Not least the central role within social policy and community work which they saw the arts playing.

Bibliography

Addams, J (1909) *Spirit of Youth and the City Streets*. New York: Macmillan.

Addams, J. (1914) *A New Conscience and an Ancient Evil*. New York: Macmillan.

Armstrong, K. (1992). *'Homespun'. The Story of Spennymoor and its Famous Settlement Told by Local People*. North Shields: Northern Voices.

Barnett, H. (1921) *Canon Barnett. His Life Work and Friends*. London: John Murray.

Barnett, S. A. (1893, reprinted 1979) *The Ideal City*. Leicester: Leicester University Press.

Bensham Grove Annual Reports 1937, 1938. Gateshead Central Reference Library.

Briggs, A. and Macartney, A. (1984) *Toynbee Hall, the First Hundred Years*. London: Routledge and Kegan Paul.

Carson, M. (1990) *Settlement Folk, Social Thought and the American Settlement Movement 1885–1930*. Chicago and London: University of Chicago.

Corlett, A. (undated, late 1980s) *Mirror for the Masses: 'A Look at Working-class Life in the 30s'*. Exhibition catalogue for the exhibition sponsored by the School of Art History, Newcastle-upon-Tyne Polytechnic.

Crawford, A. (1998) 'C. R. Ashbee in East London'. Exhibition catalogue. London: Geffrye Museum.

Cumming, E. and Kaplan, W. (1991) *The Arts and Crafts Movement*. London: Thames and Hudson.

Davis, A. F. (1967) *Spearheads of Reform. The Social Settlements and the Progressive Movement 1890–1914*. New York: Oxford University Press.

Edinburgh University Settlements Annual Report 1998.

Jeffs, T. (1998) *Henry Morris: Village Colleges, Community Education and the Ideal Order.* Nottingham: Educational Heretics Press.

Judd, J. (1999) 'The lost art of learning'. *Independent* 3 March 1999.

Lewis, J. (1990) *Art Culture and Enterprise. The Politics of Art and the Cultural Industries.* London and New York: Routledge.

Lister, D. (1999) 'We're not as dumb as they like to think we are'. *Independent* 6 March 1999.

Lloyds Weekly News 3 Feb. 1907 (cutting from Toynbee Hall library).

MacCarthy, F. (1981) *The Simple Life, C. R. Ashbee in the Cotswolds.* London: Lund Humphries.

McManners, R. and Wales, G. (1997) *Tom McGuiness. The Art of an Underground Miner.* Co. Durham: Gemini Productions.

Matarasso, F. (1997) *Use or Ornament? The Social Impact of Participation in the Arts.* Stroud: Comedia.

Miller, M. and Gray, A. S. (1992) *Hampstead Garden Suburb.* Chichester: Phillimore.

Naylor, G. (1992) 'Design craft and industry'. In Ford, B. (ed) *Victorian Britain.* Cambridge: Cambridge Press.

Picht, W. (1914) *Toynbee Hall and the English Settlement Movement.* London: Bell and Sons.

Pimlott, J. A. R. (1935) *Toynbee Hall.* London: Dent and Sons.

Pethick-Lawrence, E. (1938) *My Part in a Changing World.* London: Victor Gollancz Ltd.

Samuel, R. (1994) *Theatres of Memory. Vol. I: Past and Present in Contemporary Culture.* London: Verso.

Samuel, R., MacColl, E. and Cosgrove, S. (1985) *Theatres of the Left 1880–1935: Workers Theatre Movements in Britain and America.* London: Routledge and Kegan Paul.

Shaw, G. B. (1930) Mansfield House Archives.

Simey, M. (1999) Interview with author. Liverpool.

Steele, J. (1993) *Turning the Tide. The History of Everyday Deptford.* London: Deptford Forum Publishing.

Stocks, M. (1956) *Fifty Years in Every Street. The Story of the Manchester University Settlement.* Manchester: Manchester University Press.

Sutcliffe, T. (1999) The one-eyed hypnotist. The Thursday Review, *Independent* 4 March 1999.

Time and Talents Association (1998) Annual Review 1998.

Ward, C. (1996) *Talking to Architects.* London: Freedom Press.

10

Family centres

In the settlement tradition?

Crescy Cannan and Chris Warren

Family centres are a success story in recent social provision. Their role was enshrined in the Children Act of 1989 as having a place in the continuum of family support services, and confirmed by the Audit Commission (1994) as making a contribution to the prevention of problems in families by the support they offer to parents. Whereas only a handful existed in the 1970s, by the end of the 1980s Warren (1991) enumerated 353 family centres in England and Wales. The majority are provided by local authority social services departments but the voluntary sector is significant, not least in its insistence on the local community development role of family centres and the centrality of participation by users. This approach to family support is one mirrored in other countries, with, for instance, very strong provision in France (Cannan 1997). It meshes with current calls within the European child-care world for more integrated and holistic approaches to provision for young (and school-age) children (e.g. Henderson 1997; Moss and Petrie; 1997). What these approaches have in common is the emphasis on developing local services which meet the needs of both children and parents, though, as we shall see, there are unfinished debates about gender as well as concerns about the quality of services young children in the UK may be receiving. We raise these issues now but would like first to look at the ideals of family centres and at the models to which they subscribe, in order to compare them with settlements. We shall argue that there are some strong parallels between certain types of family centres and settlements, and that there are ways in which both can learn from each other.

What are family centres?

The Audit Commission's report was critical of local authority social services which interpreted the term 'child in need' so narrowly as almost to equate it with the much narrower definition of 'harm'. In practice, intervention was seen to focus on only the most desperate child protection cases (children at risk of significant harm). It was argued that local authorities should extend their priority to more accessible types of family support which can prevent problems, and which can avoid the stigma and isolation of families treated by services reserved for the most serious problems. This is at the heart of the nature of family centres. Their history explains the point. During the 1970s local authorities were under increasing public pressure to have more effective means of responding to what appeared to be increasing numbers of child abuse cases. At the same time, restrictions on public expenditure meant that keeping children in public care was less viable, especially as research was showing how damaging for future lives it was (cited in Cannan 1992, pp.62–5). Being in care was (and still is) associated with future family problems, with crime and imprisonment, with education and employment problems, and with homelessness. While the tendency in local authorities in the 1970s had been to respond to anxiety about child abuse by taking increasing numbers of children into care, campaigning organisations such as the Family Rights Group countered by defending the rights of parents; others pointed out the associations between poverty, race, and single parenthood and being in care (e.g. Ahmed 1987; Holman 1976). If poverty was a major factor in family breakdown and child abuse (Parton 1985, and, in the USA, Gil 1970) surely the taking into care solution was often unjust as well as unaffordable.

As local authorities started reducing the numbers of children in care, with a steep decline after the late 1970s, children's homes began to look for a new role. Many of these were run by the voluntary sector, for instance NCH Action for Children, The Children's Society, or Barnardo's. Local authority children's homes also found they were being called into question, as did day nurseries which were suffering from spending cuts but which had been used by social services departments as a way of intervening with children in need or in cases of child abuse. At the same time, the whole field of child abuse, and the question of whether professionals such as social workers were to blame for failing to prevent tragedies, became the topic of immense media interest – raising the stakes for local authorities and the anxieties of those working in the field.

There were then a number of players behind a changed approach to child protection. The local authorities and the children's charities, rights-based pressure groups and the media have been noted. There was also pressure from social work. In 1971 the small local authority children's departments and welfare services were amalgamated in the Seebohm reorganisation (named after the chair of the Committee which made the recommendations). This introduced large-scale local authority social services departments, and associated developments in training consolidated the generic base of the profession. Seebohm had encouraged community work in social services departments, with an emphasis on decentralisation and the meshing of services with local, informal care networks.

Social work expanded in this optimistic and imaginative time and became a more assertive profession. The uncritical, often unplanned and low-level care provided in day nurseries and children's homes was now considered inadequate in both political and professional terms. Similarly the rather open-ended family case-work which had been practised in both local authority services and voluntary organisations was viewed as lacking in focus and clear objectives, and while many families were thus enabled to stay together, some social workers argued that this approach did not promote family independence nor necessarily improve parenting and protection from risk of the children in these families. Later in the decade family therapy was to take root, partly encouraged by the more strategic and task-centred American responses to child abuse in that country. These connected (not always happily) in notions of community and family systems, the importance of seeing intervention, whether psychotherapeutic or more practical, as having interconnected, transactional effects along a line of family and community relationships. This ecological approach (Bronfenbrenner 1979) emphasised the child in a context, and the importance of planning interventions in ways which would strengthen that context. This is the heart of the family support idea, though this term only began to be used widely in Britain following the Children Act 1989.

Family support has addressed a lot of criticisms of the old approach to children in need and at risk of harm. It has also offered a response to the concerns of the Conservative governments in the 1970s which were identifying poor parenting as causing what Sir Keith Joseph referred to as the 'cycle of deprivation' in a call for more parent education. At that time playgroups were expanding and were held up by Joseph as examples of self-help in action and of parental responsibility. For more risky families, the Home-Start scheme was promoted. This is a project which uses volunteer mothers to visit families where parenting problems have been identified, both for friendly support and to demonstrate the value of children's play. These were seen as low-cost solutions in the late 1970s, but the rising concern around child sexual abuse in the family in the 1980s meant that local authorities were looking for something more solid, for responses both to identified abuse and for prevention. Family centres' fitful start was institutionalised in this context, and they became part of the local authority social services landscape, sometimes by direct provision, sometimes through various forms of contract and partnership with voluntary agencies, or with health or education departments.

The principles of family support, of prevention (both of family difficulties and of the separation of children from parents), of recognizing the importance of the child's continuing links with family (which includes extended kin), and of recognizing the poverty and environmental issues in family breakdown, are enshrined in the 1989 Children Act. This requires local authorities to respond to children in need in their area and to have plans for so doing. Unfortunately limited budgets have resulted in targeting services on cases of the most severe need (Tunstill 1992); hence the criticisms made by the Audit Commission, which we noted earlier. Family centres have been squeezed into a protective, regulatory role in this process. Nevertheless many, and especially but not exclusively those in the voluntary sector, continue to stress their wider, preventive goals.

So what do family centres actually do? Eva Lloyd provides a portrait of Save the Children family support centres which offer:

> ... part-time and full-time day care, holiday play schemes, out-of-school, and community health services for children, and welfare rights advice, education and training for other members of their families, as well as self-help opportunities to develop a variety of groups, credit unions and food co-ops, and some youth work. (Lloyd 1997, p.143)

Save the Children centres are located in deprived communities and stress open access, self-referral and user participation. They 'provide practical responses to locally defined need', and their anti-poverty strategy rests in a commitment to 'provide better beginnings for children and new opportunities for adults' (*ibid.*, drawing on Long 1995). This is a portrait of a community development family centre, which would ring true for many centres run by other voluntary organisations, and occasionally by local authority social services departments. The staff include social workers and workers with qualifications in youth and community work and child care. At the other extreme are client-centred (Holman 1988) or child protection (Cannan 1992) family centres, which work with clients referred by social workers or health visitors and where the centre is based more on treating or otherwise responding to serious parenting problems and providing some compensatory experience for children. These centres are generally not open to their neighbourhood and do not see local community development as part of their brief; they are predominantly staffed by social workers and child care workers, and may be centres of expertise in family therapy and in the assessment of child abuse. While the distinction between these two types of centres was fairly clear-cut through the 1980s, increasing pluralism in service provision now means that varying local compromises are arrived at, and most centres combine some elements of both models. The narrower approach is more likely where there is funding by the social services department, as their targeting on most extreme need and risk can mean that this route is easier to take than the more complex yet effective one of family support through multi-functional, multi-funded, multi-partner community development.

Community development family centres: in the settlement tradition?

While recognising that family centres have different roots from settlements, it will be clear that community development family centres look very much like many modern settlements, and indeed in some areas the two forms of provision have merged into each other. The plans for the New Albany in 1979 included a family centre concept as part of its core provision. However, they are not the same, despite similarities: neither family centres nor settlements are 'just' community centres; both have special features arising from their history, their central principles and goals, and their current place in public policy. It is these that we shall go on to explore, as a basis for comparison and in order to make some suggestions for future development.

Settlements in the UK and the United States were in their heyday in the first part of the twentieth century; the postwar (and indeed interwar) welfare state reduced them to a marginal role. This decline was underpinned by the decision to place social work training in the higher education system, which meant that from the 1960s settlements followed rather different paths from social work: the paths of community work. This has been regrettable, for the settlement tradition of commitment to local social research and social action is one which, while remaining strong in community work, has been weakened in social services departments (the main employers of social workers), where anxiety about child protection has often ruled out imaginative family services. The brief community-oriented genericism associated in England and Wales with Seebohm is also being lost in the (re)division between adult services and children and family services. Furthermore, contract cultures and managerialism are encouraging narrow, short-term, competence-based training and practice. All of this means that contemporary social work has come to be remote from the aspirations of settlement work, which has always stressed the interrelationship of social problems, the long-term, the 'hanging on in there', the value of really knowing a community in all its diversity.

So settlements may have seen their role reduced, but what they represent remains important, and this continues to invigorate and sustain community development. Settlements stand for *social* action, a term interchangeable with 'social work' in the settlement heyday. They remind of the need for social objectives to complement the contemporary focus on personal responsibility us on the one hand, and on the other, economic regeneration, both meaningless if social cohesion and the quality of life are ignored (Henderson 1997). Indeed, there is a history of voluntary organisations such as the Family Service Units (FSU) which have combined long-term, informal, practical help for families – help which connects a casework understanding of 'the problem family' with an insistence that poverty is the major difficulty facing such families. FSU has also stressed the importance of collective activities in overcoming the isolating effects of deprivation on children (Holman 1998), and such projects have embraced the combination of individual and community approaches which we claim is distinctive of family centres (see, for example, the account of the West Leeds FSU in Barford, O'Grady and Hall 1995). While social work has become increasingly regulated and regulating, it is important to remind ourselves of this social action tradition within it. Settlements and community work carry this tradition, a set of values which are important reminders to family centres and social workers struggling to contribute to and to ameliorate local life.

Settlements and social action

There are some roots and areas of work which settlements have in common with family centres. This is especially so if we begin by looking at the original aims and principles of settlements. 'The settlement movement arose out of three fundamental needs: the need for scientific research, the need for a wider life through education, and the need for leadership' (Pimlott, 1935, p.11). This account of the settlement movement and of Toynbee Hall's place within it was written in the 1930s, and so is less critical than writers today of the sometimes patronising tone of early 'settlers'. It captures a central tension in the movement: on the one hand seeking social progress by providing centres through which local people can widen their participation, and on the other fearing the spiritual vacuum into which industrialism seemed to have cast the urban working class, the settlers introduced 'higher' culture and ideals. It is not, then, about self-activity in the fullest sense, though it has often gone some way towards this in, for instance, support of the trade union movement in industrial disputes, and in promoting co-operatives. Barnett and Addams did not seek to overturn the social order of the late nineteenth century but they certainly sought to change it, and to do so in ways which would improve the material and spiritual life of the poor. Their Christian socialism (called social Christianity in the USA) and pacifism deplored violent confrontation and sought mediation and evolution instead (Carson 1990). It is the socialism of Ruskin, the early William Morris, Fabianism and Tolstoy, not Marx. They criticised the casework methods of the Charity Organisation Society (COS), prevalent at the time, for being ineffectual and degrading; they sought social as well as personal change, and while they endorsed self-help it was not the isolated self-reliance advocated by the COS, but amelioration of individual circumstances in the context of improved local social conditions and relations.

The community and the family were important institutions to Barnett and Addams, but they argued that state intervention and voluntary service, such as that established in the settlements, were needed in order for them to thrive in an industrial society. Unregulated employment, such as found in the sweated garment trades or in the docks; insanitary tenement housing, 'rack-renting' landlords; lack of street lighting, public baths or rubbish collection; poor policing; provision of open spaces – these were some of the areas where settlements were able to tip the balance in favour of the poor in the period up to the First World War (Briggs and Macartney 1984; Carson 1990; Pimlott 1935). This is what Barnett and Addams meant by leadership: it is the civic leadership of educated people moving to poor areas and then involving themselves in the growing machinery of local government in order to improve the local infrastructure.

Campaigning for better public services, supporting trade unions in their disputes, and providing legal aid for individuals (which was usually in landlord–tenant and employment cases) were radical steps to take in late Victorian society, and even in the 1920s in the United States settlement leaders were attacked as Bolsheviks, and settlements as outposts of the Soviet government (Carson 1990, p. 167). The steps were radical, though for what might be seen as conservative ends: industrialism and poverty were seen as destroying the working-class family and community, and thus as undermining the social order. Adult education and what we now term family support were central to settlement work towards these ends, and adult education continues to have a place in settlements – as it does in some community and family centres under, for instance, European Social Fund schemes. This tension between radical and conservative ends in relation to the family is still important; many early family centres emphasised their role in supporting 'family life' and obscured the fact that many of their users were single parents, and were women. Today there is more commitment to supporting diverse life styles, recognising the many forms family and personal life can take. Family support and the provision of opportunities for women are phrases whose meaning is negotiable in the best family centres – and while this notion of empowerment differs from that of the early settlers, there is a link between initiatives that aim to see fuller lives lived in impoverished areas.

Settlements and 'the higher life'

The settlements campaigned for better primary education and were instrumental in the first wave of opening access to higher education. Toynbee Hall provided adult education and was linked closely with the Workers' Education Association (WEA) after 1904, becoming the largest WEA branch in London (Pimlott 1935, p.229).

Settlements also brought culture – the 'higher life' – to the working class. Their contributions to local art exhibitions, concerts and plays meant not only that these were accessible to the working class but that the wealthy and educated were drawn to the poorer areas, thus achieving the mixing of classes so central to the settlement philosophy (Briggs and Macartney 1984, p.57). But it was also a principle in its own right: Barnett had always insisted that every person has the right to grow and to 'enjoy the best' (Johnson 1995, p.4).

> It was because of Barnett's stress on 'personal culture' as well as 'intelligent citizenship' that he wanted Toynbee Hall to be a centre of the arts as well as of social action; and in this development he had far more successes to record than disappointments. (*ibid.*)

Barnett was ahead of his time in providing exhibitions on Sundays (to which his ecclesiastical colleagues objected) and in making them accessible to children (*ibid.*). Famous people opening the exhibitions included Lord Roseberry, William Morris and Holman Hunt (Pimlott 1935, p.169), drawing press reviews and publicity.

> If the art exhibitions were to provide entertainment they were also intended as a means of education. The pictures were of the highest possible quality... Holman Hunt, Watts, Rossetti, Millais,

> Burne-Jones, and Herkomer, all the best painters of the day were
> represented, and by their best pictures. (Pimlott 1935, p.166)

Catalogues were written carefully to help the viewers understand the
pictures, and Barnett gave lectures, adapted to the tastes of his
listeners (*ibid.*). These very popular exhibitions and the subsequent
campaigns for an art gallery in Whitechapel (realised in 1901), for
public libraries, and the development of music and drama, did indeed
have an impact on the neighbourhood. Addams in Chicago also
promoted the arts, partly, like Barnett, to counter what she saw as the
vulgar and corrupting popular theatre, bars and dance halls. In
settlement tradition, however, rather than seeking to close these, she
recognised the drive of youth for pleasure and sought to establish
drama, music and folk art (important given the high population of
immigrants) as activities in which people would co-operate in contributing to the fabric of their society, and which would allow
expression of emotion and provide solace from life's hardships. Her
contribution to the arts at Hull House included highly successful
music-schools and dramatics. Settlements offered, then, not just
access to culture but opportunities that would otherwise have been
unavailable to the talented (Carson 1990, pp.115–117), and indeed
music-school settlements were to grow in Boston and New York in
the early part of the twentieth century.

When Toynbee Hall engaged prominent Arts and Crafts architects
and designers, it was partly to recreate the feel of an Oxford College,
but it also expressed a commitment in the Ruskin tradition to art's
social and moral function (Briggs and Macartney 1984, pp22–3). In
the United States

> The settlement workers offered the riches of culture to the poor as
> their unclaimed birthright. At the same time they believed that
> under the gentle tutelage of art, the poor might find the moral
> energy to begin to improve their lives. (Carson 1990, pp.116)

Perhaps out of fear of seeming patronising or elitist, such activities are
rare in family centres in England. There is little attention paid to the
arts at all by social work, either in terms of 'uplift', opportunity or

therapeutic expression. This very much contrasts with the situation in Germany or France, where the access of all to high culture is seen not just as an important social right but as contributing to social solidarity. Social-work training (especially in the educative branches of social pedagogy or *animation*) stresses practical, expressive arts and crafts as well as community arts. French *centres socio-culturels* – the equivalents of settlements but with a strong emphasis on family support – provide high-quality arts and crafts workshops and see these as important for drawing local people into the centres. Work with children and young people in deprived communities might include video or graffiti or popular music workshops, but can also include putting on a concert of classical music with trained musicians in the local cathedral (Cannan 1992). In Germany and Denmark there is a tradition of trying to create a high-quality architectural environment for children in nurseries and centres, which not only engages their imagination and enhances play, but also expresses children's value in society and develops their aesthetic senses.

The poor quality of so many modern public buildings, including family centres and nurseries, in England contrasts sadly with the notion that everyone should have a right to enjoy the best and that public and quasi-public services can take a lead by considering carefully architecture and design. The Peckham Experiment in the 1930s was an interesting example of this. With the aim of promoting health, the building was very carefully conceived to be 'an oasis of glass in a desert of brick' (Walter Gropius' verdict, quoted in Stallibrass 1989, p.24), inviting local people into the sunny, light and attractive building and encouraging their use of it. Rather like the settlements, the health centre had many clubs and facilities for families and children and became an important part of neighbourhood life.

Child and family welfare: some common roots

The Peckham Experiment was inspired partly by the shortcomings in infant and maternal health and welfare during the 1920s. As a men's settlement, Toynbee Hall was little involved in this area, but the women's and mixed settlements were important in this field in

Britain, France and the United States. This is an important link with family centres, given their role in the education of mothers. Family centres have grown from day nurseries and play groups, which, with infant welfare services, were often located in settlements, sometimes in partnership with local health services. In this there is a gendered history; in the United States women's settlements came quickly to outnumber men's. The new kind of service they expressed, linking philanthropic social work with social scientific research and social reform, provided a setting in which the rising numbers of Victorian and Edwardian women who had had a university education could find a role (Carson 1990, p.32). Women's settlements, like family centres today, were run mainly by women for women. While they provided aid to working-class mothers and their children they also became – as today – part of the system which regulates working-class family (and women's) lives. Hence, sociologically, there is a strong link between the family work of settlements and of family centres.

In Britain the infant welfare movement included 300 charitable feeding associations by 1905; these provided free meals and advice on infant care, together with access to free or subsidised milk (Thane 1996, p.63). The first school for mothers opened in St Pancras in 1907, followed quickly by others. These provided talks and classes for mothers on nutrition, hygiene and infant care, and ran clinics for infants, baby shows, sewing meetings and other social activities. Up to the First World War the majority of these were run by voluntary organisations (Lewis 1980), many located in settlements together with kindergartens, play centres and nurseries. While many have noted the patronising approach to the huge difficulties working-class women faced in rearing children – in poverty and squalor – it is also evident that the advice given was appreciated by women who had no other source of accurate information (see Carson 1990, p.85 re the USA; Thane 1996, p.63). The infant welfare movement had been stimulated by alarm at the falling birthrate and high levels of infant mortality, and the Boer War and the First World War both produced calls for measures to improve 'maternal competence'. The state began to assume responsibility for infant welfare services in the interwar period; what remained a scandalous gap, however, was the lack of services for maternal health or welfare, the lack of family allowances and the slow development of birth control services.

Much of the infant welfare service, then, can be seen in the same way as family centres now – as struggling to provide something important in a context of inadequate wider services, with a sense of filling the gaps caused by poverty and poor public services, especially housing. The same gender issues remain – is it acceptable to target women and their 'maternal competence' when women's difficulties have environmental causes? On the other hand, isn't it important to provide a place and space for women to share their difficulties, to gain what information is available to help them in bringing up their children, to have some pleasure and opportunity for self-expression? In this sense community-oriented family centres are hugely important as research on their users has shown (e.g. Smith 1992). The lesson from the settlements was that the creation of neighbourhood and women's space is important, but, to avoid falling back into the old COS style of social work, campaigning on local issues is essential. The power of groups is also important, not just for the sharing of problems, but in finding new, user-led solutions.

Settlements certainly saw the support of family life as a central objective. Competitive industrialism seemed to be destroying working-class family life – and poverty and squalor were pervasive until the Second World War in industrial areas of Britain and America. The women's settlements in the United States saw the settlement as an addition to the neighbourhood, which could provide a setting for families to spend leisure time together – something often impossible in the crowded tenements and hardly 'refined' bars or music-halls. The neighbourhood family gatherings were something previously unheard of (Carson 1990, p.85). The settlements, like family centres now, made family life more possible and satisfying than it might otherwise have been. In the interwar period settlements began to work with families with identified problems – their links with the child guidance movement and with juvenile courts are well documented by Carson (1990, pp.175–178), who also shows how in the United States settlements' work became very closely connected with mainstream social-work training in that period. Pimlott (1935, p.245) similarly describes the establishment of the local juvenile court and associated services in Toynbee Hall. Settlements then combined community work with social work, or rather their social work (in the modern sense) rested in a strong framework of a wide range of activities and services available for all local people.

> The settlements succeeded largely because their neighbours welcomed what the settlers almost apologetically offered: organised, regularly scheduled and resident-led activities. Though the neighbourhood adults often hung back from the settlement, ... the children and adolescents swarmed in and stretched the settlers' resources and imagination to their limits. ... the residents found that their clubs, classes, kindergartens, clinics, and summer camps formed a backbone of continuity that ensured settlement survival not just from year to year, but over decades. (Carson 1990, p.52)

Conclusion: common ground

While the accusation of being patronising was and still is important, at their best both settlements and family centres stress participation and self-government so that clubs and activities are run by members or users. Not always easy to put into practice, and sometimes tokenistic, this nevertheless has to be the core of centre work which ultimately tries to produce social change through the process of participation. The most successful family centres are those that are open to their community and are without stigma; within this framework successful work can be carried out with families with very grave difficulties. Part of the success lies not just in professional skills in family work, but in the integration process which coming to an open-door family centre offers to the most marginal or excluded families and their children.

Here there are two lessons. One is the importance of long-term work, of a stable presence in a community which for many family centres, especially in the voluntary sector, is threatened by short-term and insecure funding. It is extremely regrettable that recently many successful family projects and centres are closing or restricting their activities because of funding problems. Toynbee (1997) notes family support projects' success in tackling social exclusion – citing the Newpin projects, Save the Children and NCH Action for Children centres – and argues against the illogical policies which result in lack of funding for the very projects which give the opportunities that the Labour government is calling for.

The second lesson concerns the place of children. Settlements have a very strong tradition of youth work, with huge numbers of clubs and organisations involved in them. Family centres, however, have tended to base their work on younger children (because of their origins in playgroups and nurseries, as well as the emphasis on the early years as a priority for child protection). Despite family centres' place in the children's legislation, in practice the balance of work is towards parents (mothers) rather than children. The UK has poor provision for children, and many would argue that family centres could do more to alleviate this. Indeed, some saw the rise in family centre provision as linked to the demise of mainstream day care for children (Cannan 1992). True or not, family centres certainly grew in an era in which private and not public arrangements for child care were applauded. Facilities for children in family centres have tended to be sessional, in support of parent programmes or as part of explicit parent-and-child programmes. Section 17 of the Children Act 1989 has encouraged the growing assumption that the child's welfare is helped not only directly but indirectly by, for example, programmes for parents, and family centres do tend to mirror this. Nevertheless, facilities for school-age children, such as after-school clubs or groups for children with family difficulties, are increasingly to be found in them. This has relied on the energies of the workers and on local resources, and government funding initiatives. Section 17 has also encouraged a new developmental boundary and more provision up to

8 years, thus turning social services departments' attention to school-age children.

However, the variation in the type and quality of services for children, including those of school age, is a cause for concern, especially when compared with that in many other European Union countries (e.g. European Commission Network on Child Care 1996a, 1996b) which offer a greater range of provision. Settlements of course continue to work in this area, but there is great local diversity. Other European countries recognise that the modern urban child and adolescent have very limited opportunities for independence and adventure, so that summer schemes as well as regular youth activities are important in delinquency prevention. Further, they recognise, in ways which echo the settlement founders, that these schemes should not be concentrated on the most deprived but should bridge the gaps between the classes, which simultaneously means that disadvantaged children will share high-quality services with others.

We conclude that there is much in the settlement movement to inspire the family centre world. Both movements have clearly very different origins. The emergence of family centres in the era of the 'discovery' of child (sexual) abuse, and the connected reduction of social work (in local authorities) to a more regulatory and procedural activity, have had a profound influence on family centres. However, the activities of some of the early (mainly voluntary organisation) experiments reflected some of the settlement tradition of making mainstream services in health, education or community arts more widely available (see Phelan's 1983 account of The Children Society's development, and also Gibbons 1992). Save the Children's attempts to avoid regulatory social work in their focus on child care, educational and work opportunities for women (Lloyd 1977) have already been mentioned. There have been some attempts to tackle gender with experiments in programmes for men in, for instance, the Pen Green or Fulford Family Centre's attempts since the mid-1980s to integrate the community work and social work agendas. Save the Children centres have stressed the importance of providing real opportunities for women to enable them to move out of poverty. However, these examples of 'resistance' are numerically small or have proved to be short-lived. The majority of family centres, despite all manner of resistance at the margins, have been defined largely by the local authorities' need for 'assessment' and evidence within child protection procedures (Warren 1991).

What of the future? Well, we need constantly to remind ourselves about, and import, more promising messages from Europe in 'centre' development. Also, there are some optimistic possibilities in the so-called 're-focusing debate', generated by the Department of Health (DoH) and its followers. In summary, the proposition is that child-care social work has allowed itself to adopt too narrow a focus, in short, a regulatory or policing role. How might such a practice be identified with a broader framework, namely, family support? Are family support and child protection barely reconcilable cultures, or part of a continuum of practice (Parton 1997)? A community development approach to family support was recommended by the authors of the *Evaluation of the DoH Family Support Initiative* (Hartless and Warren 1995), and some local authorities have taken more seriously the encouragement to shift the balance from a protection to a family support/community development perspective (e.g. Brighton and Hove Council, London Borough of Hackney). An initial agenda for such an approach is to be found in Cannan and Warren (1997). Family centres do offer the possibility of addressing one of the criticisms of community work, that its focus on the instrumental needs and outcomes of groups has meant that it might leave behind the more fragile members of the community. In their aim of offering support and opportunity to children, young people and parents in some of the most disadvantaged areas, family centres are surely in the best of settlement tradition. What they can give to settlements is a sophisticated understanding of the ecological interrelationship of family problems and support systems; they can show how families can be strengthened by projects that generate and nourish local social networks and opportunities, and many exemplify an integrated approach to children's needs. In these cases we see social work and community work enriching rather than criticising each other in their common struggle against social exclusion and injustice.

Bibliography

Ahmed, S. (1987) 'Racism in child care'. In W. Stone and C. Warren (eds) *Protection or Prevention*. London: NCVCCO.

Audit Commission (1994) *Seen But Not Heard: Co-ordinating Community Child Health and Social Services For Children In Need*. London: HMSO.

Barford, R., O'Grady, S. and Hall, R. (1995) 'A neighbourhood centre – protection or prevention?' In Henderson, P. (ed.) *Children and Communities*. London: Pluto Press.

Briggs, A. and Macartney, A. (1984) *Toynbee Hall: The First Hundred Years*. London: Routledge and Kegan Paul.

Bronfenbrenner, U. (1979) *The Ecology of Human Development – Experiments by Nature and Design*. Cambridge, USA: Harvard University Press.

Cannan, C. (1992) *Changing Families, Changing Welfare: Family Centres and the Welfare State*. Hemel Hempstead: Harvester Wheatsheaf.

Cannan, C. (1997) 'Social Development with children and families in France'. In C. Cannan and C. Warren (eds) *Social Action with Children and Families: A Community Development Approach to Child and Family Welfare*. London: Routledge.

Cannan C. and Warren C. (1997) *Social Action with Children and Families: A Community Development Approach to Child and Family Welfare*. London: Routledge.

Carson, M. (1990) *Settlement Folk: Social Thought and the American Settlement Movement, 1885–1930*. Chicago: University of Chicago Press.

European Commission Network on Childcare (1996a) *1986–1996 – A Decade of Achievements*. Brussels: European Commission.

European Commission Network on Childcare (1996b) *Quality Targets in Services for Young Children*. Brussels: European Commission.

Gibbons, J. (ed) (1992) *The Children Act 1989 and Family Support: Principles into Practice*. London: HMSO.

Gil, D. (1970) *Violence Against Children*. Cambridge Mass: Harvard University Press.

Hartless, J. and Warren, C. (1995) *Evaluation of the Family Support Initiative*. Report to the DoH, University of Sussex. Unpublished.

Henderson, P. (1997) 'Community Development and Children: A contemporary agenda'. In C. Cannan and C. Warren (eds) *Social Action with Children and Families: A Community Development Approach to Child and Family Welfare*. London: Routledge.

Holman, B. (1998) 'Groundwork'. *The Guardian*, 15 July.

Holman, R. (1976) *Inequality in Child Care*, London: Child Poverty Action Group.

Holman, R. (1988) *Putting Families First: Prevention and Childcare, a Study of Prevention by Statutory and Voluntary Agencies*. Basingstoke: Macmillan.

Johnson, C. (1995) *Introduction to the History and Impact of the International Movement.* Derby: International Federation of Settlements and Neighbourhood Centres.

Lewis, J. (1980) *The Politics of Motherhood: Child and Maternal Welfare in England 1900–1939.* London: Croom Helm.

Lloyd, E. (1997) 'The role of the centre in family support'. In C. Cannan and C. Warren (eds) *Social Action with Children and Families: A Community Development Approach to Child and Family Welfare.* London: Routledge.

Long, G. (1995) 'Family poverty and the role of family support work'. In M. Hill, R. Hawthorne-Kirk and D. Part (eds) *Supporting Families.* Edinburgh: HMSO.

Moss, P. and Petrie, P. (1997) *Children's Services: Time for a New Approach.* London: University of London, Institute of Education.

Parton, N. (1985) *The Politics of Child Abuse.* Basingstoke: Macmillan.

Parton, N. (1997) *Child Protection and Family Support – Tensions, Contradictions and Possibilities.* London: Routledge.

Phelan, J. (1983) *Family Centres – A Study.* London: The Children's Society.

Pimlott, J. A. R. (1935) *Toynbee Hall: Fifty Years of Social Progress 1884–1934.* London: Dent.

Smith, T. (1992) 'Family centres, children in need and the Children Act 1989'. In J. Gibbons (ed.) *The Children Act 1989 and Family Support. Principles into Practice.* London: HMSO.

Stallibrass, A. (1989) *Being Me and Also Us: Lessons from the Peckham Experiment.* Edinburgh: Scottish Academic Press.

Thane, P. (1996) *Foundations of the Welfare State.* Harlow: Longman.

Toynbee, P. (1997) 'Wanted: a department for banging heads together'. *The Independent,* 8 December.

Tunstill, J. (1992) 'Local authority policies on children in need'. In J. Gibbon (ed.) *The Children Act 1989 and Family Support: Principles into Practice.* London: HMSO.

Warren, C. (1991) *The Role of Parent Advocacy in Family Centres.* MPhil Thesis, University of Southampton. Unpublished.

White, T. (1998) 'Kids' stuff'. *The Guardian,* 24 June.

⌣ entrepreneurs or sleeping giants?

Settlements in Britain today

Sarah Banks

Settlements, while having much in common, are also very diverse in their size, organisation and styles of working. This chapter seeks to give an overview of the character of a range of settlements in England and Scotland, focusing on some of the main themes relating to the nature of their work, their organisation, the continuities and disconti-nuities with the past, and future developments.

Information has been drawn from annual reports and other documentation produced by settlements, and interviews with a selection of directors and workers. All members of the British Association of Settlements and Social Action Centres (BASSAC) were contacted and asked for relevant documentation. Of the 75 members of BASSAC, 23 are historic settlements – that is, they were founded in the late nineteenth/early twentieth century with facilities for residents to live and work in 'deprived' urban neighbourhoods. The focus of this chapter is on these historic settlements – although the majority now do not offer residential facilities. Information was received from 19 of the historic settlements in membership of BASSAC, and this material forms the basis of much of this chapter. Documentation was also received from many of the other multipurpose social action centres, and has been used to set the work of the historic settlements in context.

Settlements in the 1990s

Settlements are multipurpose neighbourhood centres which are, according to BASSAC (1997a p.13), 'committed to helping local communities bring about social change'. The profile of work they do is broadly similar to that of other multipurpose centres founded more recently. Their distinctiveness lies in their past. For many there are still active links with the founders/founding organisations, which can be useful in terms of fundraising and may be apparent in the composition of their boards of trustees/management committees. Some local people have memories of the work of the settlements over many decades. For example, some of the people who attended the Young Wives' Club at Bishop Creighton House decades ago are still meeting now in their 60s and 70s as a Women's Club. At Blackfriars Settlement, the Helen Barlow Club has been running for over 60 years. The buildings the settlements inhabit are often large and old – many have rooms once used by the residents and some contain chapels, which means there may be substantial space for meeting places and offices to be used by tenant organisations. The fact that settlements have, in many cases, been in existence for a 100 or so years is very consciously used in some of their literature to give them credibility with funders and users, to indicate stability as well as a flexibility and willingness to change with the times.

The term 'settlement' is retained in the names of the majority of the organisations. A few have decided to drop it as no longer representing the nature of the work they do. For example, St Hilda's East became known as a 'Community Centre' in 1987 when the organisation changed its Memorandum and Articles of Association and became a partnership between the founding body (Cheltenham Ladies' College) and the local community (St Hilda's East Community Centre 1989, pp.32–3). In several settlements documentation reveals that a change of name has been considered, or indeed recommended (often by outside consultants), but nevertheless the old name has been retained. One relatively recently recruited director commented that the term settlement is misleading and outdated, giving the impression that 'we are rehousing people'. A recent report also recommends a name change for BASSAC, suggesting it is 'a hindrance toward a more appealing 'public' image' (Müschenborn and Rachmat 1994, p.37). Arguments against a name change focus on the importance of history and tradition and the fact that 'settlement' is an internationally recognised name reflected in the existence of similar organisations and movements worldwide.

Despite sharing a common tradition, and many similarities in the types of work they tend to do, the settlements today are extremely diverse in their size, organisational structure, sources of funding and specialisms. These range from the Birmingham Settlement, with an annual turnover of over £2 million, 23 projects, four charity shops and a strong emphasis on money advice and debt counselling, to Fern Street Settlement in London, with an income of £110,042, which focuses on pensioners' lunch clubs and children's holidays. These differences can be accounted for by many factors, including the nature of the founders, the types of neighbourhood, the influence of the personalities of particular directors, the presence or absence of other substantial voluntary sector organisations in the locality, and policies and practices of local government in terms of grant-aiding and contract giving.

Table 1 gives an overview of the levels of income and range of work identified in the annual reports of the settlements. Unless otherwise stated, the information relates to the year ended 31 March 1997. The dates of the founding of the settlements have generally been taken from the documentation and histories produced by the settlements themselves and may differ occasionally from dates given in other publications.

Table 11.1 An overview of the income and range of work of settlements, 1996–7

Settlement	Date of founding	Income 1996–7, £s	Types of work
Beauchamp Lodge Set.	1939	81,504[1]	advice, café, youth work
Bede House Association	1938	722, 561[2]	café, community development, education, youth, vol. action
Bishop Creighton House Set.	1908	343,738	café, community development, care, volunteers
Birmingham Settlement	1899	2,198,642	advice, care, nursery, training, research, shops
Blackfriars Settlement	1887	889,153	education, playground, youth, clubs
Cambridge House and Talbot	1889	1,034,029	advice, education, people with learning disabilities, youth, resources
Charterhouse in Southwark	1885	416,629[3]	care, play, volunteers, women, youth.
Edinburgh University Set.	1905	998,217	arts, care, disability, training, student placements, 2 companies
Fern Street Setttlement	1907	110,042	children's holidays, lunch clubs, pensioners' day centre
Katherine Lowe Settlement	1924	65,609	carers' support, clubs, mental health, youth
Lady Margaret Hall Set.	1897	424,579	education, health, environment
Manchester Settlement	1895	201,128	community development, clubs, play, youth housing, youth work
Oxford House	1884	523,766	arts, café, education, Somali projects, youth
Peckham Settlement	1896	177,167	advice, pensioners' clubs, playschemes, nursery

St Hilda's E. Com. Centre	1889	574,847	advice, Bengali projects, care, children, education, volunteers, youth
Salmon Youth Centre	1906	156,723	youth projects
Time and Talents Centre	1887	52,312	care, clubs, elderly, people with learning disabilties, youth
Toynbee Hall	1884	1,283,000	advice, arts, Bengali projects, cafe, care, children, shop, play, training, youth
Virginia House Settlement	1925	443,246	care, counselling, community development, youth

1   Ceased operations in 1998

2   This figure is for the 18-month period to March 1998

3   This figure is for the 9-month period to 31 March 1997

Caring and developing: the work of the settlements

The settlements characterise themselves in a number of different ways in their annual reports and publicity literature. Some quote aims and objectives which seem to have changed little from the time when they were founded. For example, the object of the Fern Street Settlement is described in the 1997 Annual Report as 'to provide for the material and moral needs of persons resident in Fern Street and the neighbourhood thereof who are in conditions of need, hardship or distress' (Fern Street Settlement 1997, p.1). Oxford House, on the other hand, reports a revised statement of purpose agreed as a result of a review in 1997: 'The purpose of Oxford House is to encourage a sense of community in a multi-ethnic society and to enhance the lives of those it serves' (Oxford House 1997, p.2). Others echo the terms used by BASSAC, calling themselves multipurpose centres or social action centres. The statement of purpose for Cambridge House and Talbot characterises the organisation as a 'multipurpose voluntary organisation working in Southwark to alleviate the local effects of poverty and to support social change' (Cambridge House and Talbot 1998, p.2). This goes beyond simply the relief of hardship and suffering to encompass the notion of social change. In the historical account of Cambridge House and Talbot it is suggested that since the late 1960s 'the principles and practice of community development have been central to the settlement's core mission' (Cambridge House 1989, p.20). Some settlements describe themselves explicitly as working in the field of community development, as the Bishop Creighton House statement illustrates: 'the settlement operates as a multipurpose centre offering community development and social support services' (Bishop Creighton House 1998, p.2). Bede House Association, in its latest literature, is described as 'a Community Development Organisation, its role is to develop services for the Bermondsey and Rotherhithe community, helping to meet identified needs' (Bede House Association 1998b). Differences in self-description are not always an indicator of marked differences in the type of work and philosophies of the settlements. However, they do give particular types of messages to funders and service users and contribute towards projecting and maintaining a settlement's identity.

Bishop Creighton's twin-pronged approach through community development and 'social support services' is typical of the work of many settlements. In the history of the Blackfriars settlement it is noted that: 'One task of recent years has been to try to find a balance between the campaigning and caring roles' (Barratt 1985, p.75). However, the tendency in the 1990s in most cases is for the balance to be tipped in favour of social support services in the form of domiciliary and day-care services for older people, people with disabilities, and child care. This shift from generic neighbourhood work towards service delivery reflects a trend in community work generally, which gained impetus following the 1990 NHS and Community Care Act (Mayo 1994; Popple 1995, pp.55–9). Nevertheless, in many pieces of work there is both a service delivery and a development function. A large number of settlements do a range of work that is somewhere between service delivery and community development through projects in the fields of education and training, youth work, advice

Table 11.2 Types of work undertaken by settlements

Care provision	Day centres, lunch clubs, domiciliary care, phone lines and a range of other work with older people, people with mental health problems, physical and learning disabilities. Special projects for smaller 'neglected' groups, e.g. the young disabled, young carers, ethnic minority elders. Child care including nurseries, after school provision, playgroups and playgrounds. Caring for the carers.
Supporting self-help	Women's groups, carers' support groups (including a young carers' project), parents projects, family support, health groups.
Community development in the self-help/care field	Supporting the establishment of new self-help groups and the development of existing groups. The development of new services arising from community needs.
Community development: neighbourhood work/capacity building	Generic neighbourhood work – support for tenants and residents groups, training for community activists. Encouraging participation in regeneration schemes often in partnership with other agencies. Development of new projects in an area.
Education/ training	Basic literacy and numeracy, computer skills, vocational qualifications, New Deal trainees. Special projects for people with disabilities, training cafés, special arts projects.
Youth work	Youth clubs, detached work, special activity projects (e.g. narrow-boats, outdoor activities centres). Ethnic minority work (e.g. with Bangladeshi or Somali young people). Work with young people with disabilities.
Advice work	Legal advice sessions, welfare rights advice, specialist advice (e.g. fuel debt, business debt), counselling, support for the establishment of advice centres and Citizen's Advice Bureaux, including provision of office space.
Opportunities for volunteers	Offering voluntary work in many projects for local people and others. Development and training of volunteers sometimes through special Opportunities for volunteering projects with paid staff to co-ordinate. A few settlements still offer opportunities for residents to live and work in the area.
Neighbour-hood resource centre	Office facilities for tenants, services such as photocopying, payroll administration for local groups. Serving as focal point for local community: cafés, art exhibitions, second-hand shops. Serving as a voice for community sector in the neighbourhood.

work, and through functioning as a 'resource centre' for local voluntary organisations and community groups. Although it is hard to categorise the work of the settlements, Table 2 is an attempt to give a broad overview of the range and types of work happening today.

Not all settlements offer all aspects of the work listed in Table 2, but they are generally involved in a varied range of services, activities, facilities and projects, as Table 1 indicates. The most common line of work tends to be youth work, followed closely by care work, which is undertaken by over half the settlements surveyed. Education/training, work with children, and advice services are also significant features of roughly one-third of settlements. Four have community cafés and three operate commercial enterprises. This broad overview shows that many of the areas of work are similar to those undertaken by the settlements during the last century, although the styles of delivery have changed (for example, some of the advice services operate via phonelines) and much of the work is targeted on specific groups (such as young people with learning disabilities or Bangladeshi elders) or specialised needs (such as immigration advice). This increasing specialisation mirrors the trends in social work and community and youth work towards targeted and focused work (Banks 1994; 1995).

The term 'care' is used broadly to cover a range of services for older people, families, children and people with disabilities. This has always been a strand of work in settlements, providing services for the most vulnerable members of the population. The work with children, especially children's holidays, was a feature of the work of settlements in the early days and still continues. In the context of the opening of a new nursery, the President of the Birmingham Settlement spoke in 1994 of 'continuity' (the settlement first opened a nursery at the beginning of the century) and the fact that 'fundamental needs like that for nursery care remain the same' (Birmingham Settlement 1994, p.1). A vast range of different types of work is undertaken in this field, ranging from domiciliary and day care centres to the 'Care and Repair' home improvement schemes operated by Manchester and Bishop Creighton settlements. This involves caseworkers and building surveyors working with vulnerable people who do not have the resources to maintain or adapt their homes.

The focus on legal and other advice work has been a constant strand since the founding of the 'Poor Man's Lawyer' scheme at Mansfield House in 1891 (Pimlott 1935, p.116–7). Many settlements have been instrumental in establishing Law Centres or Citizens' Advice Bureaux, which may then have become separate organisations in their own right. For example, the Advice Centre founded and run from Blackfriars Settlement became an independent incorporated charity running under its own name in April 1997. Some of the specialist services developed before it separated from the settlement included a pensioners project, a County Court project and outreach work with Irish pensioners in South London (Blackfriars Settlement 1997, p.10). Other settlements still provide advice sessions, often of a specialist nature. For example, one of the Somali Projects supported by Oxford House specialises in immigration work. Birmingham Settlement specialises in money advice, with a recently founded project dealing with business debt – apparently the first of its kind in the country, now operated with franchise agreements in several locations.

Work with young people is a significant feature of many settlements, although several report recent changes to the profile of their work, moving away from a predominance of youth work. For example, the Chair of the Katherine Low Settlement reports that after two major reviews 'the settlement will have changed from housing two council-run youth-oriented projects to a dynamic centre serving a wider community' (Katherine Low Settlement 1996a). Mansfield is reported in 1994 as having moved from being 'a single-sex mainly sporting club to being a multi-faceted organisation' (Mansfield Settlement 1994, p.20). Bishop Creighton Settlement lost its youth work provision with the demise of the Inner London Education Authority and has never re-established it. At the other end of the spectrum, however, is the Salmon Youth Centre (formerly the Cambridge University Mission) which focuses entirely on youth projects.

Many of the settlements have significant education and/or training projects. For example, Blackfriars operates an education centre providing part-time courses for 150 students in Southwark, with significant funding from the Further Education Funding Council (FEFC 1998). It developed out of a literacy scheme established in the 1970s and provides basic education, computer courses and English for speakers of other languages. The Edinburgh University Settlement operates several education and training projects, including the Microbeacon project – a computer training and guidance centre for adults with a range of disabilities – in collaboration with a local further education college, and funded by the city council and various trust funds. It also runs 2nd Chance to Learn, an outreach adult education project; a training centre offering vocational training and qualifications; and a Graduate Jobclub (Edinburgh University Settlement 1997). Both these projects are now offering training under the government's New Deal programme. This is a trend apparent in some of the other settlements with large training projects – such as Birmingham.

Community development, explicitly identified as such, is a much smaller part of many settlements' work than might be expected. Only a few settlements have specific neighbourhood-based community development projects. For example, Manchester Settlement runs the Beswick and Bradford Community Project which aims to 'develop and support self-help initiatives' in partnership with local people and other agencies (Manchester Settlement, 1997, p.8). Bishop Creighton began Community Networks, a new single-worker project funded for three years through the National Lottery in 1997 to build self-sustaining networks on two 'deprived' estates. The project then received funding through the Single Regeneration Budget and the European programme, URBAN, to facilitate community participation within the much larger North Hammersmith regeneration area. Bede

House Community Development Project is a women's project which aims to develop networks of local women, and addresses issues such as domestic violence, racial harassment and health education.

Other aspects of settlements' work, such as support for volunteers, self-help groups and their function as neighbourhood resource centres, are less easy to specify and sometimes lie hidden in their annual reports and accounts of work. These may often be part of the function of the 'core' rather than a specific project. Nevertheless, many settlements have developed special projects for the development and support of volunteers – often stimulated by the availability of funding through BASSAC for Opportunities for Volunteering. Bishop Creighton Settlement, for example, has a volunteer organiser, and certain services are run largely by volunteers – such as 'Careline', which involves volunteers making daily phone calls to housebound and isolated elderly people. A number of settlements state explicitly that they offer copying, printing, payroll and other services to local community groups and claim a role as development agencies in the locality. Several settlement directors and workers spoke of the 'nurturing' role of settlements in supporting new or struggling groups, often by providing office space and subsidised services. Many tenants and user groups value this service, feeling that it amounts to 'a lot more than just office space'. Indeed, Mansfield Settlement highlights the role played by its Plaistow Centre as 'a resource for growth' (Mansfield Settlement 1997, p.6).

Challenges and changes

Many of the issues facing settlements in Britain today are common across the voluntary sector, and it is important to understand settlements in this context (for an overview see Taylor 1997). The advent of the mixed economy of welfare, the contract culture, competition, the new managerialism have all had an impact on the work and management of settlements. In discussion with directors and workers a number of themes emerged which will be discussed below in relation to resourcing, organisational structures and systems and issues of culture, tradition and identity.

BUILDINGS AND BUSINESSES — A QUESTION OF RESOURCES

Buildings are a constant theme in the history of most settlements. The majority own the buildings that form their main base. Some own several on different sites. This provides a resource (particularly if there is enough space to rent out rooms and offices to other organisations) but can be a constant worry and drain on funds. Some settlements are operating from large, dilapidated and run-down buildings and debating whether to sell them. For example, at several points in the history of Blackfriars Settlement demolition was threatened and moves talked about, particularly in the 1940s and 1950s (Barratt 1985, p.21). Yet the settlement is still operating today from the one remaining original terrace in Nelson Square originally given by Octavia Hill, while the rest of the square has been demolished and rebuilt. Current plans are to sell the building and move to a site nearby. Other settlements 'solved' the problem by having their original buildings demolished and new ones built on the same site (for example, in Birmingham in 1963 and St Hilda's in 1994).

Virgina House in Plymouth undertook less drastic but very time-consuming and extensive renovation work over more than a decade at a cost of over three-quarters of a million pounds (BASSAC 1996, p.6). The director reports that when the work started in 1986 the costs were grossly underestimated – which was probably a good thing, as the project would never have been started had the full costs been known: 'If we had not taken that step then it is also doubtful that all the released energy and potential of the Settlement we have today would have come about' (*ibid.*, p.7). Some of this energy has come from a new image and new tenants, but also from an increase in revenue generated by the building and the services it contains. This rose from £16,111 in 1985/6 to £137,108 in 1995/6, when it represented roughly 30 per cent of the income of the settlement (*ibid.*, pp.17, 30). Many other settlements generate significant income through rents and hire of meeting rooms. For example, Oxford House in 1997 generated over £80,000 (16 per cent of its income) from rents and £35,000 from the hire of meeting-rooms (BASSAC 1997b, p.28).

This links to the concept of asset-based development, which is being discussed in the settlement movement at the present time, and to the theme of settlements becoming more businesslike and generating more of their income from their own resources in order to become less dependent on grants, contracts or donations for funding their work. In a recent document Oxford House is described as 'a major employer in the area and defining itself more as a small and medium sized business with social objectives' (BASSAC 1997b, p.2). The director sees the organisation as part of the 'social economy', defining this as embracing 'any organisation that trades for social purposes – including co-operatives, charities, and trade unions – and sees it as drawing on a diverse community base' (*ibid.*, p.2). He reports that a quarter of the core revenue of Oxford House is generated from its own activities, which also include a Somali–English Interpreting Service.

One of the settlements which does not own buildings, Edinburgh, instead has two trading companies which generate income for the settlement. One of these, the Bell Tower, is a graphic design unit which produces literature for the settlement at subsidised prices and undertakes outside commercial work. The other, Wilkie House, is used for settlement project work during the day and is contracted out for entertainments during the evenings, contributing 12 per cent of the settlement's annual income. According to Daniel Onifade:

> Sometimes there are discussions about whether Wilkie House, being a night club and pub, should be connected with EUS. However, the profits from this operation are fed back to the parent charity, providing money to support social projects that otherwise wouldn't get funded. (BASSAC 1997a, p.25).

Several of the buildings occupied by the settlement are also used during August as venues for the Edinburgh Festival – another way of generating income, although at the cost of some disruption to staff.

Another settlement with a separate trading company is Birmingham. Birmingham Settlement Sales Ltd, established in 1980 with one small charity shop in Sutton Coldfield, now runs four shops and contributed £66,173 to the income of the settlement in 1996–7 (Birmingham Settlement 1997, p.25). Until May 1996 the Chair of the Board was Maisie Smith, who had a long association with the settlement, being recorded as an Honorary Secretary in the 1930s and as Chair of the Settlement in the 1970s, when her 'Herculean' fundraising efforts were noted (Rimmer 1980, pp 83, 146).

The theme of adopting a 'businesslike' approach to managing settlements is not a new one, although some settlements have been slower to shift their approaches than others. In 1985 Barratt was already noting a tightening up of local authorities' policies towards grant aid (requiring more details of the organisation and how it was managed), and the contribution this had made to changing the Blackfriars Settlement's financial affairs 'from a fairly simple if always anxious matter to one resembling a business concern' (Barratt 1985, p.57).

There is no doubt that the changing nature of local government funding for voluntary sector social and community work has had a profound effect on most of the settlements in the late 1980s and 1990s as the contract culture has taken hold. None have remained unscathed, although some have weathered the storm more easily, or earlier, than others. Many settlements had relied quite heavily on local authority grants to maintain their work. Generally these grants were contributions towards the core work of the settlement. For some settlements grants have disappeared completely and been replaced by service level agreements or contracts with local authorities for specific services or pieces of work. Manchester Settlement, for example, lost its £60,000 core grant from the City Council in the mid-1990s, which precipitated yet another crisis in its long and turbulent history. The settlement nevertheless survived with several generous donations, but the experience prompted the Chair in 1995 to comment that 'the need for secure long-term funding is omni-present and acute' (Rose and Woods 1995, p.99). In other settlements the size of the core grant has been reduced considerably, meaning that, of necessity, settlements have had to rethink their funding strategies and reconsider their work priorities. The blunt statement in a leaflet produced by Lady Margaret Hall (1997b) probably reflects the position of several settlements grappling with the changes: '...1997 continues a further period of uncertainty, due to decreasing local authority funding, leaving the settlement again fighting for its survival'. The situation at Beauchamp Lodge Settlement was even more serious, resulting in a mothballing of all operations and substantial staff redundancies in February 1998. This was caused by the fact that the Lodge received no funding in 1997–8, except one grant from the London Borough's Grant Committee. In the following months, however, a business plan was developed and several grant applications were successful, including £93,000 URBAN funding, so that by September 1998 the Executive Committee was able to report 'a valid optimism for a brighter future' (Beauchamp Lodge 1998, p.1).

For some of the London settlements the demise of the Greater London Council and particularly the Inner London Education Authority (ILEA) meant a loss of funds, and in some cases loss of particular pieces of work. Youth work which had been funded directly by ILEA was particularly vulnerable, although generally this was picked up by the successor authority, the Borough Council, with whom new relationships had to be built and new priorities set.

The reaction to the shift from grants to service level agreements and contracts has been a mixed one, though many settlements are now used to the system and capitalising on it. For example, in 1996–7, St Hilda's received roughly half its income from the London Borough of Tower Hamlets for contracted services (St Hilda's East Community Centre 1997, p.24). As the director of Bishop Creighton House commented: 'At first I was totally outraged; it meant a narrowing of the work. But now we're used to it'. In the 1996–7 Annual Report it is noted that the settlement has contracts for a range of care and home improvement work with three departments of Hammersmith and Fulham Council. The Director states: 'BCH is firmly in the contract culture... This has narrowed our work in some areas but in others, such as our community centre services, it has helped to create a clearer focus and a more secure funding base' (Bishop Creighton House Settlement 1998, p.2).

Indeed, in 1996–7 Bishop Creighton House received a relatively large proportion of its income, 67 per cent (£230,075), from grants/service level agreements, and a relatively modest proportion, 8 per cent (£28,792), from fundraising/donations. It is interesting to compare this with Toynbee Hall, where only 2 per cent of income came in the form of statutory grants, compared with 37 per cent through donations and 39 per cent from property income (Toynbee Hall 1997, p.4). Fern Street, on the other hand, received 78 per cent of its total income for 1996–7 from its investments and no grants or service level agreements are recorded (Fern Street 1997, p.16). This illustrates the huge differences between settlements in the ways they fund their work, reflecting both their history and connections as well as their size and the contingencies of their relationships with local authorities and funders.

ORGANISATIONAL ISSUES – THE APPLE AND ITS CORE

The theme of 'management' is a much newer one for the settlements – indeed for the voluntary sector as a whole – than that of funds. One of the major projects of the Conservative government of the late 1980s involved reducing the role of the state and extending that of the private and voluntary sector in the delivery of welfare services (Cochrane 1994). This required substantial improvements in standards of management in voluntary organisations if they were to take up these new opportunities for expansion. Resistance was deep-rooted as the 'new managerialism', with its focus on economy, effectiveness and efficiency, seemed to cut across many of the core values of voluntarism (Deakin 1995, p.59). Nevertheless, during the 1980s and 1990s there has been an increasing literature on the theme of managing voluntary organisations and a proliferation of training courses and consultancies. For many settlements the growth in the amount of work they are doing, the complexities of funding, accountability requirements, and increasing numbers of paid staff have required a shift in approach in order to avoid becoming what Handy (1988, p.7) described as 'abodes of careworn people pushing some stone forever uphill'.

During the 1990s several underwent 'reviews' as a result of which recommendations were made for changes, including clarity in the structures and management of the organisation. For example, the report of a 'Management and Organisation Review' of one settlement produced by an external consultant in 1996 found:

> ... no clear strategy for achieving its vision; little sense its mission is shared by different stakeholders; no credible or inspiring development plan; the capacity for developing new project ideas is weak; premises are unsuitable; finances precarious; it is inward looking and over-reliant on its historical reputation.

The review of another settlement in 1997 identified issues relating to: 'not enough collaboration between projects within the settlement; little capacity to respond to changing local needs; lack of identity and clear strategic direction.'

These are accounts of organisations that appear to have lost their way – a position that most settlements have been in at some point during their long histories. Several settlements have recently been through periods of crisis – a feature of which is often a rapid turnover of directors, which in itself has a destabilising effect. The role of director in a small to medium-sized voluntary organisation is a particularly crucial one, as that person tends to cope with all the management tasks, both mundane and strategic – staffing, budgeting, planning – as well as playing other roles both internally and externally (Batsleer 1995, p.232). Not surprisingly, some of the larger settlements are now beginning to employ professionally qualified people to undertake specialist management tasks, such as personnel and accountancy. One settlement director expressed his relief that an experienced member of staff who previously worked for the Benefits Agency was now reforming the settlement's procedures for selection, recruitment and personnel issues generally. The same settlement also employs a chartered accountant who formerly worked in the oil industry. While there is little evidence of settlement directors coming into post from a background in business or public sector management, the employment of people in other roles with specialist skills from a range of backgrounds is evident. Interestingly, they all express a deep commitment to the values of the voluntary sector. The coordinator of the innovative Business Debtline operated by the Birmingham Settlement left his post as bank manager because he liked the ethos at the settlement: 'You can make a difference here'.

One of the key concerns of settlements in recent years has been the relationship of the projects run by the organisation to the 'core' or central operations. As more and more separately funded and often short-term projects have been established, in some settlements there has been a tendency towards fragmentation, with each project having its own staff and identity and the relationship with the settlement itself being unclear or forgotten. A recent review of Oxford House comments on the need for more integration between projects, stating that it 'lacks a clear role outside of the projects' (O' Connell 1997, p.6). Referring to another settlement, a member of BASSAC staff related a similar situation, describing the settlement site as 'a cluster of pearls' with each project having its own identity and logo. This was in contrast to another settlement, with a reputation for being 'well-managed', which had adopted a consistent logo and 'branded' documents.

'The Apple Needs its Core' is the evocative title of a BASSAC commissioned report which notes the difficulties faced by settlements in gaining funding for core work which includes the overall financial and administrative services, as well as the role of developing and supporting new projects. In a survey of eight settlements the variation in reported core costs as a proportion of total expenditure ranged from 19 per cent to 53 per cent (Müschenborn and Rachmat 1994, p.20). This can be explained because of the different ways settlements allocate their core costs, with many failing to attribute the full direct costs of running projects. Indeed, my interviews with directors revealed that some settlements have failed to take any or sufficient management fees from the projects to cover the real costs of administering them – although this situation is changing now.

One way of integrating individual projects has been to group them into departments or sections. This step was taken recently by the newly appointed director of Blackfriars who has created three 'service areas', each combining several projects: education, childcare and training; youth and play; and community care. A fourth area is 'settlement business' – in other words, the core. Toynbee Hall has several 'departments', some of which are individual projects, others of which combine several projects, such as the Children's Department which comprises ten projects (Toynbee Hall 1997). Virginia House is organised into two units – 'Community Services' and 'Building Services' – each of which has a manager and is also split into several teams. Each unit produces detailed annual action/work plans, outlining areas of work and objectives to be achieved over the coming year (Virginia House Settlement 1998a and b). Virginia House is regarded within the settlement movement as one of the most 'businesslike' – and indeed it is using the Business Excellence Model of the British Quality Foundation in its pursuit of a 'policy for quality' entitled 'Putting People First' (Virginia House Settlement 1997, p.3). The challenge for Virginia House and other settlements in the current climate is how to become 'business-like but not like a business' – a phrase used by Gray (1998) in relation to the challenge for public management, which applies equally to the voluntary sector.

TRADITION AND IDENTITY: 'SOLID AND ABIDING IN A CRAZY WORLD'

While seeking to survive and adapt to the changing demands of the 1990s, the importance of the settlements' history is rarely forgotten, and, indeed, can be capitalised upon. For example, on its 75th anniversary, Virginia House in Plymouth re-established its links with its founding family, the Astors, who funded the final stage of its ambitious redevelopment – the courtyard and garden (BASSAC 1996, p.18).

The relationship of the settlements with their founders is very varied. Some have lost these links completely. For example, Oxford

House no longer has any involvement with Keble College, its founding organisation. Others have preserved the links: for example, two of the five trustees of St Hilda's East are elected by the Guild of Cheltenham Ladies' College, the head of the school is *ex officio* president, the school contributes to fundraising, and sixth-form girls regularly visit the centre. The Peckham Settlement, founded by the Union of Girls' Schools for Social Service, still has strong links with many of the founding schools and their Old Girls' Associations (from Harrogate to Malvern), who not only contribute funds but also send 20 girls on placement each year. Indeed, one of the settlement's aims is:

> ... to provide opportunities for staff and pupils of schools [which founded the settlement] and others in comparable circumstances, to serve the local community and gain a better understanding of its value and the circumstances of life in Peckham. (The Peckham Settlement 1996, p.1)

Other settlements, like Virginia House, whose links with their founders had diminished, are now making a conscious effort to revive them. Lady Margaret Hall Settlement, founded by ex-students from the college of the same name in Oxford, organised a special visit to Oxford in 1997 (its centenary year) to consolidate links (Lady Margaret Hall Settlement 1997a, p.2). The Friends of Lady Margaret Hall, set up in a period of crisis in the late 1970s/early1980s (Beauman 1997, p.21), comprises many graduates of the college and in 1997 concentrated on building up contacts with the college.

As the accounts above illustrate, the links with the founders may be largely a fundraising exercise, or they may be an enduring and defining part of a settlement's identity, governance and work – sometimes seeming almost relics of a former purpose and age. Even in their heyday settlements were not universally regarded as positive features of community life. As Rose and Woods (1995, p.89) point out, they have also been seen as 'the fag end of Victorian charity and religious idealism, faintly ridiculous institutions for "do gooders" trying to bring cultural uplift to a largely indifferent working class.'

Some settlements have regarded it as important to break with some of these traditions and associations. When Lady Margaret Hall Settlement moved from its premises in Kennington to Wandsworth Road it left behind 'nearly a century of community links'. Yet a positive side to this move is also reported, as 'a completely fresh start meant a new set of relationships with local people and a visible end to the no longer viable concept of social work from a tradition of middle-class mission' (Beauman 1997, p.24).

In many settlements small relics of the past remain. The house-keeper at Blackfriars still lives on the premises and remembers the days when she used to prepare lunches for the settlement residents. She also runs two of the settlement's longstanding clubs. Until recently, the director of Bishop Creighton House was required by the management committee to be resident. When the current director declined the accommodation, a resident manager was appointed. There is another tenant occupying private accommodation in the house, and a similar situation exists at Katherine Lowe Settlement. Several other settlements, such as Toynbee Hall and Salmon Youth Centre, have short-term residents. But in most others the place of residents has been taken largely by volunteers in terms of doing the work, and tenant organisations in terms of using the space.

The composition of boards of trustees and executive or management committees often reflects traditional links with institutions and families. For example, Edinburgh University Settlement has constitutional requirements for a significant proportion of its board to be University members. Sir Adrian Cadbury is president of the Birmingham Settlement, reflecting his family's long involvement with the organisation. The tradition of 'middle-class do-gooding' by people from outside the locality where settlements are based remains stronger in some places than others. Some settlement staff expressed their frustration at the composition of their boards and described vain attempts to elect local people and service users. As one settlement worker commented, 'The trustees don't represent the local community we are working with. They are carrying a lot of baggage from the past. Most of the staff here are forward looking. Most of the trustees are backward looking.' This worker felt that the attempts of the settlement to modernise, change its image and deliver professional services were hampered by the trustees: 'You've got one hand tied behind your back all the time.' The worker recounted a story of how staff had to persuade the board that a set of cracked cups and saucers had to be replaced for health and safety reasons: 'The trustees still wanted to keep them in the basement because they had been donated.' Others seem to have made a gradual transition and now reflect a balance of representation, including local authority representatives, locally-based professionals from other organisations, and service users.

Many of the settlements' trustees and senior staff stress the importance of continuity and the continuing role for settlements, despite the changing fortunes of the areas where they are located. Periodically settlements have reviewed their roles, particularly in times of financial crisis, asking the question: 'Is there still a role for us here?' This was asked by Blackfriars quite recently, echoing the question it asked in 1941 when in serious financial difficulties during the war: 'Is it worth it?' The answer given in the annual report for that year was: 'We believe that to continue to maintain this landmark in Southwark is to contribute something solid and abiding in a crazy world' (Barratt 1985, p.19).

The Katherine Low Settlement recently went through a period of re-evaluation and questioning and undertook a needs analysis of the locality in Battersea to assess whether there was a future for the settlement there (Katherine Low Settlement 1996b). This demonstrated that there was, and that 'there are people who need the support of the Katherine Low Settlement now more than ever before'. In 1996 the Chair suggested that the past year 'will be seen as the most important watershed in the long history of the settlement', which is now transforming itself from what was basically a youth club into a social action centre (Katherine Low Settlement 1996a). The aspirations of the Chair are that it should become 'the beacon of

Battersea'. This echoes similar aspirations of the director of Oxford House to 'make it the centre of Bethnal Green again', or of Cambridge House in the 1960s to be 'a centre of community rather than a mere community centre' (Cambridge House 1989, p.20). The directors of both Oxford and Cambridge Houses stressed the importance of the settlement's role in the neighbourhood and borough, and the need to focus attention outwards, rather than inwards.

Many great claims are made by or on behalf of settlements – whether they be characterised as 'solid and abiding', pioneering and innovative, or, as Rose and Woods (1995, p.19) describe Manchester Settlement: 'a fortress of hope on the frontiers of despair'. One recently appointed director commented: 'Settlements are very complacent; we boast about things. Then I discovered all settlements boast about the same things.' Settlements may justifiably boast about certain things. Much of the work they did in the years before the welfare state was pioneering, and, as John Matthews describes in Chapter Three, had a significant influence on social policy. There may be less chance now to pioneer in such nationally significant ways as the literacy campaign, the development of child guidance clinics or citizens advice bureaux. But nevertheless many are doing very innovative work alongside provision of basic and necessary services. Birmingham is a good example, where the work on money advice has expanded into a national debtline and training project, and an innovative debt advice service for small businesses, recognising them as a vital part of the local economy and community. These co-exist alongside secondhand clothes shops, day centres for the elderly and a community nursery. As suggested in one recent annual report:

> Settlements have always been flexible. They have seen their role on the edge of society yet in the heart of it. They have been able to stand back and take an objective view and then to immerse themselves totally in a particular focus (Mansfield Settlement 1994, p.5).

Future developments

Each settlement sees its future in different ways, but several trends are common among a substantial number. Many are now talking about developing more of a community development/neighbourhood work approach – as a response both to local needs and to availability of funds. Many are in areas undergoing regeneration funded on a large scale through central government and European monies. With the recent emphasis on community involvement in regeneration, many are developing or proposing work around community capacity-building and participation. BASSAC, the national body, has taken on the running of the Pan-London Community Regeneration Consortium which adds impetus to this trend and identifies the settlement movement as having a significant role in urban regeneration (BASSAC 1998a).

Another growing area of work is involvement in the Labour government's 'New Deal' programme for the unemployed. As one director noted: 'Settlements are in an ideal position to attract New Labour funds.' The New Deal fits in well with the existing training and education programmes of many programmes of many settlements and is reminiscent of their involvement with the former Community Programme and Youth Training programmes of the old Manpower Services Commission. Some became heavily involved in this work and found it contributed significantly to their funds. Others eschewed it as compromising their independence and exploitative of the workers involved.

Although not new for settlements, another growth area is care work. Following the NHS and Community Care Act 1990 and the requirement that voluntary and private sector organisations provide some of the domiciliary and day-care services, many settlements have quite substantial contracts with local authorities for this work. Taylor (1997, p.1) notes New Labour's intention to move from the 'contract culture to a partnership culture' and the implications of this for voluntary sector organisations. This will require a clarity of mission, identifying the distinctive contribution they can make to service delivery and policy. It also requires clear costings for core work and for the contribution of volunteers, and the identification of new ways of resourcing voluntary activity. Taylor also notes the need to develop evaluation tools, ensure accountability to users and local communities, and offer adequate support for management committees. Some settlements are already living in this new world, others are moving into it, some are hovering on the edges. But none can remain unaffected by it.

BASSAC, the umbrella organisation, is now considering changing its membership criteria to include non-urban social action centres, and is planning a systematic campaign to increase membership and develop a regional presence to enable the movement to influence the new regional government structures being established (BASSAC 1998b). This is quite a development from the old days of the British Association of Residential Settlements and demonstrates how the movement has shifted as times have changed. Yet, while we might think the days of the residential settlement are now long gone, there are currently proposals from two different parts of the country to revive the idea. Liverpool Domestic Mission Society, founded in 1836 as a mission rather than a settlement, is now planning a new residential settlement based around a redundant church hall, St Dunstan's (Liverpool Domestic Mission Society (no date)). The aim of this project is both to improve the local environment and, in partnership with the University of Liverpool, to integrate higher education courses and students into the local community. Similarly, the Newcastle YMCA is working in conjunction with Northumbria University to establish a student residence based on the settlement model – an indicator of a revival of interest in the notion of university–community links and the mutual benefit to be derived from such partnerships.

What are the chances for the survival of the settlement movement? The main characteristics of settlements – tradition and independence – are both a strength and a weakness in the contemporary environment. Those that have survived so far have had to negotiate a fine line between staying true to their historic roots and changing their roles, ethos and image, as new needs and new funding regimes have emerged. They have also had to tread a careful route between remaining outside the state structure and capitalising on state funding for particular services or contracts. Over the last century many of the original settlements have ceased to exist, as their services were no longer relevant, or they hit a crisis of funding or confidence. Doubtless in the years to come some settlements will close. Yet it is also likely that, as BASSAC spreads its reach, more organisations will join the movement and the existing members will continue to transform their identities and functions, changing their names, moving premises and changing their constitutions, as all voluntary organisations tend to do. It may be more difficult to say exactly what a 'settlement' is in the future as urban and rural, new and old organisations join BASSAC. But there is no doubt that as the mixed economy of welfare seems set to continue, the role of neighbourhood-based, multipurpose voluntary organisations will gain increasing significance.

Acknowledgements

I am very grateful to the staff of BASSAC for giving interviews and allowing me access to their records. I am also grateful to the many settlements and social action centres that sent me their annual reports and other information, and to the staff who agreed to be interviewed.

The research on which this chapter is based was completed in Summer 1998.

Bibliography

Banks, S. (1994) 'Contemporary issues in youth work'. *Youth and Policy* 46, 1–4.

Banks, S. (1995) *Ethics and Values in Social Work*. Basingstoke: Macmillan.

Barratt, G. (1985) *Blackfriars Settlement: A Short History*. London: Blackfriars Settlement.

Batsleer, J. (1995) 'Management and organisation'. In J. Davis Smith, C. Rochester and R. Hedley (eds) *An Introduction to the Voluntary Sector*. London: Routledge.

Beauchamp Lodge Settlement (1998) *Report and Accounts Year Ended March 31 1998*. London: Beauchamp Lodge Settlement.

Beauman, K (1997) *The Lady Margaret Hall Settlement 1887–1997: A Century of Caring in the Community*. London: The Friends of Lady Margaret Hall Settlement.

Bede House Assocation (1998a) *Annual Report 1997–1998.* London: Bede House Assocation.

Bede House Assocation (1998b) *Bede House Association: Presentation Pack.* London: Bede House Assocation.

Birmingham Settlement (1994) *Annual Report and Summary Accounts 1994.* Birmingham: Birmingham Settlement.

Birmingham Settlement (1997) *Annual Report and Financial Statements 1997.* Birmingham: Birmingham Settlement.

Bishop Creighton House (1998) *Bishop Creighton House Settlement 1996/97.* London: Bishop Creighton House.

Blackfriars Settlement (1997) *Annual Review 1996–1997.* London: Blackfriars Settlement.

British Association of Settlements and Social Action Centres (1996) *Street Level 4: Resourcing the Stones.* London: BASSAC.

British Association of Settlements and Social Action Centres (1997a) *Annual Review 1996–7.* London: BASSAC.

British Association of Settlements and Social Action Centres (1997b) *Street Level 7: Case Studies in the Social Economy.* London: BASSAC.

British Association of Settlements and Social Action Centres (1998a) *Review 1997–8.* London: BASSAC.

British Association of Settlements and Social Action Centres (1998b) *Strategic Plan 1999–2002.* London: BASSAC.

Cambridge House (1989) *Cambridge House: The First Hundred Years, 1889–1989.* London: Cambridge House.

Cambridge House and Talbot (1998) *Annual Review 1997–8: Opportunities and Challenges.* London: Cambridge House and Talbot.

Cochrane, A. (1994) 'Restructuring the local welfare state'. In R. Burrows and B. Loader (eds) *Towards a Post-Fordist Welfare State?* London: Routledge.

Deakin, N. (1995) 'The perils of partnership: the voluntary sector and the state 1945–1992'. In J. Davis Smith, C. Rochester and R. Hedley (eds) *An Introduction to the Voluntary Sector.* London: Routledge.

Edinburgh University Settlement (1997) *Annual Report.* Edinburgh: Edinburgh University Settlement.

Fern Street Settlement (1997) *Annual Report 1997.* London: Fern Street Settlement.

Further Education Funding Council (1998) *Blackfriars Education Centre: Report from the Inspectorate 1997–8.* Coventry: Further Education Funding Council.

Gray, A. (1998) *Business-like but not like a Business: The Challenge for Public Management.* London: Chartered Institute of Public Finance and Accountancy.

Handy, C. (1988) *Understanding Voluntary Organisations.* London: Pelican/Penguin.

Katherine Low Settlement (1996a) *Annual Report 1996.* London: Katherine Low Settlement.

Katherine Low Settlement (1996b) *Katherine Low Settlement in Perspective – A Community Profile.* London: Katherine Low Settlement.

Katherine Low Settlement (1997) *Annual Report 1997*. London: Katherine Low Settlement.

Lady Margaret Hall Settlement (1997a) *Annual Review 1996/1997*. London: Lady Margaret Hall Settlement.

Lady Margaret Hall Settlement (1997b) *Lady Margaret Hall Settlement 1897–1997: An Open Door. What Does it Do?* London: Lady Margaret Hall Settlement.

Liverpool Domestic Mission Society (undated) *St Dunstan's Settlement: A Liverpool Concept*. Liverpool Domestic Mission Society/Pierhead Housing Association Limited.

Manchester Settlement (1997) *Annual Review 1997*. Manchester: Manchester Settlement.

Mansfield Settlement (1989) *New Growth in Newham: 1989/1990 Centenary Year*. London: Mansfield Settlement.

Mansfield Settlement (1994) *Still Growing in Newham*. London: Mansfield Settlement.

Mansfield Settlement (1997) *Breaking the Mould: Mansfield Settlement Annual Report 1996/97*. London: Mansfield Settlement.

Mayo, M. (1994) *Communities and Caring: The Mixed Economy of Welfare*. Basingstoke: Macmillan.

Müschenborn, D. and Rachmat, J. (1994) *The Apple Needs its Core*. London: London Business School.

O'Connell, R. (1997) *Planning the Future – A Report for Oxford House*. London: LEVELheaded training, development and research.

Oxford House in Bethnel Green (1997) *Annual Report 1997*. London: Oxford House.

Peckham Settlement (1996) *Annual Report 1995–96*.

Pimlott, J. (1935) *Toynbee Hall: Fifty Years of Social Progress 1884–1934*. London: Dent.

Popple, K. (1995) *Analysing Community Work: Its Theory and Practice*. Buckingham: Open University Press.

Rimmer, J. (1980) *Troubles Shared: The Story of a Settlement 1899–1979*. Birmingham: Phogiston Publishing Limited.

Rose, M. and Woods, A. (1995) *Everything Went on at the Round House: A Hundred Years of the Manchester University Settlement*. Manchester: Manchester University Press.

St.Hilda's East Community Centre (1989) *St Hilda's East: A Century of Community Service 1889–1989*. London: St. Hilda's East Community Centre.

St Hilda's East Community Centre (1997) *Annual Report 1996/97*. London: St Hilda's East Community Centre.

Taylor, M. (1997) *The Best of Both Worlds. The Voluntary Sector and Local Government*. York: Joseph Rowntree Foundation.

The Peckham Settlement (1996) *Annual Report 1995 and 1996*. London: The Peckham Settlement

Toynbee Hall (1997) *Annual Report 1997*. London: Toynbee Hall.

Virginia House Settlement (1997) *Putting People First: Virginia House Settlement 1997*. Plymouth: Virginia House Settlement.

Virginia House Settlement (1998a) *Building Services Action Plan 1998/9*. Plymouth: Virginia House Settlement.

Virginia House Settlement (1998b) *Community Services Unit: Annual Work-plan 1998/99 (draft)*. Plymouth: Virginia House Settlement.

List of Contributors

Sarah Banks is Senior Lecturer in Community and Youth Work in the Department of Sociology and Social Policy at the University of Durham. She is currently undertaking research on community capacity building and on ethics and the changing social professions.

Crescy Cannan is Senior Lecturer in Social Policy at the University of Sussex. She has a long-standing interest in the history of social welfare and in social activists and movements. She is currently working on environmentalism and its relationship to community development and to social policy.

Mina Carson is Associate Professor of History, at Oregon State University and researches topics in the history of social work, psychotherapy, women, and popular culture.

Ruth Gilchrist is a development worker with the Newcastle-upon-Tyne YMCA and a part-time tutor in the Community and Youth Work Studies Unit, University of Durham.

Jon Glasby is a qualified social worker and a research student at the University of Birmingham. Research interests include community care for older people, the interface between health and social care and the history of the settlement movement.

Tony Jeffs is a lecturer in the Community and Youth Work Studies Unit, Department of Sociology and Social Policy, University of Durham. He is also a member of the Editorial Board for *Youth and Policy*.

Christian Johnson was Executive Director of IFS from 1987 to 1997, after working for Birmingham Settlement as Director of Research and as Acting Chief Executive.

James Kimmis worked at the British Association of Settlements and Social Action Centres where he was a colleague of John Matthews.

John Matthews was until his recent death Head of Agency of the British Association of Settlements (BASSAC).

Michael Rose is Professor Emeritus, Modern Social History, University of Manchester.

Mark K. Smith is Rank Research Fellow and Tutor at the YMCA George Williams College, London.

Martin Walker is an activist, writer and researcher. He is the author of seven books about critical social subjects.

Chris Warren lectures in social work at Brunel University having previously taught at Sussex University. His particular interest is in community and social development as a basis for family support practice and the role of family centres in community development.

Subject Index

Author Index

This book is to be returned on or before the last date stamped below.